A REASSESSMENT OF
BIBLICAL ELOHIM

SOCIETY
OF BIBLICAL
LITERATURE

DISSERTATION SERIES

Saul M. Olyan, Old Testament Editor
Mark Allan Powell, New Testament Editor

Number 183

A REASSESSMENT OF
BIBLICAL ELOHIM

by
Joel S. Burnett

Joel S. Burnett

A Reassessment of Biblical Elohim

Society of Biblical Literature

Atlanta

A REASSESSMENT OF
BIBLICAL ELOHIM

by
Joel S. Burnett
Ph.D., Johns Hopkins University, 1999
P. Kyle McCarter, Jr., Dissertation Advisor

Library of Congress Cataloging-in-Publication Data

Burnett, Joel S. 1968–
    A reassessment of biblical Elohim / Joel S. Burnett.
       p. cm — (Dissertation series / Society of Biblical Literature ; no. 183)
    Originally presented as the author's thesis (doctoral)—Johns Hopkins
University, 1999.
    Includes bibliographical references.
    ISBN 1-58983-016-4 (alk. paper)
    1. God—Name—Biblical teaching. 2. Bible. O.T.—Criticism, interpretation,
I. Title. II. Dissertation series (Society of Biblical Literature) ; no. 183.

BS1192.6.B87 2001
221.4'47—dc21   2001049192

Printed in the United States of America
on acid-free paper

To Curtis, Ann, Jamie,
Hannah, and Wilson

Table of Contents

Acknowledgements

This study was completed and defended as my doctoral dissertation at the Johns Hopkins University in March, 1999. In preparing the manuscript for publication, I have made only the minor adjustments and corrections that are in keeping with the SBL Dissertation Series guidelines. Recent works that would have been relevant on some points include H. C. Brichto, *The Names of God: Poetic Readings in Biblical Beginnings* (1998), which came to my attention only after my dissertation had been completed and defended, and R. K. Gnuse, "Redefining the Elohist?" *JBL* 119 (2000): 201-20, which was published well after that time.

Sincere thanks are due to Professors P. Kyle McCarter, Jr., Raymond Westbrook, Jerrold S. Cooper, Glenn M. Schwartz, Betsy M. Bryan, and Richard Jasnow, and to the late Professor Delbert R. Hillers, all of the Johns Hopkins University Department of Near Eastern Studies. Their surpassing expertise and careful attention have been invaluable both to my training in the study of the ancient Near East and to this dissertation. Most especially, I would like to thank P. Kyle McCarter, Jr., whose influence is evident on every page. His instruction, guidance, and encouragement have been critical both to this project and to my development as a young scholar.

I wish to thank Leigh Andersen of SBL Publications, whose extraordinary competence and forbearance have prevailed over my technical limitations during the production process. I also thank Saul Olyan, the Hebrew Bible editor for the series, both for his prompt and courteous attention in all matters and for his very assiduous oversight in the final preparation of the manuscript.

A life-long debt of gratitude is owed to my parents, who both by instruction and by example have taught me that education is to be prized above wealth and that learning is of value for its own sake. It was with great joy that I was able to share the final months of the writing with my daughter, Hannah, and then the time of the manuscript preparation with my son, Wilson. Most of all, I thank my wife and truest friend, Jamie, who through her patience, encouragement, assistance, and hard work has contributed at every step of my scholarly life. It is to these dearest to me that I dedicate this work.

JSB
Summer, 2001

Abbreviations

AB	Anchor Bible
ABD	*Anchor Bible Dictionary*. Edited by D. N. Freedman. 6 vols. New York, 1992
ABL	*Assyrian and Babylonian Letters Belonging to the Kouyunjik Collections of the British Museum*. Edited by R. F. Harper. 14 vols. Chicago, 1892–1914
AfO	*Archiv für Orientforschung*
AJSL	*American Journal of Semitic Languages and Literature*
ANET	*Ancient Near Eastern Texts Relating to the Old Testament*. Edited by J. B. Pritchard. Princeton, 1969
ANG	Stamm, J. J. *Die Akkadische Namengebung*. Leipzig, 1939
AnOr	Analecta orientalia
AOAT	Alter Orient und Altes Testament
AOS	American Oriental Series
APN	Tallqvist, K. L. *Assyrian Personal Names*. Helsinki, 1914
ARI	Albright, W. F. *Archaeology and the Religion of Israel*. 5th ed. Garden City, N.Y., 1969
ATANT	Abhandlungen zur Theologie des Alten und Neuen Testaments
BA	*Biblical Archaeologist*
BASOR	*Bulletin of the American Schools of Oriental Research*
BDB	Brown, F., S. R. Driver, and C. A. Briggs. *A Hebrew Lexicon of the Old Testament*. Oxford, 1907
BO	*Bibliotheca orientalis*
BWANT	Beiträge zur Wissenschaft vom Alten und Neuen Testament
BWL	Lambert, W. G. *Babylonian Wisdom Literature*. Oxford, 1960
BZAW	Beihefte zur Zeitschrift für die alttestamentliche Wissenschaft
CAD	*The Assyrian Dictionary of the Oriental Institute of the University of Chicago*. Chicago, 1956–
CANE	*Civilizations of the Ancient Near East*. Edited by J. Sasson. 4 vols. New York, 1995
CAP	Cowley, A. E. *Aramaic Papyri of the Fifth Century B.C.* Oxford, 1923
CAT	Rainey, A. *Canaanite in the Amarna Tablets*. 4 vols. Leiden, 1996

CBQ	*Catholic Biblical Quarterly*
CIS	*Corpus inscriptionum semiticarum*
CMHE	Cross, F. M. *Canaanite Myth and Hebrew Epic.* Cambridge, Mass., 1973
Cooke	Cooke, G. A. *A Text-Book of North-Semitic Inscriptions.* Oxford, 1903
DDD	*Dictionary of Deities and Demons in the Bible.* Edited by K. van der Toorn, B. Becking, and P. W. van der Horst. 2d ed. Leiden, 1999
DN(N)	divine name(s)
Driver	Driver, G. R. *Aramaic Documents of the Fifth Century.* Oxford, 1957
EA	El-Amarna tablets. According to the edition of J. A. Knudtzon. *Die el-Amarna-Tafeln.* Leipzig, 1908-1915. Reprint, Aalen, 1964. Continued in A. F. Rainey, *El-Amarna Tablets 359-379.* 2d revised ed. Kevelaer, 1978
EH	El-Hofra inscriptions. According to the edition of A. Berthier and R. Charlier. *Le sanctuaire punique d'El-Hofra à Constantine.* Paris, 1952
EncMiqr	*Entsiqlopēdiā Miqrā'īt-Encyclopaedia Biblica* [= *Entsiklopedyah mikra'it*]. Edited by M. David. 9 vols. Jerusalem, 1950-
FSAC	Albright, W. F. *From the Stone Age to Christianity.* 2d ed. Garden City, N.Y., 1957
GAG	Soden, W. von. *Grundriss der Akkadischen Grammatik.* 2d ed. Rome, 1969
GKC	*Gesenius' Hebrew Grammar.* Edited by E. Kautzsch. Translated by A. E. Cowely. 2d ed. Oxford, 1910
GN(N)	geographic name(s)
gntl.	gentilic noun
HAL	Koehler, L., W. Baumgartner, and J. J. Stamm. *Hebräisches und aramäisches Lexikon zum Alten Testament.* 5 vols. Leiden, 1967-1995
HO	Handbuch der Orientalistik
HSM	Harvard Semitic Monographs
HSS	Harvard Semitic Studies
HUCA	*Hebrew Union College Annual*
IDB	*The Interpreter's Dictionary of the Bible.* Edited by G. A. Buttrick. 4 vols. Nashville, 1962

IEJ	*Israel Exploration Journal*
JA	*Journal asiatique*
JBL	*Journal of Biblical Literature*
JCS	*Journal of Cuneiform Studies*
JHNES	Johns Hopkins Near Eastern Studies
JNES	*Journal of Near Eastern Studies*
JSOTSup	Journal for the Study of the Old Testament: Supplement Series
JSS	*Journal of Semitic Studies*
KAH	*Keilschrifttexte aus Assur historischen Inhalts.* Vol. 2. O. Schroeder. Leipzig, 1922
KAI	*Kanaanäische und aramäische Inschriften.* H. Donner and W. Röllig. 2d ed. Wiesbaden, 1966-1969
KI	*Kanaanäische Inschriften (Moabitisch, Althebräisch, Phonizisch, Punisch).* Edited by M. Lidzbarski. Giessen, 1907
KS	*Kleine Schriften*
LSS	Leipziger semitische Studien
LXX	Septuagint (the Greek Old Testament)
MT	Masoretic Text (of the Old Testament)
MUSJ	*Mélanges de l'Université Saint-Joseph*
OBO	Orbis biblicus et orientalis
OLZ	*Orientalistische Literaturzeitung*
Or	*Orientalia* (NS)
OrAnt	*Oriens antiquus*
OTL	Old Testament Library
pl.	plural
PN(N)	personal name(s)
POH	Rad, G. von. *The Problem of the Hexateuch and other essays.* Translated E. W. Trueman. New York, 1966
RA	*Revue d'assyriologie et d'archéologie orientale*
RB	*Revue biblique*
RES	*Répertoire d'épigraphie sémitique*
RlA	*Reallexikon der Assyriologie.* Edited by E. Ebeling et al. Berlin, 1928-
RS	Ras Shamra
SAA	State Archives of Assyria
SBLDS	Society of Biblical Literature Dissertation Series
SBLMS	Society of Biblical Literature Monograph Series

sg.	singular
SJOT	*Scandinavian Journal of the Old Testament*
TDOT	*Theological Dictionary of the Old Testament.* Edited by G. J. Botterweck, H. Ringgren, and Heinz-Josef Fabry. Translated by J. T. Willis, G. W. Bromiley, and D. E. Green. 11 vols. Grand Rapids, 1974-
THAT	*Theologisches Handwörterbuch zum Alten Testament.* Edited by E. Jenni, with assistance from C. Westermann. 2 vols. Munich, 1971-1976
TT	Taanach Texts
TUAT	*Texte aus der Umwelt des Alten Testaments.* Edited by O. Kaiser. Gütersloh, 1984-
UF	*Ugarit-Forschungen*
VAB	Vorderasiatische Bibliothek
VT	*Vetus Testamentum*
VTSup	Supplements to Vetus Testamentum
WMANT	Wissenschaftliche Monographien zum Alten und Neuen Testament
YGC	Albright, W. F. *Yahweh and the Gods of Canaan.* London, 1968. Repr., Winona Lake, Ind., 1994
ZAH	*Zeitschrift für Althebräistik*
ZAW	*Zeitschrift für die alttestamentliche Wissenschaft*

CHAPTER 1
Introduction

A reassessment of the meaning and background of biblical *'ĕlōhîm* is warranted on three accounts. First, the amount of scholarship having *'ĕlōhîm* as its focus is relatively meager, this in spite of the term's importance not only as the usual common noun meaning "god" in Biblical Hebrew but also as the preferred designation for the god of Israel in certain portions of the Hebrew Bible, most notably Pentateuchal E and P and the "Elohistic Psalter" (Psalms 42-83). The only existing monographic study of the divine title *'ĕlōhîm* was published a century ago and exerted no lasting influence on scholarship.[1] The only other major study giving central attention to *'ĕlōhîm* is from the same era and, rather than treating the term's meaning and its significance as a title for Israel's god, concentrates on the term's appellative, that is, common-noun usage, as a *Voruntersuchung* to source-critical analysis of the Pentateuch.[2] More recent scholarly treatment of *'ĕlōhîm* has largely been confined to reference articles.[3]

---

[1]Hellmuth Zimmermann, *Elohim: Eine Studie zur israelitischen Religions- und Litteraturgeschichte nebst Beitrag zur Religionsphilosophie und einer Pentateuchtabelle* (Berlin: Mayer & Müller, 1900). Neither Zimmermann's grammatical explanation of *'ĕlōhîm* as "Totalitätsplural" (which followed Franz Eduard Dietrich, *Abhandlungen zur hebräischen Grammatik* [Leipzig: Vogel, 1846], 29) nor his thesis that all instances of *'ĕlōhîm* as a divine name, including those in E and P, were the result of editorial activity by a postexilic Elohistic scribal school was considered persuasive.

[2]Friedrich Baumgärtel, *Elohim ausserhalb des Pentateuch: Grundlegung zu einer Untersuchung über die Gottesnamen im Pentateuch* (Leipzig: J. C. Hinrichs, 1914).

[3]Bernhard W. Anderson, "God, Names of," *IDB* 2:407-17; Umberto Cassuto, "אֱלֹהִים," *EncMiqr* 1:297-321; Helmer Ringgren, "אֱלֹהִים *'ĕlōhîm*," *TDOT* 1:267-84; Martin Rose, "Names of God in the OT," *ABD* 4:1001-11; Werner H. Schmidt, "אֱלֹהִים *'ĕlōhîm* Gott," *THAT* 1:154-67; Karel van der Toorn, "God (I) אֱלֹהִים," *DDD*,

Second, while modern biblical criticism has shed light on various aspects of *'ĕlōhîm*—its etymology and grammatically plural form,[4] its theological meaning,[5] and its comparative background[6]—the lack of

---

352-65. Notwithstanding the impression given by its title, the volume of essays edited by Diana V. Edelman, *The Triumph of Elohim: From Yahwisms to Judaisms* (Grand Rapids, Mich.: Eerdmans, 1995)—apart from the editor's introductory comments on pp. 15 and 22 and the remarks on pp. 117-21 of the essay by Thomas L. Thompson ("The Intellectual Matrix of Early Biblical Narrative: Inclusive Monotheism in Persian Palestine")—has nothing to say about *'ĕlōhîm*.

[4]Though the word's etymology remains hopelessly elusive (see Ringgren, *TDOT* 1:273; Schmidt, *THAT* 1:154; Ludwig Koehler and Walter Baumgartner, *HAL* 1:47, 50-51), the grammatical treatment of the plural form in the standard reference works has yielded two compelling possibilities for its categorization: (1) the abstract plural (GKC §124; Carl Brockelmann, *Grundriss der vergleichenden Grammatik der semitischen Sprachen* [Berlin: Reuther & Reichard, 1913], §29; idem, *Hebräische Syntax* [Neukirchen: Erziehungsvereins, 1956], §19c)—this explanation bears some similarity to that of Dietrich (*Abhandlungen*) and following him Zimmermann (*Elohim*), according to whom *'ĕlōhîm*, as a term of abstraction, was based ultimately on a "Totalitätsplural" (see above)—and (2) the plural of intensity (Aaron Ember, "The Pluralis Intensivus in Hebrew," *AJSL* 21 [1905]: 207-15; Paul Joüon, *Grammaire de l'Hébreu Biblique* [Rome: Pontifical Biblical Institute, 1947], §136d). Both of these explanations have emerged in preference to the now discredited notion that the grammatical form of *'ĕlōhîm*, originally a numerical plural, is a vestige of early Israelite polytheism (see, e.g., Eduard Meyer, *Die Israeliten und ihre Nachbarstämme* [Halle: Niemeyer, 1906], 211 and n. 1; against that notion, Schmidt, *THAT* 1:154).

[5]Discussion of the theological significance of *'ĕlōhîm*'s usage in reference to the god of Israel has been carried out for the most part in the context of source criticism of the Pentateuch. Though much of the analysis has been confined to the status of *'ĕlōhîm*—being an alternative to Yahweh—as a criterion for the delineation of documentary sources (see, e.g., Abraham Kuenen, *An Historico-Critical Inquiry into the Composition of the Hexateuch* [trans. Philip H. Wicksteed; London: Macmillan, 1886], 55-58 and nn. 18-25; 140-42 and nn. 5-20; Julius Wellhausen, *Die Composition des Hexateuchs und der historischen Bücher des Alten Testaments* [Berlin: G. Reimer, 1889]; idem, *Prolegomena zur Geschichte Israels* [Berlin: G. Reimer, 1883], 7-8; Samuel Rolles Driver, *An Introduction to the Literature of the Old Testament* [New York: Meridian, 1956], 13), its association with a particular literary and theological viewpoint has always been an essential element of the debate (see Kuenen, *Inquiry*, 57 and n. 28, 140; Wellhausen, *Composition*, 18-19); after all, it was on this basis that the claim for an E source independent of the Priestly writer was introduced by D. Hermann Hupfeld, *Die Quellen der Genesis und die Art ihrer Zusammensetzung* (Berlin: Wiegandt und Grieben, 1853). Source critics have recognized among other things regarding E its emphasis on ethical rectitude and the remoteness of the deity in its presentation of the patriarchal narratives, throughout which *'ĕlōhîm* is the preferred designation for God (Otto Eissfeldt, *The Old Testament: An Introduction* [trans. Peter R. Ackroyd; New York: Harper & Row, 1965], 184; Otto Procksch, *Das nordhebräische Sagenbuch: Die Elohimquelle* [Leipzig: J. C. Hinrichs, 1906]; Georg Fohrer, *Introduction to the Old Testament* [London: S.P.C.K., 1968], 152-58; J. Alberto Soggin, *Introduction to the Old Testament*

a recent study giving central place to the expression has allowed many of these gains to become obscured, and the expression's basic meaning and significance in the Hebrew Bible remain unsettled. A general lack of clarity in current scholarship's treatment of *'ĕlōhîm* calls for a cohesive explanation of the term's meaning and background.[7]

[OTL; Philadelphia: Westminster, 1980], 105-6). This contrasts with P's keen interest in ritual, law, and genealogy expressed within a narrative framework of successive divine covenants, in which *'ĕlōhîm* is an exclusive designation for God only until the time of Abraham (Gen 17:1; see Procksch, *Elohimquelle*, 309-30; Driver, *Introduction*, 10-13; Fohrer, *Introduction*, 178-85; Soggin, *Introduction*, 135-38). Both advocates (Procksch, *Elohimquelle*, 198-99; Ringgren, *TDOT* 1:284; Werner H. Schmidt, *Old Testament Introduction* [trans. M. J. O'Connell; New York: Crossroads, 1990], 90-91) and opponents (Paul Volz and Wilhelm Rudolph, *Der Elohist als Erzähler: Ein Irrweg der Pentateuchkritik?* [BZAW 63; Giessen: Alfred Töpelmann, 1933], 20-21, 176-81; Ivan Engnell, *A Rigid Scrutiny: Critical Essays on the Old Testament* [trans. and ed. J. T. Willis and H. Ringgren; Nashville: Vanderbilt Univ. Press, 1969]; Umberto Cassuto, *The Documentary Hypothesis and the Composition of the Pentateuch* [trans. I. Abrahams; Jerusalem: Magnes, 1961], 18-41; John Van Seters, *Abraham in History and Tradition* [New Haven: Yale Univ. Press, 1975], 170-75, 183; Erhard Blum, *Studien zur Komposition des Pentateuch* [WMANT 57; Berlin: Walter de Gruyter, 1990], 25-26) of the Documentary Hypothesis have recognized that in some passages the use of *'ĕlōhîm*, in comparison with Yahweh, emphasizes more abstract and ethereal aspects of the deity.

[6]Though the comparative data for *'ĕlōhîm*, most significantly that found in the Amarna Letters, has been noted (Franz M. Th. Böhl, *Der Sprache der Amarnabriefe* [Leipziger semitistische Studien V/2; Leipzig: J. C. Hinrichs, 1909], 36; Johannes Hehn, *Die biblische und die babylonische Gottesidee: die israelitische Gottesauffassung im Lichte der altorientalischen Religionsgeschichte* [Leipzig: J. C. Hinrichs, 1913], 171-73.; Anton Jirku, *Altorientalischer Kommentar zum Alten Testament* [Leipzig: Deichert, 1923], 19; idem, "Elohim als Bezeichnung einer Gottheit," in *Reallexikon der Assyriologie* [ed. E. Ebeling and B. Meissner; Berlin: Walter de Gruyter, 1938] 2:358), attempts to integrate that evidence into the understanding of the biblical expression have been minimal (but see William F. Albright, *From the Stone Age to Christianity* [2d ed.; Garden City, N.Y.: Doubleday, 1957], 213; Walther Eichrodt, *Theology of the Old Testament* [trans. J. A. Baker; 2 vols.; OTL; Philadelphia: Westminster, 1961], 1:185-86; Anderson, "God, names of," 413; Alan W. Jenks, *The Elohist and North Israelite Traditions* [SBLMS 22; Missoula, Mont.: Scholars Press, 1977], 8-9; van der Toorn, "God," 683). Benedikt Hartmann's analysis of the political ramifications of the Late Bronze Age antecedent of *'ĕlōhîm* fails to account for the Amarna expression's use in reference not only to the Egyptian king but also to proper deities ("Elōhīm als Singular," *MUSJ* 48 [1972-1973]: 67-76).

[7]With respect to grammatical issues, the understanding of *'ĕlōhîm* is confused from the ground up by the persistence of the nebulous concept "plural of excellence" or "plural of majesty" (see, e.g., Paul Joüon and Takamitsu Muraoka, *A Grammar of Biblical Hebrew* [2 vols.; Subsidia biblica 14/1-2; Rome: Pontifical Biblical Institute, 1991], 2:§136d; van der Toorn, "God," 668-69). Though Waltke and O'Connor improve slightly upon the terminology, the alternative offered, "Honorifics and the Like," betrays

Finally, the place of *'ĕlōhîm* in the history of Israelite religion, as distinct from its character as a literary phenomenon, has received minimal attention in existing scholarship.[8] Two drastically differing

---

a lack of precision in defining the category by which *'ĕlōhîm* is to be explained (Bruce K. Waltke and Michael O'Connor, *An Introduction to Biblical Hebrew Syntax* [Winona Lake, Ind.: Eisenbrauns, 1990], 7.4.3a-f.). This vagueness in grammatical categories leads quickly into confusion over the basic meaning of the Hebrew expression, as witnessed in Bernhard W. Anderson's explanation that *'ĕlōhîm* is a "'plural of majesty' or *pluralis amplitudinis*—i.e., Elohim includes all gods; the fullness of deity is comprehended in him" ("God, names of," 416). The last part of that analysis follows Albright's explanation that in Amarna Akkadian sg. *ilānu*, a pre-Israelite antecedent of *'ĕlōhîm* (see below, Chapter 2), designates an individual deity as the head or even embodiment of the pantheon (*FSAC*, 213). Albright's explanation, which though quite reasonable proves inconsistent with a thorough review of the Amarna material (see the discussion below), provides a point of departure for the suggestion by Jenks that in (northern) Israelite usage *'ĕlōhîm* was perceived to be a plural form of the name of the god El (*The Elohist and North Israelite Traditions*, 8-9). This last claim is also made by Robert B. Coote, *In Defense of Revolution: the Elohist History* (Minneapolis: Fortress, 1991), 75, 104. The well-informed discussion of Eichrodt illustrates the difficulty that has prevailed in efforts to reach an internally consistent resolution of the issues; while Eichrodt favors the explanation of *'ĕlōhîm* as an "abstract plural," he seems to equate that category with the "plural of intensity," and also concludes, on the basis of *'ĕlōhîm*'s usage with plural verb forms, that it was secondarily plural in meaning (*Theology*, 1:184-86). A possible lack both of precision and of awareness of the pre-Israelite background is reflected in the explanation provided in a recent dictionary article that *'ĕlōhîm*'s plural form "should be understood in the sense of an intensification and eventually as an absolutization: 'God of gods,' 'the highest God,' 'quintessence of all divine powers,' 'the only God who represents the divine in a comprehensive and absolute way'" (Rose, "Names," 1006). While the comments both of Rose and of Eichrodt may be understood to be correct, they can be construed in a number of different ways and thus illustrate the need for a thorough, explicit, and cohesive assessment of all the relevant material.

[8]Both classic and more recent treatments of Israelite religion and of relevant socio-political factors virtually if not completely ignore any role played by *'ĕlōhîm*; see, e.g., William F. Albright, *Yahweh and the Gods of Canaan* (London: Univ. of London, 1968; repr., Winona Lake, Ind.: Eisenbrauns, 1994), 171; Frank M. Cross, *Canaanite Myth and Hebrew Epic: Essays in the History of the Religion of Israel* (Cambridge, Mass.: Harvard Univ. Press, 1973), 296; Rainer Albertz, *Persönliche Frömmigkeit und offizielle Religion: Religionsinterner Pluralismus in Israel und Babylon* (Calwer theologische Monographien 9; Stuttgart: Calwer, 1978); idem, *A History of Israelite Religion in the Old Testament Period* (trans. J. Bowden; 2 vols.; OTL; Philadelphia: Westminster John Knox, 1994); Herbert Niehr, *Der höchste Gott: Alttestamentlicher JHWH-Glaube im Kontext syrisch-kanaanäischer Religion des 1. Jahrtausends v. Chr.* (BZAW 190; Berlin: Walter de Gruyter, 1990); Mark S. Smith, *The Early History of God* (San Francisco: Harper & Row, 1990); Karel van der Toorn, *Family Religion in Babylonia, Syria, and Israel: Continuity and Change in the Forms of Religious Life* (Studies in the History and Culture of the Ancient Near East 7; Leiden: Brill, 1996), 284; Morton Smith, *Palestinian Parties and Politics that Shaped the Old Testament* (London: SCM Press, 1971);

interpretations of *'ĕlōhîm* with respect to Israelite religion are that the term was used as a plural form of the name of the deity El[9] and, alternatively, that biblical *'ĕlōhîm* was a purely literary expression produced by monotheistic Judaism after the exile and had never played a role in Israel's worship and cultic traditions.[10] The lack both of agreement and of clarity in the scholarly understanding of *'ĕlōhîm*'s role in the belief and worship of ancient Israel calls for a thorough discussion of this aspect of the divine designation.

Given the deficiencies that continue to characterize scholarship on *'ĕlōhîm*, a comprehensive reappraisal of biblical *'ĕlōhîm*, including philological, historical, and literary analysis of the term, is a desideratum. The aim of this study is to provide such a reassessment and thereby to demonstrate that, well before the first expressions of Israelite monotheism during the exile,[11] the title *'ĕlōhîm* played a

---

Bernhard Lang, *Monotheism and the Prophetic Minority* (The Social World of Biblical Antiquity Series 1; Sheffield: Almond Press, 1983), 22-23; Robert B. Coote, ed. *Elijah and Elisha in Socioliterary Perspective* (Semeia Studies; Atlanta: Scholars Press, 1992). The dearth of analysis on the term *'ĕlōhîm* in three works in particular is made most surprising by their titles: Karl Jaroš, *Die Stellung des Elohisten zur kanaanäischen Religion* (OBO 4; Fribourg: Universitätsverlag, 1974); Robert R. Coote, *In Defense of Revolution: the Elohist History*; and Diana V. Edelman, ed. *The Triumph of Elohim*.

[9]Jenks, *Elohist and North Israelite Traditions*, 8-9; Coote, *In Defense of Revolution*, 75, 104.

[10]E.g., Zimmermann, *Elohim*, 23-25, 66-68 and n. 2. Thompson ("Intellectual Matrix," in Edelman, *Triumph of Elohim*) sees in *'ĕlōhîm* "a coherent concept of a transcendent universal expression of ultimate reality" (p. 121 n. 17) and a "non-specific inclusive literary concept . . . which is by definition not a God of any cult, story oracle" (p. 119 n. 13); see also p. 120 n. 15, and, for the general notion that *'ĕlōhîm* is both "late" and monotheistic, the comments of Edelman, 16. The view that *'ĕlōhîm* implies universalistic or even monotheistic claims regarding the deity is expressed, with a completely different understanding of the term's history, in Procksch, *Elohimquelle*, 198-99; Cassuto, *Documentary Hypothesis*, 31; Ringgren, *TDOT* 1:284; Schmidt, *Introduction*, 90.

[11]Ezekiel, in its oracles against the nations (chs. 25-32) and against Gog and Magog (chs. 38-39), presents Yahweh as internationally transcendent; even more explicit expressions of monotheism occur in the Deuteronomistic History and in Second Isaiah: *yhwh hû' hā'ĕlōhîm baššāmayim mimma'al wĕ'al-hā'āreṣ mittāḥat 'ên 'ôd*, "Yahweh is God in heaven above and on earth below—there is no other" (Deut 4:39; see also v. 35); *lĕma'an da'at kol-'ammê hā'āreṣ kî yhwh hû' hā'ĕlōhîm 'ên 'ôd*, "so that all the peoples of the earth will know that Yahweh is God—there is no other" (1 Kgs 8:60); *yhwh 'ĕlōhê yiśrā'ēl yōšēb hakkĕrūbîm 'attâ-hû' hā'ĕlōhîm lĕbaddĕkā lĕkōl mamlĕkôt hā'āreṣ*, "Yahweh, God of Israel, enthroned above the cherubim, you are God, you alone, of all the kingdoms of the earth" (2 Kgs 19:15=Isa 37:16); *yhwh bōrē' haššāmayim hû' hā'ĕlōhîm . . . 'ānî yhwh wĕ'ên 'ôd*, (Thus says) "Yahweh, creator of heaven and

significant role in the religion of Israel. The study will begin with a philological and historical analysis of *'ĕlōhîm*'s counterparts in extrabiblical sources and then, on the basis of the results obtained, examine the meaning of *'ĕlōhîm* as a common noun in the Hebrew Bible. In the next chapter, we will make a historical-critical analysis of biblical texts which indicate that *'ĕlōhîm* played a special role in state-sponsored Israelite religion. The final chapter will address *'ĕlōhîm*'s use in Pentateuchal E, the portion of the Hebrew Bible in which *'ĕlōhîm* figures most prominently as a literary expression.[12]

---

earth—he is God! . . . 'I am Yahweh; there is no other'" (Isa 45:18).

[12]As mentioned, other major portions of the Bible in which *'ĕlōhîm* is an important designation of Israel's god are the Pentateuchal Priestly material and the so-called "Elohistic Psalter" (Pss 42-83). The former stands outside of the scope of this study due to its exilic or postexilic date (regarding which, see Driver, *Introduction*, 135-52; Cross, *CMHE*, 293; cf. Yehezkel Kaufmann, *The Religion of Israel* [trans. M. Greenberg; Chicago: Univ. of Chicago Press, 1960]; Jacob Milgrom, "Priestly ('P') Source," in *ABD* 5:454-61). The "Elohistic Psalter" is excluded from our analysis, in part, because the complexity of the issues pertaining to *'ĕlōhîm*'s place in the composition, editing, and collection of this series of psalms merits an entire study of its own. In addition, an evaluation of the historical and theological significance of *'ĕlōhîm* in this portion of the Bible would be dependent on the results of a study such as the one undertaken here.

Some of the issues raised in scholarship on the Elohistic Psalms bear mentioning. Against the longstanding (since the time of Heinrich Ewald, *The Psalms Chronologically Arranged* [London: Macmillan, 1867]) view that the prevalence of *'ĕlōhîm* in reference to God in Pss 42-83 was the result of a late (i.e., postexilic) editorial substitution of the title *'ĕlōhîm* for *yhwh*, which was motivated either by a distaste for the provincial overtones of the latter (see Fohrer, *Introduction*, 294) and/or by an emerging pious reluctance to pronounce the divine name (see Fohrer, *Introduction*, 294; Soggin, *Introduction*, 367), Robert Boling employed statistical and poetic analysis to demonstrate that the "Elohistic Psalter" represents a stylistically variant Psalms recension of a date not significantly later than that of the rest of the Psalter, in which a "fixed traditional sequence in poetic construction" shows *'ĕlōhîm* to be the preferred designation for the deity ("'Synonymous' Parallelism in the Psalms," *JSS* 5 [1960]: 221-57).

It is unclear whether *'ĕlōhîm*'s northern Israelite associations, such as will be determined by this study, have a direct bearing on the preference for *'ĕlōhîm* in Pss 42-83. The work of some scholars suggests that many Elohistic and some "non-Elohistic" Psalms were northern Israelite in origin; see Martin J. Buss, "The Psalms of Asaph and Korah," *JBL* 82 (1963): 387; Michael Goulder, *The Psalms of the Sons of Korah* (JSOTSup 20; Sheffield: Sheffield Academic Press, 1982); idem, *The Psalms of Asaph and the Pentateuch: Studies in the Psalter, III* (JSOTSup 233; Sheffield: Sheffield Academic Press, 1996); Gary A. Rendsburg, *Linguistic Evidence for the Northern Origin of Selected Psalms* (SBLMS 4; Atlanta: Scholars, 1990); William L. Holladay, "Psalms from the North," in *The Psalms through Three Thousand Years: Prayerbook of a Cloud of Witnesses* (Minneapolis: Fortress, 1993), 36-46.

CHAPTER 2

'Ělōhîm and Its Extrabiblical Counterparts

The reassessment of biblical *'ĕlōhîm* begins with a philological examination of *'ĕlōhîm*'s counterparts in extrabiblical sources. A lexical analysis of Biblical Hebrew *'ĕlōhîm* as a common noun will follow upon the results obtained from the comparative material.

THE COMPARATIVE EVIDENCE FOR BIBLICAL *'ĕlōhîm*

The comparative evidence for *'ĕlōhîm* provides a historical and philological frame of reference for understanding the Hebrew expression. The extrabiblical sources that offer a usage corresponding to *'ĕlōhîm*, i.e., the grammatically plural form meaning "gods" used as a singular, are Late Bronze Age cuneiform documents from Syria-Palestine and, from the first millennium, Northwest Semitic inscriptions and Akkadian texts from Mesopotamia. Both *'ĕlōhîm*'s plural form and its meaning are better understood in the light of the comparative data.

The Late Bronze Age Antecedent

Description of the Usage

The earliest attested parallels for *'ĕlōhîm* occur in Late Bronze Age cuneiform documents from Amarna, Qatna, Taanach, and Ugarit. The use of *ilānū*—literally, "the gods," written logographically, usually DINGIR.MEŠ(-nu)[1]—as a singular in western peripheral Akkadian is

---

[1]The "particularizing" sense of the ending *-ānū* in standard Akkadian (as argued by Albrecht Goetze, "The Akkadian Masculine Plural in *-ānū/ī* and its Semitic Background," *Language* 22 [1946]: 121-30; see also Wilfrom von Soden, *Grundriss der Akkadischen*

an exact parallel to Hebrew *'ĕlōhîm*. Our examination of the meaning, grammar, and geography of the Late Bronze expression will show that it represents the pre-Israelite antecedent of *'ĕlōhîm*.

The use of Akkadian *ilānū* as a singular in the Canaanite vassal correspondence was recognized early on in the study of the Amarna letters as a parallel to Biblical Hebrew *'ĕlōhîm*.[2] In the majority of instances (over a hundred times), the term is taken up in reference to the Pharaoh, always in a string of flattering expressions. The most common formula, of which several variations exist, reads along the lines

> LUGAL EN-ia ᵈUTU-ia / DINGIR.MEŠ-ia
> *šarri bēlīya šamšīya ilānīya*
> the king, my lord, my sungod, my god.

The phrase may occur in the introduction, within the body of the letter, or both. Less frequently, the element "my god" is written in the singular as in EA 156:1:

> a-na LUGAL EN-ia DINGIR-ia ᵈ[U]TU-ia
> *ana šarri bēlīya ilīya šamšīya*
> To the king, my lord, my god, my sungod.

In other instances, in which singular *ilānū* is used in reference not to the Pharaoh but to proper deities, the morphologically plural substantive functions grammatically as a singular. Two examples are as follows:

Grammatik [2d ed.; AnOr 33, 47; Rome: Pontifical Biblical Institute, 1969], §61i and Giorgio Buccellati, "The Case Against the Alleged Akkadian Plural Morpheme -*ĀNŪ*," *Afroasiatic Linguistics* 3 [1976]: 28-30) is not consistently operative in peripheral dialects, in which the affix appears in the normal plural forms of *ilu* "god," *ālu* "city," and *šarru* "king"; see John Huehnergard, *A Grammar of Akkadian* (HSS 45; Atlanta: Scholars Press, 1997), 20.2.

[2]See Franz M. Th. Böhl, *Der Sprache der Amarnabriefe* (Leipziger Semitistische Studien V/2; Leipzig: Hinrichs, 1909), 36; Johannes Hehn, *Die biblische und die babylonische Gottesidee: die israelitische Gottesauffassung im Lichte der altorientalischen Religionsgeschichte* (Leipzig: Hinrichs, 1913), 171-73.; Anton Jirku, *Altorientalischer Kommentar zum Alten Testament* (Leipzig: Deichert, 1923), 19; Otto Weber and Erich Ebeling, eds., *Die El-Amarna-Tafeln. Zweiter Teil: Anmerkungen und Register* (Vorderasiatische Bibliothek 2; Aalen: Otto Zeller, 1964; repr. of 1915 edition), 1190.

DINGIR.MEŠ-nu / šu-lum-ka šu-lum É-ka / li-iš-al
ilānū / šulumka šulum bītīka / lišāl
May the deity inquire concerning the welfare of you and your household.
(EA 96:4-6, an Egyptian "general" to Rib-Hadda of Byblos)

[DINGIR.M]EŠ šu-lum(!)-ka li-[iš-a]l
[ilā]nu šulumka li[šā]l
May the deity inquire concerning your welfare.
(EA 97:3, Yappaḫ-Hadda, Mayor of Beirut[?], to Šumu-Haddi, mayor[?]
detained in Egypt)[3]

In both of these passages the plural form *ilānū* is the subject of the singular verb *lišāl*. These two references from Amarna may be compared with an expression from a roughly contemporary letter found at Taanach:

EN DINGIR.MEŠ-nu / ZI-ka lí-iṣ-ṣur
bēlu ilānū / napištaka liṣṣur
May the lord, the god, protect your life![4]

In EA 129:50-52, *ilānū* is modified by a singular attributive adjective, where Rib-Hadda makes reference to *ilānī balṭi* (DINGIR.MEŠ ba-al-ṭi) his "living deity."[5] In EA 84:35, where he apparently speaks of the same deity,[6] the Byblian ruler refers to his god ^dDA.MU as *ilānū*.[7] In EA 74:56-57, *ilānū* occurs in apposition to "Our Lady," that is, the chief deity of Byblos.

Other instances of *ilānū* in apposition to a clear singular occur. In EA 189:13'-15', Aitukama of Qadesh recalls the assistance of the Egyptian king's chief god in battle:

---

[3]This identification is made by William L. Moran, ed. and trans., *The Amarna Letters* (Baltimore: Johns Hopkins Univ. Press, 1992), 384-85.

[4]Published by F. Hrozný in Ernst Sellin, *Tell Ta'annek* (Denkschriften der kaiserlichen Akademie der Wissenschaften in Wien, Philosophisch-Historische Klasse, vol. 50, no. IV; Vienna: Kaiserliche Akademie der Wissenschaft, 1904), 115; see also Anson F. Rainey, *Canaanite in the Amarna Tablets: A Linguistic Analysis of the Mixed Dialect Used by the Scribes from Canaan* (4 vols.; HO 25; Leiden: Brill, 1996), 1:147.

[5]Moran, *Amarna*, 211 n. 23; idem, "Early Canaanite *yaqtula*," *Orientalia* 29 (1960): 4 n. 3.

[6]Ibid.

[7]On the identity of this god, see Robert Steiglitz, "Ebla and the Gods of Canaan," in *Eblaitica: Essays on the Ebla Archives and Eblaite Language* (ed. C. H. Gordon and G. A. Rendsburg; Winona Lake, Ind.: Eisenbrauns, 1990), 2:81.

il$_5$-la-ak / DINGIR.MEŠ-nu-ka u ^{d}UTU-ka / a-na pa-ni-ia
illak / ilānūka u šamaška / ana panīya
. . . your god, namely your sungod, going before me.

Another example is EA 161:32-33

DINGIR.MEŠ-nu-ka ù ^{d}UTU lu-ú i-du-ú-ni$_7$
ilānūka u šamaška lū idūn-ni
May your deity, namely your sungod, bear witness for me!

In both examples the use of a singular verb of which *ilānū* is the subject confirms that *ilānū* is to be understood as a singular in apposition to another singular form.[8]

The Akkadian evidence from Ugarit requires special consideration. The relevant passages are as follows:

RS 20.33:30'-32'[9]
ù šum-ma i-na-an-din DINGIR.MEŠ a-na ŠU-ti-ni / ù lu-ú
ni-ra-aḫ-ḫi-iš ^{UZU}DUR-šu i-na KI BAR / ù i-gám-me-ru-nim l-en zé-ra-ni-ia
And if the god(s) permit(s) us—then we shall smash its *body* in the enemy's[7]
country[7] and once and for all my enemies will be annihilated.[10]

RS 25.134:20
a-ia i-din DINGIR.MEŠ-nu
May the god(s) forbid!

---

[8]See the explanation of this construction in these passages as appositional by Nadav Na'aman, "On Gods and Scribal Traditions in the Amarna Letters," *UF* 22 (1990): 255. There Na'aman also notes the clearly singular meaning of the expression "the god of the king" (DINGIR ša LUGAL, EA 179:23; 250:20, 49; 337:14) as a parallel to these references to the Pharaoh's deity. For other examples of the appositive use of the conjunction, see EA 141:13; 157:5, 40; 160:33; 192:1-2, 8, 11; 242:2, 7; 243:1-2, 6; 248:1-2, 6-7; 281:1-2; 330:5-6; cf. the Biblical Hebrew *waw explicativum* (GKC §154a n. [b]).

[9]Shlomo Izre'el and Itamar Singer, *The General's Letter from Ugarit: A Linguistic and Historical Reevaluation of RS 20.33* (Ugaritica V, No. 20; Tel Aviv: Tel Aviv Univ., 1990). The letter, from a military commander to a king of Ugarit whose name is not given, is dated to the mid-fourteenth century B.C.E. (Izre'el and Singer, *General's Letter*, 13, 180-83).

[10]Izre'el ("Early Northwest Semitic 3rd pl m Prefix: The Evidence of the Amarna Letters," *UF* 19 [1987]: 83) treats DINGIR.MEŠ in this passage as a singular; but cf. Izre'el and Singer, *General's Letter*, 26-27, 49, where it is regarded as a collective plural.

RS 15.109:55-56
DINGIR.MEŠ-nu MU-šu li-ḫal-li-iq
May the god(s) blot out his name!

The phonetic complement in the last two instances makes it clear that we are dealing here, as in the case of the Amarna evidence, not with a "logogram marker"[11] but with plural *ilānū*. In all three passages *ilānū* is the subject of a singular verb. The situation, though, is not as unambiguous as it may seem. Huehnergard explains that in Ugaritic-Akkadian plural subjects frequently occur with singular verbs,[12] a phenomenon that van Soldt calls verbal "plurals without -*ū* or -*ā*."[13] In light of this tendency at Ugarit, *ilānū* in the given passages may be understood as a numerical (collective) plural.[14]

However, other factors to be considered below favor a different conclusion. The abstract plural, the grammatical category to which Late Bronze Age singular *ilānū* at Amarna and elsewhere belongs, was in use at Ugarit (see below, Grammatical Issues).[15] The contextual usage of *ilānū* in these passages is similar to those from Amarna and Taanach (see below, The Meaning of the Late Bronze Age Expression). The location of Ugarit fits well into the geographic pattern represented by the Amarna usage (see below, Geographic Distribution of the Late Bronze Age Expression). The evidence taken as a whole favors the conclusion that singular *ilānū* at Ugarit represents the same

---

[11]Compare the comments of Aage Westenholz, who suggests that the plural ideogram MEŠ following subjects of singular verb forms "is redundant and merely indicates that the preceding sign is a logogram" ("Some Notes on the Orthography and Grammar of the Recently Published Texts from Mari," *BO* 35 [1978]: 165-66 n. 53). The suggestion that logogram markers occur occasionally at Ugarit was first made by Jean Nougayrol, *Ugaritica V* (Paris: Paul Geuthner, 1968), 146 n. 2. There is no pattern that suggests any system of logogram markers was employed in the Amarna letters; see Rainey's discussion of plural markers in *CAT* 1:27-28.

[12]John Huehnergard, *The Akkadian of Ugarit* (HSS 34; Atlanta, Ga.: Scholars Press, 1989), 145 and n. 115, 231-32.

[13]Wilfred Hugo van Soldt, *Studies in the Akkadian of Ugarit: Dating and Grammar* (AOAT 40; Kevelaer: Butzon & Bercker, 1991), 438-40.

[14]See Izre'el and Singer, *General's Letter*, 26-27, 49; Izre'el, review of Huehnergard, *Akkadian of Ugarit* in *BO* 49 (1992): 178; cf. Isre'el, "3rd pl m Prefix," 83.

[15]See in EA 45:32, 33 from Ammishtamru of Ugarit TI.LA.MEŠ ("life"), a writing which corresponds to Ugaritic *ḥym*; see below, Grammatical Issues.

phenomenon manifest in the preferred expression for "god" along the Levantine coast during the Late Bronze Age.

Both the grammatical function of *ilānū* as a singular and its use in reference to individual deities make it clear that the plural form of the word for "god" was used with a singular meaning during the Late Bronze Age in cuneiform sources from Syria-Palestine. In this respect the Late Bronze Age usage is exact in its correspondence to Hebrew singular *'ĕlōhîm* (and to Phoenician *'lm* in its use as a singular—see below, Phoenician). As others have observed, the correspondence of the Late Bronze Age form to *'ĕlōhîm* suggests that it was the historical precursor to the biblical expression.[16]

The Geographic Distribution of the Late Bronze Age Expression

The historical relationship between the Late Bronze Age usage and biblical *'ĕlōhîm* becomes even clearer in view of the geographic distribution of the former. All of the instances of singular *ilānū* at Amarna occur in letters to the Egyptian king or to an Egyptian official from vassals in Palestine and southern Syria, the only exception being EA 96:4-6 (from an Egyptian official in Canaan to Rib-Hadda). The usage seems to have radiated from the Phoenician coast. Its occurrence at Ugarit and Qatna is consistent with such a pattern. The geographic distribution of the usage and its exact correspondence both to Hebrew *'ĕlōhîm* and to Phoenician *'lm*[17] leave little room for doubt that Late Bronze Age singular *ilānū* is an Akkadian expression of a Canaanite antecedent of those Iron Age forms. A closer examination of the data reinforces this conclusion.

The Late Bronze Age usage was current along the Phoenician coast, in the cities of Tyre (EA 147:1; 148:1; 149:1; 151:2, 4; 152:4), Sidon (EA 144:1-2, 6, 8), Beirut (EA 141:1-2, 6, 10, 13, etc.) and Byblos (EA 74:56-57; 84:33, 35; 129:50-52), in the Orontes Valley at Qadesh (EA 189 rev. 13) and Qatna (EA 55:42; Temple Inventory II:1, 31, 43, 44 B; IV:rev. 9),[18] and further inland at Ruḫizzi[19] (EA

---

[16]See Hehn, *babylonische Gottesidee*, 173, 184-85 and n. 2; William F. Albright, *From the Stone Age to Christianity* (2d ed.; Garden City, N.Y.: Doubleday, 1957), 213.

[17]See below, Phoenician.

[18]On the Qatna Temple Inventories, see below, The Meaning of the Late Bronze Age Expression.

192:1-2, 8, 11). Following the coast northward from Phoenicia, the expression is found at Ugarit (RS 15.109:55-56; 20.33:30'-32'; 25.134:20). South of the Phoenician plain, it is attested at Acco (EA 235:2); from there inland at Megiddo (EA 245:3-4), Taanach (TT 2:2), and nearby Aḫtiašna[20] (EA 319:1, 9-11). Further south still, singular *ilānū* is found at Ashkelon (EA 320:1-3; 321:1-3; 322:1-2; 323:1-2; 324:1-2; 325:1-2; 326:1) and not far inland at Gezer (EA 292:1-2, 5-6; 293:5-6; 294:1-2, 4-5; 295:5-6; 297:1-2, 5-6; 298:1-2, 9-10; 299:1-2, 7-8; 378:1), Lachish (EA 328:1; 329:1-2; 330:5-6; 331:1-2, 7-8, 21-22), and at the unnamed location of Šuwardata (EA 278:1-2, 6-7; 279:1-2, 6-7; 280:1-2, 6-7; 281:1-2; 282:1-2; 283:1-2; 366:1-2).[21] The usage bears a close association with the coastal and lowland areas of Palestine and Syria. By contrast, the use of morphologically singular *ilu*, both in the address formulae and in other contexts from Amarna, is found almost exclusively in mountain and hinterland sites: Shechem (EA 252:12-13, 29-30), Ḥasi (EA 175:1, 18; 185:1, 5, 7, 15, 30; 186:9, 11, 29, etc.), Ḥašabu (EA 174:26), Guddašuna (EA 177:1),[22] Enišasi (EA 187:7, 10, 13, 24), and Mušiḫuna (EA 182:4, 13).[23]

The pattern that emerges from the evidence is impressive. The variation between the singular and plural forms corresponds quite dramatically to the topographical division between the coasts and valleys on the one hand and the mountains and hinterlands on the other, a distinction which, since the important work of Albrecht Alt on this subject,[24] has been recognized as decisive for the population and

---

[19]The remarks of Akizzi of Qatna (EA 53:36-39) indicate that Ruḫizzi (along with Lapana) was in league with Qadesh and lay somewhere between the latter and Damascus.

[20]On the location of Aḫtiašna, see Moran, *Amarna*, 350 n.1.

[21]In view of the content of EA 279 and 280, it seems that Šuwardata ruled from somewhere in the Shephelah within easy reach of Keilah.

[22]On the close association of Guddašuna and Enišasi with Ḥasi and Ḥašabu, see the nearly identical parallels in both phraseology and content—especially regarding Aitukama of Qadesh—among the letters from these cities of the Lebanese Beqaʿ.

[23]On the location of Mušiḫuna, see Moran, *Amarna*, 391.

[24]Albrecht Alt, "Settlement of the Israelites in Palestine," in *Essays on Old Testament History and Religion* (trans. R. A. Wilson; Garden City, N.Y.: Doubleday, 1968), 175-221.

culture of Canaan during the Late Bronze Age and later.[25]   The distribution of the usage suggests that the preference for *ilānū* over *ilu* spread from the coastal plain into the valley systems and finally to the highlands, the course normally observed in the flow of linguistic and cultural change in the southern Levant.[26]   The conclusion that this movement of our Late Bronze Age usage into the central highlands of Palestine resulted ultimately in Hebrew *'ĕlōhîm* requires no great leap of imagination.   Singular *ilānū* at Amarna reflects a Canaanite usage that, like so many features of language and culture, spread from the coast to the interior by way of the valley systems and that had already reached as far inland as Qatna by the fifteenth century.[27]

The Origin of the Expression

The geographic distribution of the usage suggests two possibilities for its place of origin: either (1) a location outside of Canaan, from which the usage would have gained entry by way of the port cities, or (2) the Phoenician coast itself, from which the usage would have spread inland. The most likely candidate for the former would, of course, be Egypt, whose political and cultural dominance over the southern Levant, especially the lowland areas, was definitive for the area during this period.[28]   An Egyptian origin is the explanation that has been

---

[25]On the coastland-inland division as a decisive factor for linguistic change, see Zellig Harris, *Development of the Canaanite Dialects: An Investigation in Linguistic History* (AOS 16; New Haven: American Oriental Society, 1939); more generally, on the importance of geographic zones for the history and archaeology of Syria-Palestine, see, e.g., Israel Finkelstein, *The Archaeology of the Israelite Settlement* (Jerusalem: Israel Exploration Society, 1988); Lawrence E. Stager, "The Archaeology of the Family in Ancient Israel," *BASOR* 260 (1985): 1-35; C. Nicholas Raphael, "Geography and the Bible (Palestine)," *ABD* 2:964-77.

[26]Harris, *Canaanite Dialects*, 98; on the effects of physical geography and political, economic, and sociocultural factors on linguistic change in Syria-Palestine in general, see W. Randall Garr, *Dialect Geography of Syria-Palestine, 1000-586 B.C.E.* (Philadelphia: University of Pennsylvania Press, 1985), esp. 1-21, 232-40 and the comments of William H. Moran, "The Hebrew Language in its Northwest Semitic Background," in *The Bible and the Ancient Near East: Essays in Honor of William Foxwell Albright* (ed. G. Ernest Wright; Garden City, N.Y.: Doubleday, 1961), 59.

[27]See the discussion of the Qatna Temple Inventories below, The Meaning of the Late Bronze Age Expression.

[28]See Amihai Mazar, "In the Shadow of Egyptian Domination: The Late Bronze Age (ca. 1550-1200 B.C.E.)," in *Archaeology of the Land of the Bible 10,000-586*

suggested by Benedikt Hartmann.[29] He argues that singular *ilānū* is non-Semitic in origin and that it arose from the court language of the Egyptian realm of political control including Palestine and southern Syria, where eventually the term was appropriated for religious use.[30] Hartmann's focus on political language is determined by the restriction of his discussion to references to the Egyptian king as *ilānū* in the Amarna letters; no mention is made of the term's use in references to gods. The argument's lack of explicitness regarding Egyptian origins is no doubt due to the complete absence of evidence for such origins. Egyptian texts—religious or political, from the Amarna period or any other—seem to offer no usage of *nṯrw* (the plural of *nṯr* "god") analogous to Akkadian singular *ilānū* in the Amarna letters (and at Late Bronze Age Taanach, Qatna, and Ugarit). It almost goes without saying that no such analogue is to be found in any other relevant language corpus. Hartmann denies Semitic origins for the expression simply because it is not Common Semitic; it is not attested before the Late Bronze Age and does not occur in Mesopotamian Akkadian before the seventh century (see below, First-Millennium Akkadian). He does not seem to consider whether the usage arose as a development within Canaanite, a question begged by the lack of evidence for Egyptian or other non-Semitic origins.

Upon examination of the relevant Canaanite linguistic evidence, a solution emerges. As is demonstrated below the Canaanite usage reflected in singular *ilānū* is at home within the grammar of the Iron Age expressions of that language group (see below, Grammatical Issues). Like *ilānū*, Biblical Hebrew *'ĕlōhîm* and Phoenician *'lm* are examples of the "concretized" abstract plural, a grammatical category operative in those Iron Age languages and in the Canaanite of the Amarna letters (see below). These factors indicate that the "divine plural" was an originally Canaanite development.

B.C.E. (Anchor Bible Reference Library; New York: Doubleday, 1992), 232-94; Robert S. Merrilees, "Political Conditions in the Eastern Mediterranean during the Late Bronze Age," *BA* 49 (1986): 42-50; James M. Weinstein, "The Egyptian Empire in Palestine: A Reassessment," *BASOR* 241 (1981): 1-28.

[29]"Elōhīm als Singular," *MUSJ* 48 (1972-1973): 67-76.

[30]Ibid., 74-76.

The Meaning of the Late Bronze Age Expression

As Böhl observed,[31] the juxtaposition of the plural and singular forms of the word for god in the greeting of EA 151 seems to suggest that singular *ilānū* conveys a meaning different from that of simple *ilu*. The text reads

> a-na LUGAL ᵈUTU-ia DINGIR-ia DINGIR.MEŠ-ia
> *ana šarri šamšīya ilīya ilānīya*
> To the king, my sungod, my god, my deity.
> (EA 151:1, Abimilku of Tyre to the Egyptian king)

An explanation offered as early as 1913 by Johannes Hehn[32] and a few decades later by Albright[33] is that the plural denotes a multiplicity of gods and thus equates the individual or deity so designated as the embodiment of the pantheon. While this idea may be attractive against the backdrop of Bronze Age Canaanite religion, centering as it does around the local pantheon, it is inconsistent with the use of *ilānū* in some of the texts. The most striking example is EA 198:2, which refers to the Pharaoh as *ilānī ša qaqqadīya* (DINGIR.MEŠ ša SAG.DU-[ia]), literally "the god of my head," an idiom known from Old Assyrian[34] and Old Babylonian[35] to mean "my personal deity."[36] In a letter found at Mari, Yarim-Lim of Aleppo speaks of "Adad, the god of my city, and Sin, the god of my head" (ᵈIM ì-lí a-li-ia u ᵈEN.ZU ì-lí re-ši-ia).[37] Though, theoretically, the chief god of the pantheon could be one's personal deity, especially where a king is concerned, the notion of pantheon is incompatible with the expression *ilānī ša qaqqadi* and its meaning. This incompatibility is clear in the

---

[31]*Amarnabriefe*, 36.

[32]*Babylonische Gottesidee*, 173.

[33]*FSAC*, 213.

[34] ᵈ*Sin* DINGIR *rēšīya lū rābiṣ lemuttišu ana dārêtim* "May Sin my personal god relinquish his animosity forever!" (Šamši-Adad I; KAH 1 2 vi 19, cited in CAD *ilu* 1b, p. 96b).

[35]Published in Georges Dossin, "Une lettre de Iarîm-Lim, roi d'Alep, à Iašûb-Iahad, roi de Dîr," *Syria* 33 (1956): 65 line 28.

[36]CAD 7:96 (*ilu* 1b) renders "my own god"; see Hermann Vorländer, *Mein Gott: Die Vorstellungen vom persönlichen Gott im Alten Orient und im Alten Testament* (AOAT 23; Kevelaer: Butzon & Bercker, 1975), 21, 122, 158.

[37]Dossin, "Iarîm-Lim," 65 line 28.

Mari example, in which "the god of the head" and "the god of the city" (the leader of the pantheon, himself) are used as distinct terms. Thus our grammatically plural form requires a different explanation.

Putting aside for the moment the distinction between singular and plural that is apparent in the greeting formula of EA 151, one will observe that *ilānū* is used in various contexts with the same range of meanings as *ilu*. Consistent with its use in the idiom meaning "personal god" is the appearance of *ilānū* in the blessing formulae of EA 96 and 97 and the Taanach letter (all discussed above), which stresses the deity's concern and care for the individual. As noted, Rib-Hadda refers to his personal deity ᵈDA.MU (EA 84:35) and to the Lady of Byblos (EA 74:56-57 and the restored text of 77:30-35[38]) each as *ilānū*.[39] These instances are comparable to Lab'ayu's reference to his patron god as *ilu*:

> ṣa-ab-ta-at-mì URU / ù i-li
> *ṣabtat-mi ālu / u ilī*
> The city, along with my god, was seized. (EA 252:12-13)

> LÚ.MEŠ ša ṣa-ab-tu₄ URU / i-li šu-ṣú-mì a-bi-ia
> *amēlū ša ṣabtū āla / ilī šūṣū-mi abīya*
> . . . the men who stole the city (and) my god. They are the despoilers of my father. (lines 29-30)[40]

In reference to "the God of the King," both the singular form (EA 179:23; 250:20, 49; 337:14; 366:11-16, the last two letters referring to the Pharaoh himself by the plural form *ilānū* in the greeting formula) and the plural form (EA 161:32; 189:rev. 14 [which prefers *ilu* in its greeting formula]; 245:4) are attested. Every one of these instances is concerned with military and political events understood to lie within the Egyptian deity's sphere of control. Similarly, RS 20.33:30'-32' assumes the territorial deity's jurisdiction over such matters (see above).

Either form can be used in reference to a divine statue. As noted by Na'aman, in EA 164 Aziru of Amurru, using the term *ilānīya*

---

[38]Moran, *Amarna*, 148 n. 8.

[39]Na'aman, "Gods," 255; cf. Moran, *Amarna*, 143, 148.

[40]As Moran explains, "By taking the statue or image of the family god, Lab'ayu's enemies had violated his family" (*Amarna*, 306 n. 6).

(DINGIR.MEŠ-ia), makes reference to an image of his deity, which he sends with his messenger for the purpose of oath taking.[41] In EA 55:42 Akizzi of Qatna uses the plural form in reference to the pillaged statue of his god, which he also calls *il abīya*. The preceding two references may be compared with EA 252, in which Lab'ayu, using the singular form, remarks on the image of his patron deity (see above).

Evidence from the century preceding the Amarna period shows the singular and plural forms of the word "god" to be interchangeable in Canaan. A fifteenth-century Akkadian temple-inventory from Qatna uses the expression "the god of the king," written DINGIR.MEŠ LUGAL, in the heading of the text.[42] That DINGIR.MEŠ is intended here as a singular is indicated by the fact that it is the antecedent of 3 m. s. suffix pronouns used in the opening lines' description of adornments to be placed on the cult statue of the deity, on "its right (hand)" (*ša imittīšu*, line 5) and "its left" (*ša šumēlīšu*, line 9). This writing in the plural is in contrast with singular DINGIR LUGAL in another of the Qatna inventories (IV rev. 9).[43]

Another expression noted in the Amarna letters, "the god of the father," is also found in the first Qatna inventory mentioned, where it is written DINGIR.MEŠ ša a-bi (line 43) and DINGIR a-bi (line 44, the latter instance having the variant DINGIR.MEŠ a-bi in another copy of the text).[44] In the Qatna inventories *ilu* and *ilānū* appear to be equal variants, even in technical phrases.

The evidence from Amarna, Qatna, Taanach, and Ugarit, as a whole, shows that *ilānū* is used with the same range of meanings as simple *ilu*—in reference to the personal god, the patron god of the city, the imperial god, and divine images—and is even interchangeable with the singular form in various locutions. The conclusion to be drawn is that the plural form has basically the same meaning as the singular. However, going back to EA 151, *ilānū* seems to express a different connotation. This particular sense of the plural form becomes clearer in the light of a discussion of grammar.

---

[41]"Gods," 255.

[42]Jean Bottéro, "Les inventaires de Qatna," *RA* 43 (1949): 33-34, 174-75.

[43]Ibid., 184-85.

[44]Ibid., 33, 178-79.

Grammatical Issues

Before dealing with *ilānū*, it is appropriate to address the occurrence of other plural forms in the place of an expected singular in the Amarna letters. A number of nouns fall under the heading *plurale tantum*, or collective plurals, a usage which is not uncommon in standard Akkadian: *iprē* (SAḪAR.MEŠ) "dust" (EA 233:7; 234:5; 235:6; 241:5), *ṭīṭē* (IM.MEŠ) "clay" (EA 220:6), *qaqqarē* (KI.MEŠ) "dirt" (EA 234:5), *ṣābū* (ÉRIN.MEŠ) "troop" (EA 126:25; 129:36; 138:61).[45]

Other cases (including *ilānū*) in which plural nouns occur as grammatically singular are frequently explained by recourse to a supposed "plural of amplitude," "excellence," or "majesty."[46] However, a closer review of the passages in question shows the existence of such a phenomenon in the Amarna letters to be doubtful. Weighing against this solution, first of all, is the plural writing of the word "servant" (ÌR.MEŠ, EA 47:11), a usage which Böhl ironically termed *plurale modestiae*.[47] Furthermore, the understanding of a "plural of majesty" in relationship to the Egyptian king does not hold up to scrutiny. The plural writing of "lands" is used in reference not only to Egypt (KUR.MEŠ mi-iṣ-ri-e, EA 137:28) but also to the territories belonging to Qatna (KUR.KUR-tum an-nu-ú, EA 55:8, 18; cf., in the same breath, the reference to Egypt by the singular form of the word in line 19)[48] and to Amurru (EA 45:24). The usage in question is clearly collective. The plural writing of the "mouth" of the king (ᵁᶻᵁpí-MEŠ, EA 147:20; 155:44; KA.MEŠ, EA 147:24) denotes a "logical, or inherent, dual" in reference to the body part.[49]

---

[45]von Soden, *GAG*, §61h.

[46]Böhl, *Amarnabriefe*, pp. 35-36; Na'aman, "Gods," 255; Rainey, *CAT* 1:147-48; Helmer Ringgren, "אֱלֹהִים *ʾlōhîm*," *TDOT* 1:272-73.

[47]*Amarnabriefe*, 36. Below, the passage is cited fully and the relevant grammatical category, the abstract plural, is discussed.

[48]be-lí a-na pa-ni ÉRIN.MEŠ-ka ù a-na pa-ni ᴳᴵˢGIGIR.MEŠ-ka / KUR.KUR-tum gab-bá i-pal-la-ḫé / šum-ma be-lí-ia KUR.KUR-tum an-nu-ú / a-na ša KUR-šu i-ṣa-ab-bat-šu, "My lord, the whole country is in fear of your troops and chariots. If my lord would take this country for his own country . . ." (lines 16-18; translation and reading of line 17 by Moran, *Amarna*, 127 and 128 n. 3).

[49]Celia Grave, "On the Use of an Egyptian Idiom in an Amarna Letter from Tyre and in a Hymn to the Aten," *OrAnt* 19 (1980): 209-10.

Mention of the Egyptian king's "house" by the plural (É.MEŠ, EA 5:9; É.GAL.MEŠ, EA 126:20) is logical either as a composite or an abstract plural (see below) in the sense of "household" or "dynasty." Reference to the Pharaoh as "the Sun God" by the plural form (^{d}UTU.MEŠ, EA 195:18; 281:2; 296:7) reflects a familiarity (albeit a superficial one) with the multiple manifestations of the solar deity (and other deities, often depicted in combination) in Egyptian religion.[50] Excluding of course the use of *ilānū*, this is the only deity in the entire corpus named by the plural, including references to the Pharaoh as "the Storm God" (^{d}IM, EA 108:9; 147:14; 149:7; 159:7). The inherent plurality of the Egyptian sun god is signified in a letter from Rib-Hadda, where Amun is the subject of a plural verb (EA 71:4-6).[51] The use of singular *ilu* in this passage and in EA 86:3-5 is consistent with the fact that the notion of plurality pertaining to Amun in this context is totally separate from the phenomenon denoted by *ilānū*.

Though lumping all of these cases together within the same group would be convenient, no single category presents itself as a common explanation. If a "plural of majesty" was operative in the language of the Canaanite rulers of the Amarna period, it lacks unambiguous evidence. That many of the supposed instances happen to be associated with the Egyptian king is not an unlikely coincidence in the Amarna letters.

Having established the Late Bronze Age expression's historical relationship to Biblical Hebrew *'ĕlōhîm*, one may include the biblical as well as the cuneiform evidence in the grammatical discussion. Of course, the scholarly characterization of *ilānū* as "plural of majesty/excellence/amplitude" took its point of departure from an

---

[50]See, e.g., Jan Assmann, *Egyptian Solar Religion in the New Kingdom: Re, Amun, and the Crisis of Polytheism* (trans. A. Alcock; London: Kegan Paul, 1995); Erik Hornung, *Conceptions of God in Ancient Egypt: The One and the Many* (trans. John Baines; Ithaca, N.Y.: Cornell Univ. Press, 1982), esp. 92-99; Stephen Quirke, *Ancient Egyptian Religion* (London: British Museum Press, 1992), 21-52.

[51] ^{d}a-ma-na DINGIR ša LUG[A]L [EN-k]a / ti-di-nu TÉŠ-ka i-na / pa-ni LUGAL be-li-ka, "May Aman, the god of the king, [y]our lord, establish your honor in the presence of the king, your lord" (EA 71:4-6; the same formula is found in EA 86:3-5); cf. the characterization of this verb (!) as a "plural of majesty" in William Moran, "New Evidence on Canaanite *taqtulū(na)*," *JCS* 5 (1951): 35 n. 14.

explanation of *'ĕlōhîm* in Hebrew grammar.[52] As we shall see, the reliance on this category proves to be just as groundless with respect to *'ĕlōhîm* as it is to the Late Bronze Age antecedent.

Rainey is on the right track when he states that *ilānū* as a singular seems to have been "conceived as a kind of abstract."[53] This observation cuts through much of the confusion caused by the imprecise and misleading phrases "plural of majesty," "plural of intensity," or "plural of excellence." The usage in question, as explained in GKC, is a variety of the abstract plural, which sums up "the *conditions* or *qualities* inherent in the idea of the stem."[54] Examples include *zĕqūnîm* "old age," *sanwērîm* "blindness," *'ônîm* "might," *'ēṣôt* "counsel," *ḥărāpôt* "contempt," *nĕqāmôt* "vengeance," and *nĕgîdîm* "nobility"—only a small sampling of a category that is abundantly represented in Biblical Hebrew. The use of the abstract plural at Late Bronze Age Ugarit is illustrated in the plural writing of the word "life" (TI.LA.MEŠ) in EA 45:32-33 from Ammishtamru of Ugarit, a usage which corresponds not only to Biblical Hebrew *ḥayyîm* and Phoenician *ḥym* but also to Ugaritic *ḥym*. In Phoenician, the grammatical category is represented also by **'dnm* "lordship."[55] The abstract plural, so common in Biblical Hebrew, was operative to some extent in Phoenician, in Ugaritic, and, as explained below, in the Canaanite of the Amarna letters. *'Ĕlōhîm* and its Late Bronze Age and Iron Age counterparts represent a specific kind of abstract plural.

Some abstract plurals—like Hebrew singular *'ădōnîm* "lord(ship),"[56] *bĕ'ālîm* "owner(ship),"[57] and *'ăbôt* "father(hood)"[58]

---

[52]Böhl, *Amarnabriefe*, p.35; Weber and Ebeling, *El-Amarna-Tafeln* 2:1190; Hartmann, "Elōhim," 75-76; see the citations of grammatical reference sources in the following paragraph.

[53]*CAT* 1:147.

[54]GKC §124 d, g; cf. Edward C. Mitchell and Emil Kautzsch, *Gesenius' Hebrew Grammar* (trans. B. Davies; Andober: Warren F. Draper, 1884), §108 2.b; Aaron Ember, "The Pluralis Intensivus in Hebrew," *AJSL* 21 (1905): 207-15; Joüon and Muraoka, *Grammar*, §136 d.

[55]*KAI* 26 A 10; see Stanislav Segert, *A Grammar of Phoenician and Punic* (Munich: C. H. Beck, 1976), 174, 282; cf. Herbert Donner and Wolfgang Röllig, *Kanaanäische und aramäische Inschriften*, Band II. *Kommentar* (Wiesbaden: Otto Harrassowitz, 1964), 40; John C. L. Gibson, *Textbook of Syrian Semitic Inscriptions*, vol. 3. *Phoenician Inscriptions* (Oxford: Clarendon, 1982), 47.

[56]Gen 40:7; Gen 24:9; Exod 21:4, 6, 8, 32; Deut 23:16; Judg 19:11, 12; 1 Kgs 16:24; Ps 123:2; Job 3:19; Prov 25:13, etc.; see the dictionaries.

and Phoenician singular *'bt* "father(hood)"[59]—can be used in reference to a single individual or object that is exemplary of the quality named and to which a corresponding status applies.[60] The term "concretized abstract plural" is preferable to others that have been mentioned, because it is more precise and not susceptible to the mistaken notion that the plural form implies a quality of might, excellence, or superiority which may or may not characterize the referent of the word.[61]   Again, in the case of the abstract plural, the emphasis conveyed by the plural form pertains not to the object denoted but to the meaning of the substantive itself.   Thus the suffix form of *bĕtûlîm* in Lev 21:13 (*wĕhû' 'iššâ bibtûlêhā yiqqāḥ*, "And he shall take a wife in her virginity") does not mean "mighty virgin" but "virginity," emphasizing the *idea* associated with the stem, i.e., an abstraction.   In Deut 22:14, 15, 17 the same abstract plural is used in a concretized sense in reference to the "*evidence* of virginity": *wĕhôṣî'û 'et-bĕtûlê hanna'ǎrâ 'el-ziqnê hā'îr*, "And they shall bring the evidence of the young woman's virginity to the elders of the city" (v. 15).   Here the abstract plural is used in reference to a concrete object representing the status of "virginity."   This use of *bĕtûlîm* is an example of the concretized abstract plural.   An example in which an abstract plural is used in reference to a person is found in Dan 9:23, where the angel Gabriel tells Daniel that he has been given a divine order to impart special understanding to Daniel, "because you are one highly esteemed [precious, desirable]" (*kî ḥǎmûdôt 'attâ*).   Daniel's special status before God as one who is "highly esteemed" is denoted by the concretized use

---

[57]Exod 21:29; Isa 1:3; etc.; see the dictionaries.

[58]Ps 109:14; note the parallel between *'ăwōn 'ăbōtāyw* "the iniquity of his father(s)" and *ḥaṭṭa't 'immô* "the sin of his mother."

[59]*KAI* 26 A i 12; Gibson, *Textbook*, 3:58; cf. Donner and Röllig, *KAI*, 2:40; see below, Phoenician.

[60]See Walther Eichrodt's discussion of a similar idea in *Theology of the Old Testament* (trans. J. A. Baker; 2 vols.; OTL; Philadelphia: Westminster, 1961), 1:185.

[61]A term comparable to the one adopted here is Otto Eissfeldt's reference to the grammatical category "substantivisches Abstraktum" or "konkretes Substantiv" in connection with the title *yhwh ṣĕbā'ôt* ("Jahwe Zebaoth," in *Kleine Schriften* 3 [Tübingen: J. C. B. Mohr, 1966], 106, 110-13). See below for further discussion of Eissfeldt's remarks in this connection.

of the abstract plural *ḥămûdôt* "desirableness," "preciousness."[62] The person or object denoted by the abstract plural partakes of a certain status indicated by the noun. The same understanding pertains to other instances in which the abstract plural refers to an individual. That singular *'ădōnîm* and *bĕ'ālîm*, and, to some extent, *'ābôt* and *ḥămûdôt* designate individuals who are characterized by might or superiority is accidental, but corresponding plurals in reference to less prominent figures seem to be lacking. It has been argued that *tĕrāpîm*, the term for a household divine image, is disparaging in its basic meaning, but the etymology has yet to be explained satisfactorily.[63]

While Biblical Hebrew does not offer an example of *'ăbādîm* "slaves/servanthood" as a concretized abstract plural in reference to an individual, its counterpart is attested in Late Bronze Age Canaanite. In EA 47:10-11, the Canaanite vassal tells the Egyptian king

a-na-ku a-na LUGAL ᵈUTU-ši / [EN-i]a lu-ú ÌR.MEŠ-ma
anāku ana šarri šamši [bēlī]a lū ardū-ma
I am truly a servant to the king, the Sun, [m]y [lord].

Like singular *ilānū*, this Amarna example clearly reflects the concretized abstract plural in Canaanite, from which the usage so commonly attested in Hebrew was derived.

The evidence from Late Bronze Age cuneiform, Phoenician, and Biblical Hebrew indicates that the concretized abstract plural was a Canaanite linguistic development. According to this grammatical category, the plural form denoted an individual person or thing representing a certain status expressed as an abstraction. Hebrew *'ĕlōhîm*, Phoenician *'lm*, and their Canaanite antecedent reflected in Late Bronze Age singular *ilānū* are best translated "divinity" or "deity," two English words in which the abstract noun is used in

---

[62]Eissfeldt ("Jahwe Zebaoth," 106, 110-13) mentions, in addition to this passage, PNN with the plural ending *-ôt* as examples of the "substantivisches Abstraktum" or "konkretes Substantiv." Though the PNN mentioned by Eissfeldt—which include *lappîdôt* "torches," *ṭabbā'ôt* "signet rings," *mĕrāyôt* "rebelliousness," and *šĕlōmôt* "peace," "peaceableness" and which, on the basis of the feminine plural ending, are relevant for the discussion of *ṣĕbā'ôt*—can be understood as abstractions, the exact referent of the quality or quantity denoted within each PN is uncertain, and thus these should be left aside as evidence relevant to our discussion.

[63]See Ludwig Koehler and Walter Baumgartner, *HAL*, 4:1651-53.

reference to an individual who represents the quality named and who holds that status.[64] As the interchangeableness of *ilānū* and simple *ilu* in the Qatna inventories suggests,[65] the distinction between the two as implied in EA 151 is one more of style than of meaning. Though the two forms of the word conveyed the same general sense, the abstract plural, as a more elaborate form of expression, was likely perceived as a more elegant and sophisticated usage.

Conclusions

The grammar, meaning, and geographic distribution of singular *ilānū* in cuneiform sources from Qatna, Taanach, Ugarit, and Amarna show it to have been the Late Bronze Age forerunner of biblical *'ĕlōhîm*. The Canaanite term reflected in Late Bronze Age singular *ilānu*, like its Iron Age reflex in Hebrew *'ĕlōhîm*, is an instance of a concretized abstract plural, a category well represented in Biblical Hebrew, which means "deity"—nothing more and nothing less. This understanding is critical to any historical or theological interpretation either of the Late Bronze references or of the biblical materials, including the E and P contributions to the Pentateuch and the "Elohistic Psalter." It also provides a point of departure for the investigation of *'ĕlōhîm*'s counterparts from the first millennium.

First-Millennium Parallels

Phoenician[66]

Like its Hebrew counterpart *'ĕlōhîm*, Phoenician *'lm* is an Iron Age expression derived from the Late Bronze Age Canaanite usage. As

---

[64]Other examples of the concretized abstract in English are "majesty," "lordship," and "honor," as titles of address—e.g., "your majesty," "your lordship," etc. As is the case with "deity" and "divinity," these are, semantically speaking, not strictly analogous to our Canaanite concretized abstract plurals, for the English examples are euphemisms employed to avoid inappropriately direct speech in reference to a revered individual or to avoid a specific term or name for a god.

[65]See above, The Meaning of the Late Bronze Age Expression.

[66]Most of the references cited below are discussed in Wolfgang Röllig, "El als Gottesbezeichnung im Phönizischen," in *Festschrift Johannes Friedrich* (ed. R. von Kienle et al; Heidelberg: Universitätsverlag, 1959), 403-16.

mentioned in the previous discussion, the Phoenician expression is an example of the concretized abstract plural. Though it appears more frequently in later Phoenician, '*lm* is preserved in an eighth-century inscription from Karatepe (*KAI* 26).[67]

It may be surprising that in the surviving epigraphic material from the first half of the first millennium B.C.E. singular '*lm* is attested in only one inscription, that one being from outside Phoenicia itself (though Karatepe is written in "proper" Tyro-Sidonian Phoenician). Otherwise, the term appears only in later Phoenician, usually from outside of the Phoenician homeland. Even more surprising, though, is that in the entire corpus not a single unambiguous instance of singular '*l* as a common noun is preserved. This paucity of occurrences of the common noun meaning "god" or "deity" is due no doubt in part to the accidents of preservation but also in part to context. The surviving texts are almost always memorials or records of some sort and not theological treatises. Where a deity is mentioned, it is usually by name, the label "god" or "deity" being unnecessary.[68] Where the singular appellative is employed, though, it is in the plural form '*lm*, the numerical plural being '*lnm*.[69]

Karatepe. Like Biblical Hebrew 'ĕlōhîm, Phoenician '*lm* is a concretized abstract plural. Another example of this usage in Phoenician is '*bt* in Karatepe (*KAI* 26) A i 12 (mentioned above, Grammatical Issues): *w'p b'bt p'ln kl mlk bṣdqy*, "Also every king treated me as a father because of my righteousness."[70] Examples of more general abstract plurals in Phoenician include *ḥym* "life" and

---

[67]Donner and Röllig, *KAI*, 2:40, 41-42; Röllig, "El," 404-5; and Gibson, *Textbook*, 3:57 n. 8; 64 n. 16. On singular '*lm* in Phoenician in general, see Zellig Harris, *A Grammar of the Phoenician Language* (AOS 8; New Haven: American Oriental Society, 1936), 60 (which was published before the discovery of the Karatepe inscriptions); Röllig, "El," 403-6; and Segert, *Phoenician*, 174-75.

[68]Cf. the convention attested in Egyptian and Palmyrene Aramaic, according to which the title "the god" often accompanies a given DN; see Delbert R. Hillers, "Palmyrene Aramaic Inscriptions and the Bible," *ZAH* 11 (1998): 34.

[69]Röllig, "El," 403-6, 407; see also Harris, *Grammar*, 60; Segert, *Phoenician*, 112, 175.

[70]See Gibson, *Textbook*, 3:58; cf. Donner and Röllig, *KAI*, 2:40.

from Karatepe *'dnm "lordship."[71] In three instances from Karatepe, 'lm expresses a general abstraction ("divinity") used in the adjectival genitive. The first of these is in the phrase "divine beings" (bn 'lm; KAI 26 A iii:19), a parallel to Biblical Hebrew běnê 'ēlîm (Ps 29:1; 89:7) and běnê hā'ĕlōhîm (Gen 6:2, 4; Job 1:6; 2:1). The second instance is found in the version of the text inscribed on a statue of the chief god of Azatiwada, the ruler celebrated in the inscription; it pronounces a curse upon anyone who would remove the ruler's name "from this divine statue" (bsml / '[l]m z; KAI 26 C iv:15-16). Line 19 of this same section also mentions "the divine statue (sml h'lm) which Azatiwada made." The importance of these references for our discussion is that they demonstrate that the use of Phoenician 'lm (like Biblical Hebrew 'ĕlōhîm) as a singular was dependent on its expression of a more general abstraction (i.e., "divinity"). It is the application of this abstract expression in a concretized sense that makes it suitable in reference to a single god ("deity"). A discussion of examples of the latter from Karatepe follows.

In the inscription, Azatiwada gives credit for the prosperity and peace that he has secured for his realm to "Ba'l and the Deity" (b'l w'lm; KAI 26 A i:8; ii:6; iii:11; C iv:12), i.e., to the dynastic god and the local patron god. That 'lm here refers to a single deity is made clear both by the use of 'ln(m) as the form of the numerical plural in the expression "all the gods of the city" (kl 'ln qrt; A iii:5)[72] and by the substitution of a specific DN elsewhere in place of 'lm (ršp sprm "Resheph ṢPRM"; KAI 26 A ii:10-11, 12).[73] Though the interpretation of this god's name is debated,[74] one can safely deduce from his role—shared with Ba'l-KRNTRYŠ, Azatiwada's personal god—in assuring the region's welfare and in commissioning the

---

[71]KAI 26 A i 10 bt 'dny bn'm wp'l 'nk lšrš 'dny n'm (And I established) "the house of my lordship in delightfulness, and I dealt pleasantly with the 'root' of my lordship"; Segert (Phoenician, 174, 282) characterizes 'dny here as an abstract plural; cf. Gibson, Textbook, 3:47, who treats the form as sg. 'dn + first-person common singular suffix pronoun -y, "my lord"; cf. Donner and Röllig, KAI, 2:40, who, though not recognizing the plural form, acknowledge the abstract meaning.

[72]Albertus van den Branden ("Les inscriptions phéniciennes de Karatepe," Melto 1 [1965]: 65), characterizes the expression of the singular by 'lm as "une sorte d'expression consacrée par l'usage, une sorte de cliché théologique."

[73]Donner and Röllig, KAI, 2:40, 41-42.

[74]Ibid.; van den Branden, "Karatepe," 68.

reconstruction of the city (renamed Azatiwadiya; *KAI* 26 A ii:10-12) that he is the local patron deity.[75]

The term *'lm* is used in reference to Azatiwada's dynastic god in the following lines from the exemplar inscribed on a statue of Baal:

> *wyšb / 'nk h'lm z b'l krntryš*
> And I caused this deity, Ba'l-KRNTRYŠ, to dwell (in the city).
> (*KAI* 26 C iii:15-16)[76]

Also, the blessing that accompanies the statue refers to offerings to be brought before "every image of this god" (*[']lm / kl hmskt z*; *KAI* 26 C iv:2-3).[77] Singular *'lm* at Karatepe parallels *'ĕlōhîm* as a concretized abstract plural in reference to a particular "deity." The Phoenician expression, like Biblical Hebrew *'ĕlōhîm*, is an Iron Age reflex of the Canaanite usage attested at Amarna.

Late Phoenician and Punic. Singular *'lm* persists in Phoenician and Punic long after the eighth century. The expression sometimes appears in apposition to a DN. Examples are *'lm nrgl*, "the deity Nergal" (*KAI* 59.2; third century B.C.E., Piraeus), and *'lm 'wgsts* (*KAI* 122.1, 14-16 C.E., Leptis Magna). Like appellative *'ĕlōhîm*,[78] Phoenician *'lm* can be used in reference to a goddess: *bbt 'lm 'štrt*, "in the temple of the deity, Ashtart" (*Le Muséon* 51: 286 line 6; 345-315 B.C.E., Cyprus); *lrbty l'lm 'drt 'š 'lm 'štrt w'lnm 'š*, "to my Lady, to the majestic deity Isis, the deity Ashtart and the deities who . . ." (*KAI* 48.2; first century B.C.E., Memphis). (Note in the last example the use of the form of the numerical plural *'lnm* in distinction to singular *'lm*.)

The late inscriptions provide abundant evidence that concrete singular *'lm* was derived from a general abstract usage of the plural form.[79] These include numerous technical phrases constructed with the adjectival genitive use of *'lm*. Examples are *b'lytn 'š 'lm*, "Ba'lyaton, man [i.e., "representative"] of the divine" (Cooke 150.5; fifth-fourth

---

[75]Compare van den Branden, "Karatepe," 65, but see 37, 50.

[76]Compare *yšb 'nk bn / b'l krntryš*, "I caused Ba'l-KRNTRYŠ to dwell in it (the city)" (*KAI* 26 A ii:18-19).

[77]On the translation of this difficult line, see Gibson, *Textbook*, 3:52-53, 64.

[78]See below, *'Ĕlōhîm* as a Common Noun.

[79]On the abstract nature of *'lm* in later Phoenician, see the comments of George Albert Cooke, *A Text-Book of North-Semitic Inscriptions* (Oxford: Clarendon, 1903), 99.

century B.C.E.; cf. Biblical Hebrew *'îš [hā]'ĕlōhîm*); *bn 'lm*, "divine being" (= Caesar Augustus; *KAI* 120.1; Leptis Magna, 8 B.C.E.; cf. Biblical Hebrew *bĕnê [hā]'ĕlōhîm*); *bt 'lm*, "house of the divine" (i.e., "temple"; *KAI* 60.2, 3, 4-5, 5; Piraeus, 96 B.C.E. [?]; cf. Biblical Hebrew *bêt [hā]'ĕlōhîm*); *mqm 'lm*, "establisher of the divine," a title attested in numerous inscriptions;[80] *ksp 'lm*, "divine treasury" (*KAI* 60:6; Piraeus, 96 B.C.E. [?]); *glb 'lm*, "divine tonsurer" (*CIS* I 257.3; 258.4-5; 259.3; 588.4-5); *'mt 'lm*, "female servant of the divine" (*CIS* I 378.3); *[m]yqṣ 'lm*, "designated of the divine"(?)[81] (*CIS* I 3921.1); *m'š 'lm*, "divine votive statue" (*KAI* 118.1; Ras el-Haddagia, 15-17 C.E.); *kl mrzḥ 'lm*, "every (participant in) the cultic meal of the divine" (*CIS* I 165.16); also the PN *klb 'lm*, "'Dog'-of-the-Divine" (*CIS* I 49). The use of the abstraction "the divine" as a concrete noun in reference to particular deities is attested in *CIS* I 165.13; 167.8 (*pnt 'lm*, "the presence of the deity") and in *KAI* 19:2-3 (Ma'ṣūb, 222 B.C.E.: *h'lm ml'k mlk / 'štrt*, "the deity, the Messenger of MLK-'ŠTRT").

Röllig points out a group of inscriptions in the dialect of El-Hofra which, due to an interchange of nasals *m* and *n*, represent singular *'lm* by *'ln*.[82] These consist of the following: *l'ln l'dr lb'l 'dr*, "to the deity, to the majestic one, to majestic Ba'l" (EH 5.1); *l'ln lb'l 'dn*, "to the deity, to Ba'l the lord" (*JA* 1917: 1.57); *l'dn l'ln 'qdš*, "to the lord, to the holy deity" (*RES* 327.1); *l'dn l'ln lb'l ḥmn*, "to the lord, to the deity, to B'L ḤMN" (*RES* 328.1).

More ambiguous are possible construct and suffix forms of *'lm* represented in the following inscriptions: *KAI* 19.4 (Ma'ṣūb, 222 B.C.E.) reads *b'šrt 'l ḥmn*, "in the shrine of the deity of ḤMN." Weighing in favor of understanding *'l* as representing a plural construct form rather than a morphological singular is the consideration that the patron deity of the city was feminine.[83] Singular *'lm* with suffix may be represented in the following forms: *l'ly 'štrt*, "for his deity Ashtart" (*CIS* I 4.5); *l'ly ršp mkl*, "for his deity Resheph-MKL" (*CIS*

---

[80]A. M. Honeyman, "Larnax tēs Lapēthou: A Third Phoenician Inscription," *Le Muséon* 51:286 line 1; *KI* 64.3; 87.3; *RES* 13.2; 537.3; 1569; *CIS* I 227.4; 262.1; 377.4; 3351; Cooke 57.4; *KAI* 44.2, all cited in Röllig, "El," 412 n. 7. For this interpretation of the title, see Honeyman, "Larnax," 288-89.

[81]For this interpretation, see Röllig, "El," 413 n. 9.

[82]Röllig, "El," 405, discusses other instances in these inscriptions in which *n* occurs in place of expected *m* and *vice versa*; all the following are referenced by Röllig.

[83]Cooke, *Text-Book*, 49.

I 90.1); *l'ly l'šmn*, "for his deity, for Eshmun" (*KI* 8:9; Sidon, mid-fifth century B.C.E.).

An important piece of evidence for the understanding of *'ĕlōhîm*'s Phoenician counterpart comes from an Akkadian document. In Esarhaddon's treaty with King Baal of Tyre,[84] the list of witnessing deities indigenous to Phoenicia and inland Syria (DINGIR.MEŠ e-bir ÍD, rev. II: 8) includes the writing ^dBa-a-a-ti-DINGIR.MEŠ *Bayti-ilāni* (rev. II:6) "for the usual Canaanite Beth-El, proving that the plural of *ilu* is used in Phoenician for the singular, precisely as *elōhim* is frequently used in Hebrew."[85]   Not only does this reference parallel *bêt 'ĕlōhîm* in the etymology of the GN Bethel in Gen 28:17-22, but it also accords with the observation noted above that plural *'lm* is the standard form of the appellative meaning "god," "deity" in Phoenician.

Though *'lm* is sparsely preserved in inscriptions from Phoenicia itself, the usage cannot be attributed to foreign influence. Not only is no such influence to be identified, but the Phoenician usage itself cannot be localized to a particular area outside of Phoenicia; it is attested in Libya, Egypt, Cilicia, and the Aegean. Phoenician *'lm* was obviously at home in the language that was spread throughout the eastern Mediterranean through Phoenician maritime activity.   The implication of its use in Phoenician inscriptions in reference to non-Phoenician gods is that it was the standard expression for "god" or "deity" in Phoenician.

Phoenician singular *'lm*, like its Hebrew counterpart, could be used both to express a general noun of abstraction ("divinity") and to designate a particular god as "deity," i.e., as a concretized abstract plural. Examples of both usages of the singular common noun are found not only in later Phoenician and Punic but also in the eighth-century inscriptions from Karatepe. These observations are consistent with the character of *'lm* (and of *'ĕlōhîm*) as an Iron Age reflex of the Canaanite expression reflected in the Amarna letters and in other Late Bronze Age cuneiform documents.

---

[84]Simo Parpola, ed. *Neo-Assyrian Treaties and Loyalty Oaths* (SAA 2; Helsinki: Helsinki Univ. Press, 1988), 24-27 column IV 6', 8'.

[85]Stephen Langdon, "A Phoenician Treaty of Assarhaddon: Collation of K. 3500," *RA* 26 (1929): 193.

Aramaic

Though the existence of an expression corresponding to Biblical Hebrew *'ĕlōhîm* in Aramaic is not certain, three possible instances merit discussion. Two of these, one from an inscription of Bar-Rakib and the other from the proverbs section of *Ahiqar*, are northern Syrian in origin and belong to dialects that otherwise exhibit Canaanite influence (see below). A third is found in an administrative letter from Elephantine. A fourth text, which does not represent a true counterpart to *'ĕlōhîm*, warrants mentioning as it is sometimes suggested as an example of such a usage.

Bar-Rakib. A possible instance of the plural noun for "god" used as a singular in Aramaic is found in an inscription from Zenjirli, in which Bar-Rakib, the king of Sam'al-Ya'udi, makes reference to *'lhy byt 'by* (*KAI* 217.3, second half of the eighth century).[86] Weighing in favor of reading morphologically (construct) plural *'lhy* as a plural are references to a group of deities in another inscription from Zenjirli. Panammu I, the great-grandfather and predecessor of Bar-Rakib as king of Ya'udi, attributes his success, including the acquisition of the throne, to the providence of "the gods Hadad, El, Resheph, Rakib-El and Shemesh" (*'lhw . hdd . w'l . wršp . wrkb'l . wšmš, KAI* 214.2-3; cf. simply "the gods" *'lhy*,[87] in lines 4, 12, 13).[88]

---

[86]While the Bar-Rakib inscriptions (*KAI* 216-218) are usually classified as Old Aramaic, some contend that these represent early Imperial Aramaic under the Assyrian Empire (see Harold Louis Ginsberg, "Aramaic Dialect Problems," *AJSL* 50 [1933]: 3-4; Gibson, *Textbook*, 2:88). For their classification as Old Aramaic, see Joseph Fitzmyer, "The Phases of the Aramaic Language," in *A Wandering Aramean: Collected Aramaic Essays* (Chico, Calif.: Scholars Press, 1979), 61, 63-70; Stephen A. Kaufman, "Languages (Aramaic)," *ABD* 4:173; Rainer Degen, *Altaramäische Grammatik der Inschriften des 10-8 Jh. v. Chr.* (Wiesbaden: F. Steiner, 1969), 4-5; Stanislav Segert, *Altaramäische Grammatik* (Leipzig: VEB Verlag Enzyklopädie, 1983), 38; and Frank M. Cross and David Noel Freedman, *Early Hebrew Orthography: A Study of the Epigraphic Evidence* (New Haven: American Oriental Society, 1952), 21, 29-34, 63-64.

[87]The forms *'lhw* (*KAI* 214.2) and *'lhy* (lines 4, 12, 13, 19; *KAI* 215.23), reflect the nominative and oblique masculine-plural-absolute case endings, respectively, in the dialect of Ya'udi (found in *KAI* 214 and 215); see Donner and Röllig, *KAI*, 2:214, 217, 229; Gibson, *Textbook*, 2:63.

[88]See also lines 11, 18.

On the other hand, favoring the interpretation of *'lhy* as a singular and the translation of the phrase as "the (patron) deity of my father's dynasty" are references by Bar-Rakib himself to a single dynastic god, Rakib-El.[89] Within the same group of deities, which are also mentioned by Panammu I (Resheph being replaced by "all the gods of Ya'udi"), Bar-Rakib distinguishes Rakib-El as "lord of the dynasty" (*hdd . w'l . wrkb'l . b'l . byt . wšmš . wkl . 'lhy . y'dy, KAI* 215.22). This designation is anticipated by the late-ninth-century Phoenician inscription of Kilamuwa, an earlier king of Ya'udi who speaks of "Rakib-El, lord of the dynasty" (*rkb'l . b'l . bt, KAI* 24.16). In another inscription, Bar-Rakib mentions "my lord Rakib-El" (*mr'y . rkb'l, KAI* 216.5). The notion of a single deity as dynastic patron god was apparently a firmly established tradition for the kingship of Sam'al-Ya'udi. Thus one would expect Bar-Rakib to speak of a single "god of my father's dynasty." The evidence is consistent with the possibility that *'lhy* in *KAI* 217.3 has a singular meaning.

Provided the form does indeed represent an authentic example of our usage, Canaanite origins are beyond doubt. This point holds regardless of whether one assumes a division between Canaanite and "Old Aramaic" (and/or its predecessor). As witnessed in the Late Bronze Age evidence from Amarna and elsewhere, the geographic distribution of the usage shows its place of origin to have been the Phoenician coast (see above). The Phoenician inscription of Kilamuwa (*KAI* 24) attests to a strong Canaanite linguistic presence in the area of Sam'al-Ya'udi prior to Bar-Rakib. The Canaanite (i.e., Phoenician) coast as the ultimate origin of such a usage in Sam'al-Ya'udi, viewed either as a borrowing from one dialect to another or as a result of "genetic" diffusion across a linguistic continuum, would hardly be disputable.

Ahiqar. Another possible but uncertain instance of an Aramaic equivalent of *'ĕlōhîm* appears in the proverbs section of *Ahiqar*:

---

[89]See the comments of Donner and Röllig, *KAI*, 2:34, 225; cf., though, the conclusion that *'lhy* in *KAI* 217.3 is plural (p. 235).

['l tdrk q]ŝtk w'l thrkb ḥtk lṣdyq lmh 'lhy' ysgh b'drh wyhtybnhy 'lyk
[Do not bend] your [b]ow and do not cause your arrow to ride to a
righteous man lest the god(s) proceed(s) to his help and turn(s) it back
against you. (line 126)[90]

The plural form *'lhy'* is the subject of two singular verbs in this
passage. While some have opted to treat the plural form as a scribal
lapse for singular *'lh'*,[91] others have recognized in this passage a use
of the plural form *'lhy'* "gods" as a singular.[92]

In response to these two solutions, James Lindenberger contends
that "it is not possible to translate the subject *'lhy'* as 'god' or 'the
god.'"[93] Against the other possibility mentioned (i.e., *'lhy'* as scribal
lapse for singular *'lh'*), Lindenberger makes the point that the singular
form appears nowhere else in the text.[94] He proposes, alternatively,
that it is the two singular verb forms that are to be understood as the
result of a scribal lapse and suggests emending them to *ysgwn* and
yhtybwnh.[95] This may be a satisfactory explanation for only one verb
but not for two, notwithstanding Lindenberger's comment that "the
second error could have been produced by the first."[96] In objection
to reading *'lhy'* as a plural with a singular meaning, Lindenberger

---

[90]Citations and transcriptions of *Ahiqar* follow the edition of Bezalel Porten and Ada
Yardeni, eds., *Textbook of Aramaic Documents from Ancient Egypt: Newly Copied,
Edited and Translated into Hebrew and English*, vol. 3, *Literature, Accounts, Lists*
(Winona Lake, Ind.: Eisenbrauns, 1993), 23-53 and Foldouts 1-9.

[91]Felix Perles, "Zu Sachaus 'Aramäischen Papyrus und Ostraka,'" *OLZ* 14 (1911):
502; Arthur Ernest Cowley, *Aramaic Papyri of the Fifth Century B.C.* (Oxford:
Clarendon, 1923), 241; Pierre Grelot, "Les proverbes Araméens d'Aḥiqar," *RB* 68
(1961), 187; offering this as one possibility, Segert, *Altaramäische Grammatik*, 334, 440.

[92]Paul Jouön, "Notes grammaticales, lexicographiques et philologiques sur les
papyrus araméens d'Égypte," *MUSJ* 18 (1934): 27; Pontius Leander, *Laut- und
Formenlehre des Ägyptisch-Aramäischen* (Hildesheim: Georg Olms, 1966), 92 §45j; with
less certainty, Segert, *Altaramäische Grammatik*, 334, 440; cf. Takamitsu Muraoka and
Bezalel Porten, *A Grammar of Egyptian Aramaic* (HO 32; Leiden, 1990), §47d.

[93]"Ahiqar (Seventh to Sixth Century B.C.): A New Translation and Introduction,"
in *The Old Testament Pseudepigrapha* (ed. J. H. Charlesworth; 2 vols.; New York:
Doubleday, 1985), 2:503 note b.

[94]*The Aramaic Proverbs of Ahiqar* (JHNES; Baltimore: Johns Hopkins Univ. Press,
1983), 118; the same point is made by Jouön, "Notes," 27.

[95]*Aramaic Proverbs*, 118; "Ahiqar," 503 note b.

[96]*Aramaic Proverbs*, 118.

invokes "universal usage" in Aramaic.[97] In light both of the Zenjirli passage (discussed above) and of other instances of plurals used as singulars in Aramaic,[98] the last point may be overstated. Lindenberger's argument that the "polytheistic character of the text" rules out a reference to a single unnamed god does not hold in view of the tendency in ancient Near Eastern wisdom literature[99] to refer to an unspecified deity as "the god."[100] Reference to "the deity in question" is quite consistent with a polytheistic framework. When specific deities are named elsewhere in the wisdom portion of *Ahiqar*, only one deity is mentioned in a given saying.[101]

In support of Lindenberger's solution, the absolute plural form *'lhn* ("gods") appears elsewhere in the text as the subject of plural verbs (lines 163, 172). All things considered, there is no more reason for emending the text with respect to the verbs than there is for doing so with respect to their subject.[102] While the reading of *'lhy'* in line 126 as a counterpart to Biblical Hebrew *'ĕlōhîm* may not be dismissed out of hand, neither is it to be affirmed with certainty; it is merely one possible solution.[103]

---

[97]"Ahiqar," p. 503 note b.

[98]Leander's list of "Pl. mit Sg.-Bedeutung" (*Ägyptisch-Aramäischen*, 92 §45j) is not limited to Egyptian Aramaic; these include *dmn* "worth," **z'ryn* "limited number" (*Ahiqar* line 106), *hyn* "life," *qdšn* "holiness" (*Ahiqar* line 95), *rhmn* "mercy," and *šlyn* "peace," the last example being cited also by Cowley, *CAP*, 241. Segert (*Altaramäische Grammatik*, 333), under the heading "Plurale mit singularischer Bedeutung" (6.3.2.3) cites the abstract plurals *hyn* "Leben" and *nš(y)n* "Weiblichkeit," the latter in reference to individuals (see, e.g., *CAP* 9.12: *nšn rbh* "a great lady"); cf. Muraoka's and Porten's characterization of *nšn* in reference to one woman as "enigmatic" (*Egyptian Aramaic*, §§47c; 76cf; discussed below, *Egyptian Papyri*).

[99]Lindenberger characterizes the *Ahiqar* proverbs as "a deposit of the traditional wisdom of Aram" meriting its "proper place alongside the wisdom of Mesopotamia, Egypt, Israel, and other nations of the ancient world" (*Aramaic Proverbs*, 25) and notes that these proverbs "have a special intrinsic interest because of their similarities to Biblical and ancient Near Eastern wisdom traditions" (p. 15).

[100]See Henri Frankfort, *Ancient Egyptian Religion: An Interpretation* (New York: Harper & Row, 1967), 67; Hornung, *The One and the Many*, 50-60; also, the indefinite use of "the god" in *Ludlul bēl nēmeqi* and in "The Babylonian Theodicy" (both discussed below, First-Millennium Akkadian. Wisdom Texts).

[101]E.g., El (lines 91, 97, 109); Shamash (lines 92, 107, 138, 189).

[102]See Jouön, "Notes," 27.

[103]Another possibility is that *'lhy'* represents a collective reference to "the gods," as the subject of singular verbs, though a clear instance of such a usage would be unparalleled in Northwest Semitic; see references to "the gods" at Zenjirli, Tell

The linguistic character of the proverbs would be consistent with the appearance of such a usage from Canaanite. Lindenberger observes that this dialect in some respects resembles Old Aramaic more than it does Imperial Aramaic, to which the narrative section of *Ahiqar* belongs.[104] He also lists a number of features in the text that are common to Canaanite languages, in terms of morphological, lexical, semantic, and idiomatic usage.[105] Both of these factors, along with the group of DNN mentioned in the text, indicate that the *Ahiqar* proverbs, like Bar-Rakib's inscription, originated in northern Syria, "a geographical area in which Aramaic and Canaanite were in close contact."[106]

The Canaanite linguistic and cultural influence evident both in the *Ahiqar* proverbs and in the Bar-Rakib inscription would be consistent with the occurrence of Biblical Hebrew *'ĕlōhîm*'s counterpart in each. However, the reading of a plural "gods" with a singular referent while possible is uncertain in both texts. The fact that both texts shared a similar geographic, cultural, and linguistic background in no way increases the likelihood that the usage occurs in either case—two uncertain examples do not result in more certainty!

Egyptian Papyri. A third possible instance of an Aramaic parallel to *'ĕlōhîm* is a passage from the letters of the Persian satrap Arsham (Driver 13.2), which is translated by Driver "so act as to please his majesty and 'Aršam" (*kn 'bd kzy l'lhy' wl'ršm thd[y]*).[107] Here *'lhy'* is rendered "his majesty" on the basis of two factors: (1) the correspondence between the phrase *l'lhy' wl'ršm* in this letter and *mn mlk' wmny* "by the king and by me" in a letter from Arsham (Driver 2.1, 3) and (2) the function of *'lhy'* as an ideogram for Middle Persian

---

Fekherye, and Deir 'Alla, all cited below (see Deir 'Alla).

[104]*Aramaic Proverbs*, 19, 288-90; according to Lindenberger, "some of the closest linguistic affinities of the collection are with the latest phase of Old Aramaic and the earliest of Imperial Aramaic, a transition which occurred around 700 B.C." (p. 20); he acknowledges, though, the methodological difficulties in such hard and fast dialectical and chronological divisions (and transitions) for the language (pp. 291-94); see also "Ahiqar," 481-82.

[105]*Aramaic Proverbs*, 287-88.

[106]Ibid., 290; also "Ahiqar," 482.

[107]Godfrey Rolles Driver, *Aramaic Documents of the Fifth Century* (Oxford: Clarendon, 1957), 37.

bagān "majesty" in Pahlavi documents.[108] Provided this reasoning holds, it may have more of a bearing on Persian than on Aramaic and may involve a different phenomenon altogether.[109] More likely, though, the association depends on an abstract notion of "deity" expressed by the plural. Of relevance are other Aramaic plural forms having a singular meaning.[110] Contact with Phoenician would account for the appearance of an originally Canaanite usage in Egyptian Aramaic.[111] The passage is to be considered another *possible* example of "gods" as a singular in Aramaic.

This is in contrast with the Passover letter of Hananiah (*CAP* 21.2), which opens with the greeting *šlm 'ḥy 'lhy' [yš'lw]*, "May the god(s) [seek] the peace of my brothers." Though *'lhy'* in this greeting, when spoken by a Jew, could have been intended as a singular (even with a plural verb)[112] or simply overlooked as belonging to a stereotyped expression,[113] its original meaning in the formula was clearly plural.[114]

---

[108] Driver, *Aramaic Documents*, 85; also Wilhelm Eilers, "Neue aramäische Urkunden aus Ägypten," *AfO* 17 (1956): 335; cf. J. David Whitehead, "Some Distinctive Features of the Language of the Aramaic Arsames Correspondence," *JNES* 37 (1978): 134 and n. 103.

[109] For instance, the Persian notion of "majesty" may correspond to an aspect of true plurality expressed by the Aramaic word.

[110] See Leander, *Ägyptisch-Aramäischen*, 92 §45j; specific examples are enumerated above (see discussion of *Ahiqar*). Muraoka and Porten describe the use of *nšn* in reference to a singular woman (e.g., *nšn rbh* "a great lady," *CAP* 9.12), often prefixed to the name of a woman in legal documents, as "enigmatic" and note that it is applied once to a slave woman and thus cannot be considered a "plural of majesty" (*Egyptian Aramaic*, §§47c; 76cf). Against the suggestion that *'lhy'* here may be a singular, they contend that "there does not seem to exist a sound basis for postulating a special case of the plural of majesty for the word [*'lh*] 'god'" (§47d).

[111] See *'lm* in inscriptional Phoenician from Egypt as late as the Roman Period (above, Phoenician).

[112] Bezalel Porten, *Archives From Elephantine: The Life of an Ancient Jewish Military Colony* (Berkeley: Univ. of California Press, 1968), 160; Driver, *Aramaic Documents*, 85; see also the translation of Wilhelmus C. Delsman in *TUAT* 1:253.

[113] Harold Louis Ginsberg, *ANET*, 491 n. 3; Cowley, *Aramaic Papyri*, 63.

[114] Porten, *Archives*, 159; see *CAP* 39.1 *'lhy' kl yš'lw* "may all the gods seek" (your welfare); Emil Gottlieb Kraeling, *The Brooklyn Museum Aramaic Papyri: New Documents of the Fifth Century B.C. from the Jewish Colony at Elephantine* (New Haven: Yale Univ. Press, 1953) 13.1, *'lhy' kl' [yš'lw]*; also *CAP* 56.1 *'lhy' yš'lw*; 37.1-2 [*'lhy'*]/*yš'lw*.

The Aramaic texts discussed present three possible instances of a counterpart to Biblical Hebrew *'ĕlōhîm*. The Linguistic borrowing from Canaanite would account for each instance: the first two, from Bar-Rakib and the *Ahiqar* proverbs section, are found in texts that exhibit a marked Canaanite linguistic and cultural influence, and the third, in the Arsham letter, could quite plausibly be the result of contact with Phoenician, or possibly with Hebrew. Nonetheless, all three cases are far from certain and, without further evidence, judgment should be reserved as to their identification as true parallels to *'ĕlōhîm*.

Deir 'Alla[115]

The Balaam inscription from Deir 'Alla provides evidence of special relevance to biblical *'ĕlōhîm*. The similarities of the Deir 'Alla tradition to the material in Numbers 22-24 is well documented.[116] The central figure in both is Balaam, son of Beor, a seer who receives

---

[115]The *editio princeps* of the ink-on-plaster inscriptions is Jacob Hoftijzer and G. van der Kooij, eds., *Aramaic Texts from Deir 'Alla* (Documenta et monumenta Orientis antiqui 19; Leiden: Brill, 1976); the line numbers of the passages cited here follow the arrangement of the main fragments of Combination I by André Caquot and André Lemaire, "Les textes Araméens de Deir 'Alla," *Syria* 54 (1977): 189-208; see further the arrangements and readings by Jo Ann Hackett, *The Balaam Text From Deir 'Allā* (HSM 31; Chico, Calif.: Scholars Press, 1980), 25-30; P. Kyle McCarter, Jr., "The Balaam Texts from Deir 'Allā: The First Collation," *BASOR* 239 (1980): 49-60; cf. Manfred Weippert, "The Balaam Text from Deir 'Allā and the study of the Old Testament," in *The Balaam Text from Deir 'Alla Re-evaluated: Proceedings of the International Symposium held at Leiden, 21-24 August 1989* (ed. J. Hoftijzer and G. van der Kooij; Leiden: Brill, 1991), 153-58.

The date of the inscription is disputed. Franken, following Monique Vilders and revising earlier estimates, dates the associated pottery to the first half of the eighth century or earlier (Hendricus Jacobus Franken, "Deir 'Alla re-visited," in Hoftijzer and van der Kooij, *Proceedings*, 8-9). Paleographic dating of the inscription has ranged from the mid-eighth century or earlier (Joseph Naveh, "The Date of the Deir 'Allā Inscription in Aramaic Script," *IEJ* 17 [1967]: 256-58) to the early seventh century (Frank M. Cross, "Notes on the Ammonite Inscription from Tell Sirān," *BASOR* 212 [1973]: 14).

On the difficulty of a linguistic classification for this inscription, see P. Kyle McCarter, Jr., "The dialect of the Deir 'Alla texts," in Hoftijzer and van der Kooij, *Proceedings*, 87-99; cf., in the same volume, Dennis Pardee, "The linguistic classification of the Deir 'Alla text written on plaster," 100-105.

[116]See Hoftijzer and van der Kooij, *Deir 'Alla*, 183-302; McCarter, "Balaam Texts"; Hans-Peter Müller, "Die aramäische Inschrift von Deir 'Allā und die älteren Bileamsprüche," *ZAW* 94 (1982): 214-44; Weippert, "Study of the Old Testament," 151-84; Jo Ann Hackett, "Deir 'Alla, Tell. Texts," *ABD* 2:129-30.

revelations in the night and announces the divine intent. As McCarter notes, the similarities in language between passages from Deir 'Alla and from the Hebrew Bible "suggest stereotyped patterns" indicating that the Deir 'Alla texts "draw upon the literary tradition in which Israel and Judah participated."[117] The parallels are striking:[118]

1. *wy'tw 'lhn 'lwh blylh . . .*
wy'mrw lbl'm br b'r
Gods came to him in the night . . .
Then they said to Balaam, son of
Beor . . .(Deir 'Alla I.1, 2)

1. *wayyābō' 'ĕlōhîm 'el-*
bil'ām wayyō'mer
God came to Balaam and
said . . . (Num 22:9)

1. *wayyābō' 'ĕlōhîm 'el-*
bil'ām laylâ wayyō'mer lô
God came to Balaam at
night and said to him . . .
(Num 22:20)

2. *wyqm bl'm mn mhr*
And Balaam rose in the
morning . . . (Deir 'Alla I.3)

2. *wayyāqom bil'ām babbōqer*
And Balaam rose in the
morning . . . (Num 22:13, 21)

3. *wlkw r'w p'lt 'lhn*
Now come, see the deeds of the gods!
(Deir 'Alla I.5)

3. *lĕkû-hăzû mip'ălôt 'ĕlōhîm*
Come, see the deeds of God!
(Ps 46:9)

3. *lĕkû ûrĕ'û mip'ălôt 'ĕlōhîm*
Come and see the deeds of God!
(Ps 66:5)

Most significant for the topic in question is the correspondence between *'ĕlōhîm* and *'lhn* in examples 1 and 3. Balaam is introduced at Deir 'Alla as *ḥzh 'lhn*, "seer of the gods/the divine" (I.1). While Hoftijzer compares the phrase with biblical construct expressions in which *nābî'* is in construct with DNN,[119] even more apt are

---

[117]McCarter, "Balaam Texts," 53, 57.

[118]The following parallels and their translations are taken from McCarter, "Balaam Texts," 57 (parallels 1 & 2), 53 (parallel 3); the last comparison is also made by Hoftijzer, *Deir 'Alla*, 192.

[119]*nĕbî'ê yhwh* (1 Kgs 18:4, 13), *nĕbî'ê habba'al* (1 Kgs 18:19, 22, 25, 40; 2 Kgs 10:19), *nĕbî'ê hā'ăšērâ* (1 Kgs 18:19); Hoftijzer and van der Kooij, *Deir 'Alla*, 184.

comparisons with the biblical PN *ḥăzî'ēl*, "Vision of El" or "Vision of God/the Divine,"[120] and with expressions in Biblical Hebrew and Phoenician in which *(hā)'ĕlōhîm* and *'lm* function as an adjectival genitive.[121] The inscription clearly belongs to the same theological thought world as the Hebrew Bible.

"The gods" are mentioned in I.5-6, which reads *'l[h]n.'tyḥdw./ wnṣbw.šdyn.mw'd*, "the gods gathered, and the Shaddayin took their places in the assembly" (I.5-6). Notwithstanding the correspondence between the biblical and inscriptional passages cited, the last passage leaves no doubt that Deir 'Alla *'lhn* is to be understood as a plural. As McCarter notes, the *'lhn* introduced in the opening lines of Deir 'Alla are not specified.[122] The two corresponding clauses spanning lines 5 and 6 could be understood as a parallelism, in which case "the Shaddayin" in this context is an alternate expression for "the gods" (i.e., the same unspecified gods who come to Balaam in the night and disclose the divine will). Alternatively, the second clause may provide additional, more specific information about the first,[123] in which case, as McCarter explains, the Shaddayin are "a sub-group of the gods."[124] Either way, the identity of "the gods" in the Deir 'Alla inscription is nonspecific.

Related to the nonspecificity of the gods at Deir 'Alla is Balaam's status as a foreigner. Noting the similarity between the references to Balaam's "people" in Deir 'Alla I.4 (*'m*) and Num 24:14 (*'ām*), McCarter explains that in both contexts Balaam is regarded as being from somewhere else.[125] Balaam's essential character as a foreigner is most appropriate, in view of the archaeological

---

[120] *'Ĕlōhîm* does not appear in PNN and is probably represented by the PN element *'ēl* (see below, *'Ĕlōhîm* as a Common Noun).

[121] E.g., Biblical Hebrew: *'îš (hā)'ĕlōhîm* "man of God/of the divine," *mal'ak hā'ĕlōhîm* "messenger of God/of the divine," *'ebed hā'ĕlōhîm* "servant of God/of the divine," (see below, The Abstract Nature of *'ĕlōhîm*); Phoenician: *bn 'lm* "divine being(s)," *'š 'lm* "man of the gods/of the divine," *mqm 'lm* "establisher of the divine," *glb 'lm* "divine tonsurer," *klb 'lm* "'dog' of the divine," *'mt 'lm* "female servant of the divine" (see above, Phoenician).

[122] "Balaam Texts," 56.

[123] As in Job 1:6: *wayyābō'û bĕnê hā'ĕlōhîm lĕhityaṣṣēb 'al-yhwh wayyābô' gam-haśśāṭān bĕtôkām*, "The divine beings came to present themselves before Yahweh, and the Adversary came among them."

[124] "Balaam Texts," 57.

[125] Ibid.

interpretation of the setting of the Deir 'Alla texts. Franken suggests that the sanctuary in which the plaster texts were displayed was located in "a market area with an international character" and that it may have been, like the Late Bronze Age sanctuary before it,

> a meeting point for traders and caravan owners from different regions, all with their own deities and rituals. Many kinds of priests from a wide variety of backgrounds may have been permanently stationed there, to sanction sales contracts or bless goods that were being traded.[126]

That a foreign seer would be central to a religious inscription displayed in a sanctuary catering to international worshipers is quite fitting.

Equally fitting is the generic way of referring to the divine as "the gods," a designation which, by virtue both of its plurality and its nonspecificity, would have lent itself to the accommodation of a diversity of deities and worshipers. Though Aramaic inscriptions make reference to "the gods," it is usually as a kind of shorthand for a group of deities already named in the given context.[127]   In light both of this fact and of the context of the inscription at Deir 'Alla, the nonspecific use of *'lhn* there seems to have been intentional. The language about the gods is inclusive in its indefiniteness. This inclusivity is essential to the inscription's expression of what Franken identifies as "religious concepts in agreement with the international character of the trade."[128]   The designation *'lhn* facilitated an inclusive dynamic of religious identification at Deir 'Alla.

Though Deir 'Alla *'lhn* "the gods" is a numerical plural and thus not an exact grammatical and semantic counterpart to Biblical Hebrew *'ĕlōhîm*, it is an important parallel to the biblical expression, especially

---

[126]Hendricus Jacobus Franken, "Deir 'Alla, Tell. Archaeology," *ABD* 2:137; see also, idem, "Deir 'Alla re-visited," 10-15.

[127]As noted above, *'lhy* in *KAI* 214.4, 12, 13 refers to "the gods Hadad, El, Resheph, Rakib-El and Shemesh" (*'lhw . hdd . w'l . wršp . wrkb'l . wšmš*, lines 2-3); *'lhn* in Sefire I (*KAI* 222) A:30; B:31; C:15 and III (*KAI* 224) line 24 refers to the witnessing deities of the treaty, enumerated in *KAI* 222 A:8-12 and referenced elsewhere as "all the gods of the treaty" (*kl 'lhy 'dy, KAI* 222 B:23; 224:4, 14, 17, 23); cf. the indefinite meaning in the expression "before gods and before man" in *KAI* 215.23 (*qdm . 'lhy . wqdm . 'nš*) and in Tell Fekherye, line 14 (*'l . 'lhn . w'l . 'nšn*; Ali Abou-Assaf, Pierre Bordreuil, and Alan R. Millard, eds., *La statue de Tell Fekherye et son inscription bilingue assyro-araméenne* [Paris: Editions recherche sur les civilisations, 1982], p. 23).

[128]"Deir 'Alla re-visited," 15.

as it occurs in the Balaam material in Num 22-24. Along with other aspects of the Balaam inscription, the nature of the term *'lhn* as a usage of international currency is an element of religious and literary tradition represented in the Hebrew Bible.

First-Millennium Akkadian

Parallels to biblical *'ĕlōhîm* are found in first-millennium Akkadian texts in which the word for god is written as a plural (DINGIR.MEŠ or DINGIR.DINGIR). As the following analysis will indicate, the appearance of this usage—which grammatically speaking is out of place in standard Akkadian—beginning in the seventh century is best explained as the result of a scribal borrowing from the west. Analysis of the usage in various kinds of documents, dating from Sargonid to Persian times, shows the expression to be not an orthographic idiosyncracy but a plural used as a singular.

Assyrian Royal Correspondence. A number of these instances of "gods" as a singular occur in Sargonid royal correspondence. Before examining those references themselves, it is instructive to note other occurrences of the "concretized" abstract plural in these letters. The plural EN.MEŠ (*bēlū* "lords/lordship") is clearly used as a singular. In a letter to the Assyrian king, Urad-Gula quotes a proverb that begins

> LÚ ša AŠ UGU pi-i ša EN.MEŠ-šú / ⌐i-du⌐-lu-ú-ni
> *amēlu ša ina muḫḫi pî ša bēlēšu / idullū-ni*
> As to the man who proceeds according to the command of his lord . . .
> (SAA 10.290 [= *ABL* 118]:9-10)

A second instance of *bēlū* as abstract plural in reference to a single individual is *ABL* 402:10:

> ÌR ša É EN.MEŠ-šú / i-ra-'a-a-mu / ù AŠ UGU É EN.MEŠ am-ru
> *ardu ša bīt bēlēšu / ira''amu / u ina muḫḫi bīt bēlē amru*
> A servant who loves the house of his lord and is found to be in subjection to the house of his lord . . .[129]

---

[129]Cf. *ABL* 290: ¹ᵈÌR šá É EN-šú i-ram-mu (*arad ša bīt bēlīšu irammu*, lines 12-13) and i-na UGU É EN-ka (*ina muḫḫi bīt bēlīka*, line 9).

This usage of *bēlū* calls to mind not only Biblical Hebrew *'ădōnîm* but also Phoenician **'dnm* "lordship."[130]   As in Biblical Hebrew, the concretized abstract plural here denotes a certain status for the referent. Such is the case in another example of this grammatical category from the Sargonid correspondence, singular *zērû* "progeny." *ABL* 442: rev. 1-2 reads

> at-ta NUMUN.MEŠ DU / ša ᴵᵈ30.PAP.MEŠ.IRI₄
> *atta zērē kīnu / ša Sin-aḫḫē-erība*
> You, O legitimate scion of Sennacherib . . .

Here the singular meaning indicated by context is reinforced by the singular adjective modifying the plural noun form.

The most commonly attested instance of a plural form used as a singular in these texts is singular DINGIR.MEŠ (*ilānū/ilū*).   In five attested instances, the Assyrian king uses the phrase, "Ashur, my deity," written AN.ŠÁR DINGIR.MEŠ-ia/DINGIR.MEŠ-e-a (*ABL* 287:rev. 8; 290:12; 292:6; 297:6; 1170:10-11).   The king's use of the expression occurs in an oath formula (AN.ŠÁR DINGIR.MEŠ-e-a at-te-me, *ABL* 287:rev. 8; AN.ŠÁR DINGIR.MEŠ-ia at-te-mi, *ABL* 1170:10-11—"By Ashur, my deity, I swear!") and in the context of comments about warfare and territorial control:

> AŠ ŠÀ GÍR.AN.BAR / AN.ŠAR DINGIR.MEŠ-e-a KUR ul-li-ti gab-bi
> IZI tu-šá-ki-la
> *ina libbi patri parzilli / aššur ilē-a māti ullīti gabbi išāti tušakkilā*
> With the iron weapon of Ashur, my deity, you wiped out that entire land
> with fire. (*ABL* 292:5-6; 297:6-7)

The term is also used in the context of the influence of the king's god over life-or-death administrative decisions:

> AN.ŠAR DINGIR.MEŠ-ia-a / ú-raq-an-ni-i
> *aššur ilēya / uraqqanni*
> Ashur, my deity, would prevent me (from having a certain official
> executed). (*ABL* 290:12-13)

---

[130]*KAI* 26 i 10 (discussed above, Phoenician), though this occurrence is not in reference to an individual.

It is in the light of these references that the oath of Urad-Nanaya in a letter to Esarhaddon (SAA 10.319 [= *ABL* 392]: rev. 9-11) is to be understood:

> DINGIR.MEŠ-ka šúm-ma me-me-ni / UZU.Á.2-šú AŠ UGU / ú-me-du-u-ni
> *ilēka šumma memēni / idāšu ana muḫḫi / ummedūni*
> By your deity! If anyone lays a hand on him . . .[131]

That the plural form DINGIR.MEŠ is used as a singular is clear in SAA 10.54 (= *ABL* 433):6-7, where it is paired with a singular verb:

> UD-2-KAM /   DINGIR.MEŠ [ša L]UGAL i-na-ṣur
> *šania ūma / ilū [ša š]arri inaṣṣur*
> On the second day, the deity of the king shall stand guard.

Another occurrence of DINGIR.MEŠ with a singular verb form is found in the proverb cited by Urad-Gula in the letter to the Assyrian king (noted above):

> LÚ ša AŠ UGU pi-i ša EN.MEŠ-šú / ⌜i-du⌝-lu-ú-ni DINGIR.MEŠ še-e-du /
> [. . .].MEŠ-šú KASKAL.2 SIG₅ ir-ra-di-šú
> *amēlu ša ina muḫḫi pî ša bēlēšu / idullū-ni ilū šēdu /*
> *[. . .]-šu ḫarrāni ṭābi iraddišu*[132]
> As to the man who proceeds in accordance with the word of his lord,
> (his) *šēdu* deity, his [. . .], will lead him on a favorable road.[133]
> (SAA 10.290 [= *ABL* 118]:9-11)

Singular DINGIR.MEŠ, along with *bēlū* and *zērū*, in the Neo-Assyrian royal correspondence resembles the concretized abstract plural found in Biblical Hebrew, in Phoenician, and in Late Bronze Age Canaanite attested at Amarna, Taanach, Qatna, and Ugarit. This usage

---

[131]Cf. Parpola's rendering of DINGIR.MEŠ as a plural in *Letters from Assyrian and Babylonian Scholars* (SAA 10; Helsinki: Helsinki Univ. Press, 1993), 319; cf. the interpretation of Robert H. Pfeiffer, *State Letters of Assyria* (AOS 6; New Haven: American Oriental Society, 1935), 289, including the reading of DINGIR.MEŠ as a singular.

[132]This verb is G durative third-person masculine singular; cf. iq-qa-bi for *iqabbi* in *ABL* 370:rev. 9; see Emil Behrens, *Assyrisch-Babylonische Briefe Kultischen Inhalts aus der Sargonidenzeit* (LSS 2; Leipzig: J. C. Hinrichs, 1906), 6 n. 2.

[133]See Robert H. Pfeiffer, "Three Assyriological Footnotes to the Old Testament," *JBL* 47 (1928): 184; cf. Parpola, SAA 10.290; Behrens, *Briefe kultischen Inhalts*, 6 n. 2.

is out of character for Akkadian, in which, as a rule, masculine abstract plurals do not occur[134] and a concretized abstract plural does not occur at all. As demonstrated, the latter phenomenon is a Canaanite development. The appearance of the usage in seventh-century Assyrian is most likely the result of a peripheral borrowing from the west by way of scribes of western origins[135] and/or through the appropriation of an exotic and sophisticated language usage from a conquered population group. Suggestive of the latter possibility is ᵈBa-a-a-ti-DINGIR.MEŠ (*Bayti-ilānī*) for Bethel in the Esarhaddon-Baal treaty (mentioned above),[136] which dates to the beginning of the period of the earliest occurrences of singular DINGIR.MEŠ in Akkadian. This document represents the kind of circumstances under which Assyrian scribes may have been exposed to the Phoenician manner of expressing the term "deity." Perhaps a more viable possibility is Aramean mediation of the originally Canaanite expression,[137] which—provided the instance represents an authentic example of the usage—would be illustrated by the reference from the inscription of Bar-Rakib (see above, Aramaic), himself a vassal of Tiglathpileser III.

Wisdom Texts. Babylonian wisdom literature provides further evidence of the use of the expression within Akkadian scribal circles, beginning in the eighth or seventh century. Copies both of *Ludlul bēl nēmeqi* and of "The Babylonian Theodicy," some from the libraries of Ashurbanipal (*Ludlul* II.25; "Theodicy" 49, 82, 241) and from those of Sultantepe (*Ludlul* II.25, 33) and Ashur ("Theodicy" 219, 237,

---

[134]See von Soden, *GAG* §61f; though, abstract plurals with the feminine ending are not uncommon (see *GAG* §61h). As von Soden contends, -*ūtu*, the regular ending for abstract nouns, was originally identical with that of masculine plural adjectives (§56s).

[135]For discussion of western scribes in the service of the Assyrian empire, see Haim Tadmor, "The Aramaization of Assyria: Aspects of Western Impact," in H. Nissen and J. Renger, *Mesopotamien und seine Nachbarn*, part 2 (Berlin: G. Reimer, 1982), 449-71; see, of course, Sennacherib's "Judahite"-speaking Rabshakeh in 2 Kgs 18:19-35 (= Isa 36:4-20), an account which relies on the verisimilitude of an Assyrian official's being fluent in a Canaanite language.

[136]See above, Late Phoenician and Punic.

[137]On Aramaic influence on Neo-Assyrian, see Richard Caplice, "Languages: Akkadian," in *ABD* 4:172; on Aramean cultural influence on Mesopotamia, see Paul E. Dion, "Aramaean Tribes and Nations of First-Millennium Western Asia," in *CANE* 2:1287-92.

241), preserve the plural writings DINGIR.MEŠ and DINGIR.DINGIR in reference to a single deity.[138] In some instances, the plural orthography occurs in the same places where DINGIR (*Ludlul* II.12, 25, 33; "Theodicy" 49, 237, 241) appears in other copies; in other cases, the plural appears without a variant ("Theodicy" 82, 219, 295).

The subject matter of both of these wisdom texts concerns reflection upon appropriate behavior vis-à-vis the deity. The principle to be tested is stated in short by the friend of the sufferer in "The Babylonian Theodicy":

> n[a]-ṭil pa-an DINGIR-ma ra-ši la-mas-[sa]
> n[a]-ak-di pa-li-iḫ ᵈINNIN ú-kám-mar ṭuḫ-[da]
> He who waits on his god has a protecting angel,
> The humble man who fears his goddess accumulates wealth.
> (lines 21-22)[139]

In these lines, the words for "god" and "goddess" are placed in parallel. Compare the plural writing for "god" in an Ashurbanipal manuscript, where the same terms are placed in parallel in lines 80-81 and in lines 82-83:

> ki-du-de-e DINGIR.MEŠ la šum-ṣu-r[i] taḫ-ši-ḫu ka-bat-tuk
> ki-nu-te me-si ᵈiš-ta-ri x [. . .]
> In your mind you have an urge to disregard the divine ordinances.
> [. . .] the sound rules of your goddess.

> ki-i qí-rib AN-e šib-qí DINGIR.MEŠ [. . .]
> qí-bít pi-i ᵈil-ti ul iš-še-[. . .]
> The plans of the god [. . .] like the centre of heaven,
> The decrees of the goddess are not [. . .].

Such is the case also in lines 295-96 (these lines being preserved only in later—i.e., post-seventh-century[140]—copies):

---

[138]Wilfred G. Lambert, *Babylonian Wisdom Literature* (Oxford: Clarendon, 1960), 67, 37, 26, 38-39, 40-41, 63, 69, 74-75, 76-77, 82-83, 84-85, 88-89. The transliteration and translation of these texts will be taken from Lambert.

[139]Ibid., 70-71.

[140]Ibid., 26, 63.

ri-ṣa liš-ku-nu DINGIR.MEŠ/DINGIR.DINGIR šá id-da-[an]-ni
ri-ma li-ir-šá-a ^diš-tar šá x [. . .]
May the god who has thrown me off give help,
May the goddess who has [abandoned me] show mercy.

Though a plural verb form accompanies the plural writing for "god,"
the same is true for singular "goddess" in both extant copies of the
text. The subject matter of the poem, as set out in summary fashion
in lines 21–22 (quoted above) and as treated throughout the work,
requires the consideration of a single, though unspecified, deity.[141]

In line 219, the friend advises granting the god his due:

ri-di-ma us DINGIR.MEŠ ú-ṣur ma-si-šu
Follow in the way of the god, observe his rites.
(preserved in a copy from Ashur)

The use of DINGIR.MEŠ as the antecedent of a third-person masculine
singular pronoun shows that it is clearly a singular. Seventh-century
copies of the text offer the plural writing as a variant to singular
DINGIR in other copies, in lines 237 and 241:

ša la DINGIR.MEŠ is-ḫap-pu ra-ši ma-ak-ku-ra
The godless cheat (the one) who has wealth. (line 237)

ša-a-ra ṭa-a-ba šá DINGIR.MEŠ ši-te-'-e-ma
Seek the kindly wind of the god. (line 241)

The plural writing DINGIR.DINGIR appears in place of the singular
in a rhetorical question placed in the mouth of the sufferer:

[aq-qà]t-ti-i pak-ki DINGIR.DINGIR ú-zu-un-šu ib-š[i]
Did it (the onager) pay attention to *the giver of assured* divine oracles?
(line 49)

Both grammar and context show that the plural writing of the
noun *ilu* functions in "The Babylonian Theodicy" as a variant
expression of the word meaning "god" or "deity." The same holds
true with respect to the instances attested in *Ludlul bēl nēmeqi*. A

---

[141]See also the comments of Lambert, *BWL*, 67.

post-seventh-century copy of the text from Babylon[142] gives the plural
in parallel with singular "goddess":

> ki-i šá tam-qí-tum a-na DINGIR.MEŠ la uk-tin-nu
> ù AŠ ma-ka-le-e ᵈiš-tar-ri la zak-ru
> Like one who has not made libations to his god,
> Nor invoked his goddess at table . . . (II.12-13)

A similar parallel appears a few lines later, "god" being rendered by
the plural orthography in several copies, including two from
Ashurbanipal's libraries:

> u₄-mu pa-la-aḫ DINGIR.MEŠ ṭu-ub lìb-bi-ia
> u₄-mu ri-du-ti ᵈiš-tar né-me-li ta-at-tur-ru
> The day for reverencing the god was a joy to my heart;
> The day of the goddess's procession was profit and gain to me.
> (II.25-26)

Following an enumeration of honorable acts, the speaker despairs,

> lu-u i-di ki-i it-ti DINGIR.MEŠ i-ta-am-ku-ra an-na-a-ti
> I wish I knew that these things were pleasing to one's god! (II.33)

The reading DINGIR.MEŠ in this passage is preserved in a seventh-
century manuscript from Sultantepe, as a variant to the singular writing
in other copies.

The plural writing for *ilu* in both *Ludlul bēl nēmeqi* and "The
Babylonian Theodicy" is shown by its use with singular grammatical
forms, by context, by parallelism, and by textual variants to be both
interchangeable with the singular and a variant expression of the word
meaning "god" or "deity."[143] Thus the usage shows itself to be the
same expression attested in the roughly contemporary Sargonid
correspondence.

---

[142]Ibid., 26.

[143]Cf. the conclusion that the plural form is used strictly in the context of the
personal god (Lambert, *BWL*, 67), and, for a similar conclusion regarding texts discussed
in the following section of the text, see Marie-Joseph Seux, *Hymnes et prieres aux dieux
de Babylonie et d'Assyrie* (Paris: Cerf, 1976), 143 n. 1, 314 n. 19.

Ritual Texts. Other evidence from the same period is found in eighth-seventh century copies of "šu.ila"-prayers, in which the plural writing DINGIR.MEŠ/.ME is used in various contexts with the basic meaning "deity."[144] With the exception of Madānu 1, line 2, all of the instances cited occur as variants to singular DINGIR.

As in wisdom literature, the plural writing can occur as a counterpart to singular "goddess" in the discussion of the individual's relationship to the divine:

> DINGIR.MEŠ u ᵈU.DA[R] ze-nu-tu₄ šab-su-tu₄ [u ki]-it-mu-lu-tú
> ⌞li-is⌟ -li-mu KI.MU
> May the god and goddess who are incensed, angry, and disgruntled be reconciled to me. (Nergal 2, line 23)

With respect to the same concerns, the plural form is associated with the term *šēdu*:

> ᵈALAD₂ na-ṣi-ru DINGIR.MEŠ mu-šal-li-mu šu-zi-iz AŠ SAG-ia₅[145]
> Place at my head a protective *šēdu*, a safeguarding deity. (Nusku 4, line 47)

The same expression, *ilū mušallimu*, is used clearly as a singular in another prayer, in the context of divine protection:

> lit-tal-lak DINGIR.ME mu-šal-li-mu ina Á-MU lu ka-a-a-an
> May a safeguarding deity always walk at my side. (Šamaš 1, line 124)

A text devoted to Madānu (labeled "Madānu 1" in Mayer), though extolling the god's benevolence toward humankind, speaks of the deity's sphere of influence as transcending that of the personal god. The speaker refers to him as DINGIR.MEŠ kib-ra-a-ti, "Gottheit der ganzen Welt" (line 2), and ᵈDI.KUD DINGIR.MEŠ réme-nu-ú šá bul-lu-ṭu i-ram-mu, "barmherziger Gott, der gern Leben schenkt" (line

---

[144]Werner Mayer, *Untersuchungen zur Formensprache der Babylonischen "Gebetsbeschwörungen"* (Studia Pohl: Series Maior 5; Rome: Pontifical Biblical Institute, 1976), 464-65; the transliterations of these texts are taken from Mayer, unless noted otherwise.

[145]Transliteration taken from Erich Ebeling, *Die Akkadische Gebetsserie "Handerhebung"* (Deutsche Akademie der Wissenschaften zu Berlin, Institut für Orientforschung 20; Berlin: Akademie-Verlag, 1953), 40.

12).[146]   The general meaning "deity" or "god" is clear both in reference to "Zaqar, the god of dreams" (AN.ZA.GÀR DINGIR.MEŠ šá MÁŠ.GI₆.MEŠ; Sin 1, line 25) and in the expression "god and king" (DINGIR.MEŠ u ⌊LUGAL⌋, where the plural writing occurs as a variant to singular DINGIR; Ea 1a, line 10). Singular *ilū/ilānū* in eighth-to-seventh-century copies of the "šu.ila"-prayers is used interchangeably with singular *ilu* and with various nuances of the meaning "god" or "deity."

A Babylonian Royal Inscription.   An inscription of Nabonidus commemorating the restoration of the temple of Sin at Ur,[147] extols the deity as

> ᵈSin EN DINGIR.MEŠ ša AN-e u KI-tim
> LUGAL DINGIR.MEŠ DINGIR.MEŠ ša DINGIR.MEŠ
> a-ši-ib AN-e GAL.MEŠ EN è-giš-šir-gal
> ša qi-rib URI₂ᵏⁱ EN-ia

> Sin, lord of the gods of heaven and the netherworld,
> king of the gods, god of gods,
> dwelling in the great heaven, lord of Ekishnugal
> in Ur, my lord (i 28-31)

> ᵈSin be-lí DINGIR.MEŠ
> LUGAL DINGIR.MEŠ ša AN-e u KI-tim
> DINGIR.MEŠ ša DINGIR.MEŠ
> a-ši-ib AN-e GAL.MEŠ

> Sin, lord of the gods,
> king of the gods of heaven and earth,
> god of gods,
> dwelling in the great heaven. (ii 3-6)

As the *nomen regens* of the superlative construction DINGIR.MEŠ ša DINGIR.MEŠ (*ilū ša ilū*, "god of gods"),[148] singular DINGIR.MEŠ in reference to Sin here is used in apposition to the terms *bēlu* and *šarru* and is paired with the singular form *ašib*. This passage shows

---

[146]The translations are those of Mayer, *Untersuchungen*.

[147]Stephen Langdon, ed. *Die Neubabylonischen Königsinschriften* (VAB 4; Leipzig: J. C. Hinrichs, 1912), 252-53.

[148]Cf. Biblical Hebrew *'ĕlōhê hā'ĕlōhîm*, Deut 10:17; Ps 136:2; *'ēl 'ēlîm*, Dan 11:36.

singular DINGIR.MEŠ to be appropriate in the context not only of the personal god but of the supreme deity. The meaning is similar in the following text.

Hymn Texts. An Achaemenid-period copy of a hymn to Nergal[149] preserves the following passage:

> qar-ra-du ŠEŠ.MEŠ-šú DINGIR.MEŠ NIR.GÁL
> šu-tur EN UGU DÙ ᵈÍ.GÌ.GÌ
> ᵈGIR₄-KÙ DINGIR.MEŠ e-til-lu
> šu-tur EN e-li kal-la ᵈÍ.GÌ.GÌ

> Warrior among his brothers, princely god,
> Lord surpassing all the Igigi-gods,
> Nergal, princely god,
> Lord surpassing all the Igigi-gods . . . (lines 1-4)

> DINGIR.MEŠ šá ḫu-u-du šá-lum-mat uz-zu-zu
> ᵈGIR₄-KÙ me-lam-mu na-mur-rat ka-sir
> DINGIR.MEŠ šá ḫu-u-du šá-l[um-m]at [u]z-zu[-z]u

> The god who is furious in joy(?) (and) fearsomeness,
> Nergal has fastened on a vestment of divine splendor and awesomeness,
> The god who is furious in joy(?) (and) fea[rsomeness]! (lines 6-8)[150]

The succession of epithets in lines 1-4 places *ilānū* in apposition to *qarradu* and *bēlu*, and, in lines 6 and 8, *ilānū* is paired with the masculine singular adjective *uzzuzu*. The deity is described here as superlative among the gods of the pantheon.

Another hymn preserved in a Persian-period manuscript refers to the spouse of the goddess Gula as

> DINGIR.MEŠ el-li šá AŠ šar-ru-tum as-mu
> the pure god, who is suited for kingship. (line 157)[151]

---

[149]Published in Jean Nougayrol, "Textes et documents figurés," *RA* 41 (1947): 38-41.

[150]The translation is that of Benjamin R. Foster, *Before the Muses: An Anthology of Akkadian Literature* (2d ed.; 2 vols.; Bethesda, Md.: CDL Press, 1996), 2:613-14.

[151]Wilfred G. Lambert, "The Gula Hymn of Bulluṭsa-rabi (Tab. VIII—XXIII)," *Or* 36 (1967): 105-32, whose translation is given here.

Here singular *ilānū* is seen to be appropriate in the description of a deity as exalted among the gods.

The use of singular *ilānū/ilū* in various contexts in various kinds of Akkadian texts from the first millennium shows the term to cover the same range of meanings as singular *ilu* ("god," "deity") with which it is interchangeable.

Personal Names.[152]   This last observation—i.e., that *ilū/ilānu* is basically equivalent to *ilu* in use and meaning in Akkadian—is reinforced by evidence from Neo-Babylonian and Late Babylonian onomastica, in which the plural writing for "god" is interchangeable with the singular.   Though offering a different explanation, Stamm cites some examples, including, from the reign of Neriglissar, *dSin*-DINGIR and *dSin*-DINGIR.MEŠ, and, from Nabonidus' reign, *dNabû-nūr*-DINGIR and *dNabû-nūr*-DINGIR.MEŠ, as variant writings of the same individuals' names.[153]

Stamm's suggestion of "orthographische Ungenauigkeit" as an explanation for the variance begs the question of why such an "imprecision" evidently pertains only to the word for "god" and not to other PN elements.   A likely explanation is that singular *ili* and (morphologically) plural *ilī* would have been close enough in pronunciation that the plural form, as it became more common as a variant form of the term meaning "god," eventually and gradually made its way into personal names, which being conservative in nature are more resistant both to grammatical and to theological change.

---

[152]The element "(the) gods" with sg. verbs in a number of PNN expresses a numerical (collective) plural (i.e., "the Pantheon") and represents a separate usage: Old Akkadian, Iš-dup-DINGIR.DINGIR, I-ti-DINGIR.DINGIR, I_3-lu-da-lil$_2$, I_3-lu-DINGIR (all cited in J. J. M. Roberts, *The Earliest Semitic Pantheon: A Study of the Semitic Deities Attested in Mesopotamia Before Ur III* [JHNES; Baltimore: Johns Hopkins Univ. Press, 1972], 134); Old Babylonian, *ibašši-ilānī* (Knut L. Tallqvist, *Assyrian Personal Names* [Helsinki: Societas Scientiarum Fennica, 1914], XXXV); Middle Assyrian, *ilānī-aḫa-iddina* (TR 3016:6 in *Iraq* 30 [1968]: 82), *ilānī-[eriš]* (Ass. 6096 ch², published in Ernst Weidner, "Aus den Tagen eines assyrischen Schattenkönigs," *AfO* [1935]: 39, restored by Simo Parpola, "The Assyrian Tree of Life," *JNES* 52 [1993]: 187 n. 97); Neo-Assyrian, *Gabbu-ilānī-šarru-uṣur* (Ass. 8890:9 and rev. 5, cited in Parpola, "Tree of Life," 187 n. 97); *Gabbu-ilānī-eriš* (Tallqvist, *APN*, 78).

[153]Johann Jakob Stamm, *Die Akkadische Namengebung* (Leipzig: J. C. Hinrichs, 1939), 71-72 and nn. 2 and 3. Stamm suggests that an "orthographische Ungenauigkeit" is responsible for the variation (p. 71).

Consistent with this explanation are instances in which *ilu*-names from an earlier era are rendered with the plural writing in Neo-Babylonian texts. Stamm compares Old Babylonian Ì-lí-*rēmanni* with Neo-Babylonian DINGIR.MEŠ-ri-man-ni.[154] Lambert cites the Kassite-period name EGIR-DINGIR-dam-qa (*arkāt-ili-damqā*), which during the Late Babylonian period is written ár-kát-DINGIR.MEŠ-SIG$_5$.[155] Hehn offers the following comparisons: Old Babylonian *iddin-ilum*, cf. Neo-Babylonian *ilānī-iddin*; Old Akkadian *ilu-ittia*, cf. Late Babylonian *ilū-ittia*.[156] With respect to the occurrence either of the singular or of the plural in the spelling of the same person's name (as noted by Stamm), if both terms have the same meaning and sound virtually if not completely identical, it is not surprising that both variants should appear, even within the same document.

Other Neo-Babylonian PNN containing singular DINGIR.MEŠ are attested. Hehn cites the following: *ilū-qa-nu-ú-a, mušallim-ilū, ilū-a-di-nu*.[157] The Murašu documents from fifth-century Nippur include the following names:[158] ᶦsi-lim-DINGIR.MEŠ,[159] ᶦrab-bi-DINGIR.MEŠ (and its variant ᶦra-ab-bi-DINGIR.MEŠ), ᶦli-nu-uḫ-ŠÁ-bi-DINGIR.MEŠ, ᶦ·ᵍⁱˢMI.DINGIR.MEŠ (*ṣilli-ilī*), ᶦin-DINGIR.MEŠ (*īn-ilī*), and ᶦNUMUN.KI.I.DINGIR.MEŠ (*zēr-itti[?]-ilī*). The Neo-Babylonian onomastica attest to what had become a common practice in Akkadian of writing "god" as a plural in PNN.[160] Coogan identifies twenty-eight such names for eighty different individuals, containing DINGIR.MEŠ both in initial and in final positions.[161] The plural writing in these West Semitic PNN would have been consistent with the meaning of the PN element, in that, at least in Hebrew and Phoenician, the standard word for "god" is in the plural form and that,

---

[154]Ibid., 72 n. 1.

[155]Lambert, *BWL*, 67.

[156]Hehn, *babylonische Gottesidee*, 169.

[157]Ibid.

[158]Michael D. Coogan, *West Semitic Personal Names in the Murašû Documents* (HSM 7; Missoula, Mont.: Scholars Press, 1976), 43-44.

[159]Cf., from the same corpus, ᶦsi-lim-ᵈEN.LÍL, ᶦsi-lim-ᵈEN, ᶦᵈEN-si-lim, etc.; ibid., 44.

[160]Coogan, *West Semitic Personal Names*, 43-47; Hehn, *babylonische Gottesidee*, 171.

[161]Coogan, *West Semitic Personal Names*, 44-47.

in the Hebrew Bible, *'ēl*-names are etymologized by *'ĕlōhîm*.[162] The superimposition of an Akkadian grammatical form that is not present in an original West Semitic PN but consistent with its meaning (as represented by the writing DINGIR.MEŠ for *'ēl*) also occurs in the precative verbal prefix in DINGIR.MEŠ-*lindar*, a name which, for lexical reasons, is to be identified as West Semitic.[163]

In a few instances in West Semitic PNN, the singular form does appear both in names in which the plural is otherwise attested (ᴵDINGIR-li-in-dar and ᴵDINGIR-in-dar for ᴵDINGIR.MEŠ-li-in-dar, *barīk*-DINGIR for *barīk*-DINGIR.MEŠ, *ya'darnī*-DINGIR for *ya'darnī*-DINGIR.MEŠ, and *raḥīm*-DINGIR for *raḥīm*-DINGIR.MEŠ)[164] and in names with the theophoric element *bêt'ēl*, written with singular and plural forms—e.g., ᴵᵈÉ.DINGIR.ZALAG-' (*bêt-'ēl-nūrī*), ᴵÉ. ⌐DINGIR⌐-ḫa-da-ri (*bêt-'ēl-'adar*), ᴵᵈÉ.DINGIR.MEŠ-da-la-' (*bêt'ēl-dalā*), and ᴵÉ.DINGIR.MEŠ.A.KAL(/DIR).RI (*bêt-'ēl-'ādir* or *bêt-'ēl-'addīr*).[165] As noted for other PNN, this variance does not reveal a mere lack of precision in Babylonian orthography, according to which "both the singular and the plural of *ilu* could be written either DINGIR or DINGIR.MEŠ."[166] Coogan's invocation of "the use of DINGIR and DINGIR.MEŠ as free variants" in explanation of the phenomenon in earlier Akkadian (even in the Amarna letters, where the phonetic complement indicating the plural form is often included) accounts neither for the writings DINGIR.ME and DINGIR.DINGIR in place of the singular (see above)[167] nor for the fact that (outside of PNN) examples of singular *ilu* occurring in place of an expected plural are apparently not attested. The variance within the onomastica of the Murašû documents shows that *ilū/ilānū* had become interchangeable with *ilu* in Akkadian as the noun meaning "god." This conclusion is

---

[162]E.g., PNN: Israel, Gen 32:28; GNN: Bethel, Gen 28:17; Peniel, Gen 32:28.

[163]Coogan, *West Semitic Personal Names*, 45.

[164]Ibid., 46.

[165]Ibid., 48-49.

[166]Ibid., 46, following Stamm, *ANG*, 71.

[167]Coogan, *West Semitic Personal Names*, 58 n. 19. Coogan does not seem to be aware of those instances, based on his mention only of "the analogous use of DINGIR.DINGIR in Old Akkadian personal names"; on the latter, see the footnote at the beginning of this section on PNN.

in keeping with the rest of the evidence from first-millennium Akkadian.

Conclusions

The plural writing for "god," having been introduced into Akkadian by the seventh century, came to be employed as a variant of singular *ilu*. Its appearance in various types of Akkadian texts during the Neo-Assyrian, Neo-Babylonian, and Persian periods, taken as a whole, shows the expression to have had a significant usage. Its abrupt appearance, along with other concretized abstract plurals, in Sargonid Royal correspondence makes it likely that the Akkadian usage was borrowed from the west and was derived ultimately from the Canaanite expression attested in the Amarna letters and eventuating both in Hebrew *'ĕlōhîm* and in Phoenician *'lm*.

Summary

Biblical Hebrew *'ĕlōhîm* is an example of a Canaanite linguistic development, namely, the concretized abstract plural, according to which the nominal plural form expresses an abstraction in reference to an individual or thing that holds a particular status named by the abstract category in question. Thus the plural of the noun "god" occurs with the meaning "deity." The Late Bronze Age forerunner of *'ĕlōhîm* is attested in the Amarna vassal correspondence and in other cuneiform texts from Syria-Palestine. The Iron Age reflex of this Canaanite expression occurs not only in Hebrew but also in Phoenician. A few Aramaic texts present possible instances in which the Canaanite usage, having passed into certain dialects of Aramaic, appears in the latter. The first-millennium Akkadian counterpart of *'ĕlōhîm* is most likely the result of linguistic borrowing from the west, ultimately from the Canaanite group of Northwest Semitic languages. It is important to recognize that the use of *'ĕlōhîm*'s counterparts in these other languages conveys the general sense "god" or "deity" without any specific nuance in meaning. This consideration is foundational to an understanding of the significance of Biblical Hebrew *'ĕlōhîm*.

'Ĕlōhîm AS A COMMON NOUN

The investigation of biblical 'ĕlōhîm as a designation for Israel's god requires consideration of the word's usage as a common noun. Comprehensive word studies of 'ĕlōhîm, the results of which need not be duplicated here, can be found in the standard reference works.[168] Our lexical analysis of 'ĕlōhîm will begin with two aspects that were found to be significant with respect to its counterparts in the extrabiblical sources: the term's generic meaning and its abstract character.[169] As our examination of the comparative material has shown, 'ĕlōhîm's pre-Israelite antecedent was used in the same contexts and with the same range of meanings as the singular form of the word meaning "god," and, like the Late Bronze usage, the Iron Age counterparts to 'ĕlōhîm were used with the general sense "god" or "deity." The comparative evidence has also led to the conclusion that 'ĕlōhîm and its extrabiblical equivalents are best understood as concretized abstract plurals. These considerations call for a comparison of 'ĕlōhîm with other words for "god" in Biblical Hebrew and for an examination of 'ĕlōhîm's character as an abstract noun. Afterwards we will discuss three contexts in which the use of 'ĕlōhîm as a common noun is especially significant: in religious and legal technical language, in connection with patron deities, and in the depiction of international settings. We will also examine instances in which pl. 'ĕlōhîm, "gods," occurs where the sg. 'ĕlōhîm would be expected.

'Ĕlōhîm in Comparison with Other Words for "god"

As might be expected on the basis of the Late Bronze comparative evidence, the common noun usage of 'ĕlōhîm covers the same range of meanings as that of other, less frequently occurring words used in reference to Israel's god, 'ēl and 'ĕlôăh. Although, as we shall see, 'ĕlōhîm's particular history resulted in its distinct significance as a divine title,[170] it is important to note at this point that 'ĕlōhîm's

---

[168]See *HAL*, 1:50-52; Helmer Ringgren, *TDOT* 1:267-84; Werner H. Schmidt, "אֱלֹהִים *ᵉlōhîm* Gott," *THAT* 1:154-67.

[169]See above, The Late Bronze Age Antecedent.

[170]See below, Chapter 3. The Title *'ĕlōhîm* in Israelite Religion.

generic meaning is born out by its reciprocity with other terms for "god" in Biblical Hebrew.

Like *'ĕlōhîm*, both *'ēl* and *'ĕlôăh* are used in reference to "a god" in a general sense: *'ēl 'aḥēr*, "another god" (Exod 34:14); *'ēl lō' yôšîa'*, "a god who does not save" (Isa 45:20); *'ēl-ḥāpēṣ reša'*, "a god who delights in doing harm" (Ps 5:5), etc.; *'ĕlôah mā'uzzîm*, "a god of fortresses" (Dan 11:38).

All three words are used in reference to the gods of other peoples: *dāgôn 'ĕlōhêhem*, "Dagon, their (the Philistines') god" (Judg 16:23); *kĕmôš 'ĕlōhêkā*, "Chemosh, your deity" (Judg 11:24); *zû kōḥô lĕ'lōhô*, "whose strength is his god" (Hab 1:11); *'ēl zār*, "strange god" (Ps 44:21); *'ēl nēkār* (Deut 32:12; Mal 2:11; Ps 81:10) and *'ĕlôah nēkār* (Dan 11:39), "foreign god"; *'ĕlôah 'ăšer lō'-yĕdā'ûhû 'ăbōtāyw*, "a god whom his ancestors did not know" (Dan 11:38).

Both *'ĕlōhîm* and *'ēl* are used in reference to a divine image: *'ĕlōhê zāhāb*, "a god of gold" (Exod 32:31); *'ĕlōhê massēkâ*, "a molten god" (Exod 34:17); *habbōṭĕḥîm bappāsel hā'ōmĕrîm lĕmassēkâ 'attem 'ĕlōhênû*, "they who trust in an idol, who say to a molten image, 'You are our god'" (Isa 42:17); *mî yāṣar 'ēl ûpesel nāsak*, "Who has fashioned a god and cast an idol?" (Isa 44:10); *yip'al-'ēl wayyištāhû*, "He makes a god and worships it" (v. 15); *ûšĕ'ērîtô lĕ'ēl 'āśâ lĕpislô*, "The rest (of the wood) he makes into a god, into his idol" (v. 17); "Those who lavish gold from a purse and weigh silver on the scale—they hire a goldsmith, and he makes it into a god (*'ēl*)" (46:6).

All three words are used in the same way with respect to Yahweh's uniqueness as "God." This point is illustrated by the questions posed in 2 Sam 22:32 (*kî mî-'ēl mibbal'ădê yhwh*, "Who is God but Yahweh?"), in Ps 18:32 (*kî mî-'ĕlôah mibbal'ădê yhwh*, "Who is God but Yahweh?"), and in Isa 44:8 (*hăyēš 'ĕlôah mibbal'āday*, "Is there a god besides me?"), and by the statement in 2 Kgs 5:15 (*kî 'ên 'ĕlōhîm bĕkŏl-hā'āreṣ kî 'im-bĕyiśrā'ēl*, "There is no god in all the earth except in Israel").

'Ĕlōhîm is used in many of the same phrases as *'ēl* and *'ĕlôah*, as the following comparisons illustrate: *'ĕlōhê yiśrā'ēl* (Josh 22:24; 2 Kgs 19:15) and *'ēl yiśrā'ēl* (Ps 68:36); *'ĕlōhîm ḥay* (2 Kgs 19:4, 16; Isa 37:4, 17), *'ĕlōhîm ḥayyîm* (1 Sam 7:26, 36; Jer 10:10; 23:36), and *'ēl ḥay* (Josh 3:10; Hos 2:1; Pss 42:3; 84:3) "living god"; *lō' 'ĕlōhîm* (Hos 8:6), *lō'-'ēl* (Deut 32:21; Isa 31:3), and *lō' 'ĕlôah* (Deut 32:17)

"no god"; *'ĕlōhê ya'ăqōb* (2 Sam 23:1; Isa 2:3; Mic 4:2; Pss 20:2; 46:8; etc.), *'ēl ya'ăqōb* (Ps 146:5), and *'ĕlôah ya'ăqōb* (Ps 114:7) "god of Jacob"; *rûaḥ 'ĕlōhîm* (Gen 1:2; 41:38; Exod 31:3; 1 Sam 10:10; etc.), *rûaḥ-'ēl* (Job 33:4), and *rûaḥ 'ĕlôah* (Job 27:3) "divine wind/breath"; *'ĕlōhê haššāmayim* (Gen 24:3, 7; Jonah 1:9; Ezra 1:2; Neh 1:4; etc.) and *'ēl haššāmayim* (Ps 136:26) "god of heaven"; *'ĕlōhê 'ābîkā* (Gen 46:3; 50:17; Exod 3:6; etc.) and *'ēl 'ābîkā* (Gen 49:25) "god of your father"; *'ĕlōhê hā'ĕlōhîm* (Deut 10:17; Ps 136:2) and *'ēl 'ēlîm* (Dan 11:36) "god of gods"; *'ĕlōhê 'ĕmet* (2 Chr 15:3) and *'ēl 'ĕmet* (Ps 31:6) "true/faithful god"; *'ĕlōhê yĕšû'ātî* (Ps 88:2) and *'ēl yĕšû'ātî* (Isa 12:2) "the god of my deliverance"; *'ĕlōhê 'ôlām* (Isa 40:28) and *'ēl 'ôlām* (Gen 21:33) "god of eternity"; *'ĕlōhîm ṣaddîq* (Ps 7:10) and *'ēl-ṣaddîq* (Isa 45:21) "righteous god."

In the following passages *'ēl* and *'ĕlōhîm* are used interchangeably within the same context.

> *wĕ'ên 'ôd 'epes 'ĕlōhîm / 'ākēn 'attâ 'ēl mistattēr 'ĕlōhê yiśrā'ēl*
> There is no other, no god (*'ĕlōhîm*) (besides Israel's god). / Truly you are a god (*'ēl*) who hides himself, O god (*'ĕlōhîm*) of Israel. (Isa 45:14-15)

> *'ēl 'ānî môšab 'ĕlōhîm yāšabtî . . '. wĕ'attâ 'ādām wĕlō'-'ēl wattittēn libbĕkā kĕlēb 'ĕlōhîm*
> (The prince of Tyre says,) "I am a god (*'ēl*); I sit on the throne of a god (*'ĕlōhîm*) . . ." But you are a mortal and not a god (*'ēl*), though you regard your heart as the heart of a god (*'ĕlōhîm*). (Ezek 28:2)

> *'ĕlōhîm 'ānî . . . wĕ'attâ 'ādām wĕlō'-'ēl*
> (Will you still say,) "I am a god (*'ĕlōhîm*)" . . . though you are a mortal and not a god (*'ēl*)? (v. 9)

In Dan 11:36-38, *'ĕlōhîm*, *'ēl*, and *'ĕlôah*, all three, are used interchangeably:

> He will magnify himself above every god (*'ēl*), and he will speak extraordinary things against the greatest god (*'ēl 'ēlîm*) . . . He will not regard the god of his ancestors (*'ĕlōhê 'ăbōtāyw*) or the one beloved by women, and he will not regard any other god (*'ĕlôah*) but will magnify himself above all. He will honor instead a god (*'ĕlôah*) of fortresses, a god (*'ĕlôah*) his ancestors did not know.

These examples demonstrate clearly that 'ĕlōhîm as a common noun is used with the same range of meanings and in the same contexts as 'ēl and 'ĕlôăh, other words having the generic sense "god."

While 'ĕlōhîm's general meaning makes it synonymous with these other terms, its use with other nuances of meaning shows it to have an even broader semantic range than the alternatives. In a few instances, the notion of "the divine" applies to "superhuman" beings, rather than gods as commonly perceived in the Hebrew Bible. For instance, Ps 8:6 says of humankind, "You have made him a little lower than a god ('ĕlōhîm)," the latter occupying a place in the order of creation somewhere between Yahweh and humans. Elsewhere, the spirit of the deceased Samuel is called an 'ĕlōhîm by the medium at Endor (1 Sam 28:13). In Ps 45:7-8, the king is addressed as 'ĕlōhîm. In Exod 4:16, Yahweh tells Moses, hû' yihye(h)-lĕkā lĕpe(h) wĕ'attâ tihye(h)-lô lē'lōhîm, "He [Aaron] shall be as a mouth for you, and you shall be to him as a god," and in 7:1, nĕtatîkâ 'ĕlōhîm lĕpar'ō(h), "I have made you as a god to Pharaoh." The employment of 'ĕlōhîm to the exclusion of other words for "god" in these contexts shows the former to be more flexible in meaning than the alternatives.

In its usage in various contexts, 'ĕlōhîm represents neither a single specialized nuance of "god" nor a particular type of deity. Rather, as the preferred word for "god" in Biblical Hebrew, it has the basic sense "god" or "deity" and is quite flexible in its application. Ironically, as we shall see, this generic sense of 'ĕlōhîm proved advantageous in the term's use as a substitute for a specific DN, a phenomenon which resulted ultimately in the use of 'ĕlōhîm as an important religious title.[171]

The Abstract Nature of 'ĕlōhîm

As noted, though 'ĕlōhîm is roughly synonymous with other words for "god," it is somewhat more flexible in its usage. This aspect of 'ĕlōhîm corresponds to another one that distinguishes it from those terms, namely, that it is essentially an abstract noun.[172] The abstract

---

[171]See below, Chapter 3. The Title 'ĕlōhîm in Israelite Religion.
[172]See above, Grammatical Issues.

nature of *'ĕlōhîm* is given expression in its usage as an adjectival genitive, i.e., where *'ĕlōhîm* occurs as the *nomen rectum* in various construct expressions.   An analysis of these expressions not only confirms the abstract character of *'ĕlōhîm* but also sheds light on the implications of that abstract quality for *'ĕlōhîm*'s meaning and usage as a common noun.

The locution to be considered follows the pattern *X 'ĕlōhîm* and is used mainly in technical expressions.   An example is *bĕnê (hā) 'ĕlōhîm*, "divine beings" (Gen 6:2, 4; Job 1:6; 2:1; 38:7).   That *'ĕlōhîm* in this phrase does not in itself refer to a specific god but to "the divine" in general is clear from the variant form of the expression, *bĕnê 'ēlîm*, literally "sons of gods" (Pss 29:1; 89:7).   The phrase *'îš (hā) 'ĕlōhîm* (1 Sam 2:27; 9:6; 1 Kgs 13:1; etc.), though usually occurring in reference to a representative of Israel's God, designates one as a "man of the divine" or holy man and, in and of itself, does not refer to Yahweh.   The phrases *mar'ôt 'ĕlōhîm*, "divine visions" (Ezek 1:1; 8:3; 40:2), and *ma'ănē(h) 'ĕlōhîm*, "divine reply" (Mic 3:7), identify forms of supernatural communication and, though used with Yahweh in view, do not in themselves denote the revelations of a particular god.   The *ḥerdat 'ĕlōhîm*, "divine trembling," that overcomes Israel's enemy in 1 Sam 14:15 is, as defined in BDB, a "terror ascribed to supernat[ural] causes,"[173] a phenomenon also called "divine terror" (*ḥittat 'ĕlōhîm*) in Gen 35:5.[174]   The *rûaḥ 'ĕlōhîm*[175] ("divine wind" or "divine spirit") both manifests the divine presence (Gen 1:2) and imbues a human agent with supernatural ability (41:38; Exod 31:3; Num 24:2; 1 Sam 10:10; etc.). Superhuman wisdom is called *ḥokmat 'ĕlōhîm*, "divine wisdom" (1 Kgs

---

[173]Francis Brown, ed. *The New Brown-Driver-Briggs-Gesenius Hebrew and English Lexicon with an Appendix Containing the Biblical Aramaic* (Peabody, Mass.: Hendrickson, 1979), 353.

[174]Cf. the hypostatization of the divine dread in the epithet *paḥad yiṣḥāq* (Gen 31:42) and "the dread of Yahweh" (*paḥad yhwh*), which is associated with the specific deity (1 Sam 11:7; Isa 2:10, 19, 21; etc.). For more on *paḥad yiṣḥāq*, see below, *'Ĕlōhîm* in the Patriarchal Traditions of E. On the phenomenon of hypostatization, see below, The Title *'ĕlōhîm* in the National Cult.

[175]Cf. *rûaḥ-'ēl*, which parallels *nišmat šadday*, "the breath of Shaddai," in Job 33:4 and *rûaḥ 'ĕlôah* in 27:3.

3:28). The deity's displeasure is expressed in the "divine curse" (*qillat 'ĕlōhîm*, Deut 21:23). The fact that no corresponding variants along the lines *X yhwh* occur for any of these expressions suggests that we are dealing with established technical phrases originally pertaining to matters in no way peculiar to any one god but to "the divine" in general, as expressed by the abstract term *'ĕlōhîm*.

As would be expected in the context of the Hebrew Bible, though, some of the expressions following the pattern *X 'ĕlōhîm* occur with corresponding phrases of the pattern *X yhwh*. Expressions for the divine abode, *har (hā) 'ĕlōhîm* (Exod 3:1; 4:27; 18:5; 24:13; Ezek 28:14, 16; 1 Kgs 19:8; Ps 68:16; cf. *har yhwh*, Gen 22:14; Num 10:33 and, explicitly in reference to Zion, Isa 2:3; 30:29; Mic 2:4; Zech 8:3; Ps 24:3) and *gan(-hā) 'elōhîm* (Ezek 28:13; 31:8, 9; cf. *gan-yhwh*, Gen 13:10; Isa 51:3), do not in themselves name a particular deity, although the biblical context warrants translating these expressions "mountain of God" and "garden of God," respectively. While references to temples and sanctuaries are usually to those of specific deities and are thus designated as *bêt yhwh* (1 Kgs 6:37; etc.), *bêt dāgôn* (1 Sam 5:2, 5), or *bêt 'ĕlōhāyw* ("the house of his god," Ezra 1:7), the phrase *bêt 'ĕlōhîm* ("house of a god/gods/the divine," Judg 17:5) denotes a sanctuary in general, a sense which is conveyed in the title *nĕgîd bêt hā 'ĕlōhîm*, "Overseer of the Temple" (Neh 11:11; 1 Chr 9:11; etc.; no corresponding title containing *bêt yhwh* or the like occurs). The phrase *dĕbar 'ĕlōhîm*, "divine message" (Judg 3:20; 1 Sam 9:27; etc.), may be compared with the much more frequent *dĕbar yhwh*, "word of Yahweh," and *nĕ'ūm yhwh*, "utterance of Yahweh."

"Divine fire," *'ēš 'ĕlōhîm*, can be an unwelcome manifestation of the deity's power (2 Kgs 1:2; Job 1:16; cf. *'ēš yhwh*, Num 11:1, 3; 1 Kgs 18:38). What is significant about the comparisons noted is that, although the option *X yhwh* existed, *X 'ĕlōhîm* was so frequently preferred. While the biblical context and the corresponding phrases containing *yhwh* make it clear that these *'ĕlōhîm*-expressions were used with the god of Israel in mind, the common and in some cases predominant use of *'ĕlōhîm* in these phrases indicates that we are dealing with fixed technical expressions for which the general meaning conveyed by *'ĕlōhîm* was appropriate.

The use of *'ĕlōhîm* as an adjectival genitive in these various phrases demonstrates how the character of *'ĕlōhîm* as an abstract noun results in its generic meaning, "deity, divinity," a quality that is well illustrated in the expression *'ĕlōhîm wa'ănāšîm*, "god and man" or "the divine and the human" (Judg 9:9, 13; *'im-'ĕlōhîm wĕ'im-'ănāšîm*, Gen 32:29). What is more, our overview of these expressions confirms what has been noted already, namely, that *'ĕlōhîm*'s abstract character gives it a greater flexibility than the other terms for "god" mentioned above (*'ēl* and *'ĕlôah*). With the exception of two instances (both from Job), these genitive expressions occurred without corresponding variants containing those terms. Thus *'ĕlōhîm* by virtue of its abstract nature proves more suitable than the alternative common nouns for use in these phrases designating things associated with "the divine."

This abstractness and greater flexibility of *'ĕlōhîm* is clearly seen in the noun's usage in reference either to a god or a goddess, as in 1 Kgs 11:33, which lists *lĕ'aštōret 'ĕlōhê ṣidōnîm lĕkĕmôš 'ĕlōhê mô'āb ûlĕmilkōm 'ĕlōhê bĕnê 'ammôn*, "Ashtart, the deity of the Sidonians; Chemosh, the deity of Moab; and Milcom, the deity of the Ammonites." By contrast, neither *'ēl* nor *'ĕlôah* would be appropriate in reference to a female deity. The general sense of *'ĕlōhîm*, which is derived from its abstract nature, will have relevance for the use of *'ĕlōhîm* as a divine title (see below).

Appellative *'ĕlōhîm* in Technical Language

We have seen that *'ĕlōhîm*'s abstract nature gives it a flexibility and general meaning that are suitable to technical language. Two areas of technical usage in which *'ĕlōhîm* has an important role as a common noun are religious and legal language. An examination of the technical usage of *'ĕlōhîm* in these established contexts provides insight into its role as a designation for Israel's God.

To "curse God," an offense which involves both religious and legal spheres, is an unspeakable behavior, as witnessed both by the occurrence of *brk* "bless" as a euphemism for *qll* "curse" in 1 Kgs 21:10, 13; Job 1:5; 2:9, and by the emendation necessary for identifying the transgression that Eli's sons have committed in 1 Sam 3:13. That this is a general expression and, in itself, not in reference to a particular deity, is apparent from the Covenant Code's prohibition of this act: *ʾĕlōhîm lōʾ tĕqallēl wĕnāśîʾ bĕʿammĕkā lōʾ tāʾōr*, "You shall not revile a deity nor curse a leader among your people" (Exod 22:27).[176] As the parallel expression to *ʾĕlōhîm* in this injunction, the indefinite phrase *nāśîʾ bĕʿammĕkā* makes clear that the former is to be understood in the most indefinite sense. No indication of a more specific variation on the phrase, such as "to curse Yahweh," is evident. In 1 Kgs 21:10, 13, Naboth is wrongly executed on the false charge of "cursing god and king" (*brk ʾĕlōhîm wāmelek*), an offense that is essentially and literally (taking into account the euphemistic use of *brk*) synonymous with that named in Exod 22:27. It hardly requires explaining that the identity of the king reputedly cursed here, Ahab, is known not from the given expression but from the background circumstances; the same is true of the god in question. Thus the expression "to curse (a/the) god" is an intrinsically general one and becomes specific only by virtue of a particular context.

The nonspecific sense of *ʾĕlōhîm* is also essential to the utterance "There is no god" (*ʾēn ʾĕlōhîm*, Pss 10:4; 14:1; 53:2), the claim made by one who denies accountability to the divine for his actions. Again, no corresponding expression naming Yahweh is attested. In this example, as in the prohibition against "cursing a god," *ʾĕlōhîm* is employed in generic religious language, with the apparent intent that specificity be determined by the logic of context.

The general meaning of *ʾĕlōhîm* is observable in other examples of religious technical language. Expressions relating to divination include "to inquire (*šʾl*) of the deity" (Judg 18:5; 20:18; 1 Sam 14:37; etc.)[177] and "to seek (*drš*) the deity" (Exod 18:15; 1 Sam 9:9; 2 Sam 12:16; etc.).[178] While in many of these examples it is clear from context that it is Yahweh's will that is being sought, the expressions themselves refer to consulting the divine in a general way. Due to the specific cultic setting of these expressions, it is not surprising that they

---

[176]For discussion of *ʾĕlōhîm*'s use here and elsewhere in the Covenant Code, see Cyrus H. Gordon, "אלהים in its Reputed Meaning of Rulers, Judges," *JBL* 54 (1935): 139-44.

[177]Cf. "to inquire (*šʾl*) of Yahweh," Judg 1:1; 20:23; 1 Sam 23:2; etc.

[178]Cf. "to seek (*bqš*) Yahweh," Gen 25:22; 1 Kgs 22:8; etc.

should occur alternatively with the more concrete and specific "Yahweh."

Correct behavior is a natural result of "knowledge of the divine" (*da'at 'ĕlōhîm*, Prov 2:5; Hos 4:1; 6:6) and the "fear of the divine" (*yir'at 'ĕlōhîm*, Gen 20:11; 2 Sam 23:3; Neh 5:9, 15; cf. *yir'at yhwh*, Isa 11:2, 3; 33:6; Pss 19:10; 34:12; 111:10; Job 28:28; 2 Chr 19:9; and in numerous instances in Proverbs; *yir'at šadday*, Job 6:14). That *da'at 'ĕlōhîm* does not have an attested counterpart containing Yahweh (but cf. *da'at 'elyôn*, Num 24:16) suggests that *yir'at yhwh* is a concrete variant of a more general expression. Like the other examples of technical language reviewed thus far, the prominence of *'ĕlōhîm* in established expressions dealing with activities and phenomena not peculiar to Yahweh but applicable to gods or to "the divine" in general emphasizes the word's generic and flexible meaning.

The same holds true in other examples from the Covenant Code. The indeterminate use of *'ĕlōhîm* in the Exod 22:27 prohibition against cursing a deity (see above) implies that the identity of no specific god was assumed in the original context of this relatively early collection of biblical law. Elsewhere in the Covenant Code, *hā'ĕlōhîm* (with the definite article) refers to unspecified domestic or communal deities whose authority in legal matters is recognized.[179] In the law of the Hebrew slave (Exod 21:2-6), the servant who wishes to remain in his master's household permanently must be brought to *hā'ĕlōhîm*, perhaps at the doorpost of the house (v. 6). The law of deposit (22:6-8) provides that disputes between two parties be settled by *hā'ĕlōhîm* (the subject of the plural verb *yaršî'ūn* in v. 8). In these two instances, *hā'ĕlōhîm* designates a specific deity or deities only to the extent that it contains the definite article and so refers to "the god(s) in question" (see also 21:13), a reference which can be made only by virtue of the nonspecific meaning of *'ĕlōhîm*.

In the Covenant Code we see more strikingly an aspect of *'ĕlōhîm* which is at work in other instances of its technical usage, namely that *'ĕlōhîm*, though generic in meaning, regularly has a

---

[179]Compare the identification of *hā'ĕlōhîm* in these passages with *tĕrāpîm* (*penates*) both by Gordon, "אלהים in its Reputed Meaning," 139-43 and by Anne E. Draffkorn, "Ilāni/Elohim," *JBL* 76 (1957): 216-24.

specific referent that is determined by context. In this way 'ĕlōhîm behaves much like a title, a relatively general designation for a specific individual, e.g., "the President," "Grandma," "the Pope." Such is the case with "the god in question" in the Covenant Code but also in the expressions "to inquire of the god (in question)," "the fear of the god (in question)," etc.

The analysis of 'ĕlōhîm in technical language has shown not only that it is general and flexible in meaning but that the appellative is frequently taken up in a religious or legal setting in place of or in preference to the name of a specific deity whose identity is understood from context. This usage of 'ĕlōhîm demonstrates the way in which the common noun easily lent itself to use as a title.

Patron Deities

The appearance of 'ĕlōhîm in epithets for patron deities gives insight into its use as a religious title. Before examining these epithets, it will be useful to consider the notion of the patron god as reflected in the literary traditions of the Hebrew Bible. A recognition of the patron deity as a concept operative in the literature of ancient Israel will prove informative both to our discussion of appellative 'ĕlōhîm and to an understanding of the word's use a title for Israel's god.

The Concept of the Patron Deity in the Hebrew Bible

In ancient Israel and in the ancient Near East in general, the patron god was not a specific type of deity but any god who, by virtue of a unique association with a particular individual, social group, or place, was understood to act as its divine representative and to advance its welfare.[180] In the Hebrew Bible reference is made to the patron deity by use of the general term *'ĕlōhîm*.

Expressions containing *'ĕlōhîm* denote the patron deity of the individual: "the god of Shem" (*'ĕlōhê šēm*, Gen 9:26), "the god of Elijah" (*'ĕlōhê 'ēlîyāhû*, 2 Kgs 2:14), and "the god of David" (*'ĕlōhê dāwīd*, 20:5). The personal god is portrayed colorfully in the ancestral narratives as "the god of Abraham" (*'ĕlōhê 'abrāhām*, Gen 26:24; 28:13 etc.), "the 'fear' of Isaac" (*pahad yiṣḥāq*, Gen 31:42), and the god of Jacob ("to the god who answered me in the day of my distress and has been with me wherever I have gone," *lā'ēl hā'ōne(h) 'ōtî bĕyôm ṣārātî wayhî 'immādî badderek 'ăšer hālāktî*, Gen 35:3). Though it was not always the case, an individual's personal god was usually the same as his family god,[181] as implied both by Ruth's words to Naomi, "Your people shall be my people and your god, my god," (*'ammēk 'ammî wē'lōhayik 'ĕlōhāy*, Ruth 1:16), and by Naomi's statement that her other daughter-in-law had returned "to her people and to her god" (*'el-'ammāh wě'el-'ĕlōhêhā*, v. 15).[182] Thus it is not surprising that the same deity should be identified as the personal god of Abraham, Isaac, and Jacob (*'ĕlōhê 'abrāhām yiṣḥāq wěya'ăqōb*, Exod 3:16). The continuing association with the same personal deity from one generation to the next is recognized where Joseph's house steward, in addressing Joseph's brothers, refers to "your god and the god of your father" (*'ĕlōhêkā wē'lōhê 'ābîkem*, Gen 43:23). The concept of the personal/ancestral deity is operative where Laban tells Jacob, "It is in my power to do you harm, but the god of your father

---

[180]The concept of patron deities is discussed within the analysis of such works as Vorländer, *Mein Gott*; Rainer Albertz, *Persönliche Frömmigkeit und offizielle Religion: Religionsinterner Pluralismus in Israel und Babylon* (Calwer theologische Monographien 9; Stuttgart: Calwer, 1978); Henri Cazelles, "Der persönliche Gott Abrahams und der Gott des Volkes Israel," in *Der Weg zum Menschen: Zur philologischen und theologischen Anthropologie für Alfons Deissler*, ed., R. Mosis and L. Ruppert (Freiburg: Herder, 1988), 46-61; Karel van der Toorn, *Family Religion in Babylonia, Syria, and Israel: Continuity and Change in the Forms of Religious Life* (Studies in the History and Culture of the Ancient Near East 7; Leiden: Brill, 1996).

[181]See Vorländer, *Mein Gott*, 12-14, 84, 155-58; van der Toorn, *Family Religion*, 71-87, 255-65.

[182]In this case, returning to one's "people" (*'am*) meant going back to "her mother's house" (*bêt 'immāh*, v. 8).

(*'ĕlōhê 'ăbîkā*, LXX; cf. *'ăbîkem*, MT) spoke to me last night,"
(31:29) and where the two men invoke witnessing deities for a treaty:
'ĕlōhê 'abrāhām wĕ'lōhê nāhôr yišpĕṭû bênênû, "The god of Abraham
and the god of Nahor judge between us" (v. 53).[183] Each man calls
on the god of his ancestor as his own god.[184] The use of *'ĕlōhîm* in
these examples expresses the patron deity's special relationship to the
given individual and kin group.

The term *'ĕlōhîm* is also used in references which emphasize a
god's association with a particular place. An example of the patron
deity of a city is "Baal-Zebub, the god of Ekron" (*ba'al zĕbûb 'ĕlōhê
'eqrôn*, 2 Kgs 1:2, 3, 6, 16). Failure to give appropriate reverence to
the patron deity of the territory that one inhabits brings adverse
consequences, as experienced by foreign settlers in Samaria whose
ignorance of the "custom of the god of land" (*mišpaṭ 'ĕlōhê hā'āreṣ*,
2 Kgs 17:26) resulted in fatal lion attacks. A god's inextricable
relationship to a specific territory is best recognized by Naaman, who
proclaims, "There is no god in all the earth but in Israel" (*'ên 'ĕlōhîm
bĕkol-hā'āreṣ kî 'im-bĕyiśrā'ēl*, 2 Kgs 5:15) and requests two mule-
loads of soil from there so that he can worship Yahweh when he
returns to Damascus (v. 17). *'Ĕlōhîm* is the appropriate term to be
used to denote the territorial patron deity.

Appellative *'ĕlōhîm* is also suitable in reference to the national
patron god. The understanding of the national deity's activity on
behalf of his people is illustrated both by Jephthah's words to the
leader of a foreign nation in Judg 11:24: "Do you not possess that
which Chemosh your god (*kĕmôš 'ĕlōhêkā*) causes you to possess, and
do we not possess that which Yahweh our god (*yhwh 'ĕlōhênû*) places
before us to possess?" and by those of the Philistines at Ashdod in 1

---

[183]The plural *yišpĕṭû* in the MT (cf. the LXX and Sam., which render the verb in
the singular) agrees with the implication of Laban's mention of "the god of your father"
(v. 29), namely, that he and Jacob worship different ancestral deities. The MT's *'ĕlōhê
'ăbîhem*, "the god of their father" (v. 53), is certainly a gloss (note both the change in
person and the dislocation of this appositive) intended to explain the plural form of the
verb that it follows.

[184]That Abraham and Nahor, who were brothers, apparently had not worshiped the
same god is consistent with the fact that one did not necessarily serve "the god of his
father."

Sam 5:7: "The ark of the god of Israel (*'ĕlōhê yiśrā'ēl*) must not remain with us, for his hand is hard against us and against Dagon, our god (*dāgôn 'ĕlōhênû*)." Israel is punished by its god for worshiping the deities of other nations enumerated in 1 Kgs 11:33: *lĕ'aštōret 'ĕlōhê ṣidōnîm likmôš 'ĕlōhê mô'āb ûlĕmilkōm 'ĕlōhê bĕnê 'ammôn*, "Ashtoreth, the goddess of the Sidonians; Chemosh, the god of Moab; and Milcom, the god of the Ammonites." The concept of national and ethnic deities is operative in 2 Kgs 17:29-31, which describes how the population groups that the Assyrians settled in Samaria brought with them the veneration of their own gods:

> Every nation made its own gods and deposited them in the sanctuaries of the high places which the people of Samaria had made, every nation in the cities in which they lived. And the men of Babylon made Succoth-Benoth; the men of Cuth made Nergal; the men of Hamath made Ashima; and the Avvites made Nibhaz and Tartak. The Sepharvites burned their children in the fire to Adrammelek and Anammelek, the gods of Sepharvaim.

Assyrian propaganda at the walls of Jerusalem (2 Kgs 18:28-35; 19:10-13) included warnings about the futility of dependence on the national deity against the Sennacherib's armies: "Do not let your god (*'ĕlōhēkā*) in whom you trust deceive you . . . Did the gods of the nations that my fathers destroyed deliver them?" (19:10, 12). As a common noun, *'ĕlōhîm* is regularly employed to denote the unique status of the national deity, a usage which will prove essential to the development of *'ĕlōhîm* into an important title.[185]

In connection with the concept of the patron deity, *'ĕlōhîm* designates the god who stands in special relationship to a particular individual, group, territory, or nation. This aspect of *'ĕlōhîm* is illustrated by its appearance in certain biblical epithets for patron deities. Two such epithets that are prominent among the literary and religious traditions preserved in the Hebrew Bible relate to the portrayal of the patriarchal and the national god, respectively.

---

[185]See below, Chapter 3. The Title *'ĕlōhîm* in Israelite Religion.

"The God of the Fathers"

The ancestral narratives portray the patron deity of Israel's eponymous ancestors as "the god of the fathers" (*'ĕlōhê 'ăbōtêkem/'ăbōtām*). This designation facilitates the merging of various traditions about the deities of the patriarchs—some of these explicitly naming a local manifestation of El: *'ēl 'elyôn* of Jerusalem (Gen 14:18-22); *'ēl 'ôlām* of Beer-sheba (21:33); *'ēl rŏ'î* of Beer-lahai-roi (16:13); *'ēl šadday* (Gen 49:25)—to depict a single ancestral god.[186] The patriarchal deity can be referred to (1) as "the god of the father" (*'ĕlōhê 'ăbî/-ka/-kem*, Gen 31:2, 29, etc.), (2) as "the god of Abraham," "Isaac," and/or "Jacob" (Gen 31:53), or (3) by a combination of the first two types of expressions (e.g., *'ĕlōhê 'abrāhām 'ābîkā*, Gen 26:24; 28:13 etc.; *'ĕlōhê 'ăbî 'abrāhām wē'lōhê 'ăbî yiṣḥāq*, Gen 32:10).[187] Designating the family god not by name but as "the *'ĕlōhîm* of PN" or "the *'ĕlōhîm* of the father(s)," the equivalent of which is attested as a DN substitute in Old Assyrian texts,[188] allows these various traditions to be integrated into the depiction of a single ancestral deity.

The portrayal of a single god of the patriarchs is consistent with the Hebrew Bible's depiction of Israelite origins in terms of ethnic identity. The depiction of the inherited veneration of the ancestral god establishes continuity and cohesion in the religious component of Israelite origins. The patriarchal lineage of Israel is traced not only by genealogical descent but also by the worship of the ancestral deity. Only those who worshiped this god can be counted among the nation's forebears. Yet the general designation of this god as "the patriarchal *'ĕlōhîm*" allows various and distinct traditions of ancestral gods to be

---

[186]Compare Alt's view of "the God of the Fathers" as a type of otherwise nameless nomadic deity, originally distinct from the local deities of the *El*-religion indigenous to Canaan ("The God of the Fathers," in *Essays on Old Testament History and Religion* [trans. R. A. Wilson; Oxford: Basil Blackwell, 1966], 1-77; trans. of *Der Gott der Väter* [Stuttgart: Kohlhammer, 1929]; cf. Frank M. Cross, "The God of the Fathers," in *Canaanite Myth and Hebrew Epic: Essays in the History of the Religion of Israel* [Cambridge, Mass.: Harvard Univ. Press, 1973], 3-12).

[187]Here we follow the analysis of Werner H. Schmidt, "אֱלֹהִים *ᵉlōhîm* Gott," *THAT* 1:157-58.

[188]See Cross, *CMHE*, 9-10.

included into a composite representation of this deity. In the terminology of family religion, the designation of a single ancestral *'ĕlōhîm* facilitates both the inclusion of various traditions and the amalgamation of these into the representation of a single deity. This is not to mention E's designation of the patriarchal deity simply as *'ĕlōhîm*.[189]

The use of *'ĕlōhîm* serves not only the forging of a single "god of the fathers" but also the identification of the patriarchal god with the national deity Yahweh, the god of the Exodus.[190] This equation is made in Exodus 3, in the call of Moses by *yhwh 'ĕlōhê 'ăbōtêkem 'ĕlōhê 'abrāhām 'ĕlōhê yiṣḥāq wĕ'lōhê ya'ăqōb*, "Yahweh, the god of your fathers, the god of Abraham, the god of Isaac, and the god of Jacob" (v. 15).[191] The phrase "god of our/your/their fathers," a summary form of the titles "the god of the father" and "the god of PN," asserts the continuity between the national worship of Yahweh and the earlier religion of the patriarchs.[192]

The use of these *'ĕlōhîm* epithets in reference to the patriarchal deity demonstrates both the association of the term *'ĕlōhîm* with the concept of the patron deity (i.e., the deity in close relationship to an individual or group) and the flexibility of *'ĕlōhîm* as a generic term, a quality which made it favorable for use in place of a specific DN. We now consider another title in which *'ĕlōhîm* is used in reference to a patron deity.

"The God of Israel"

The epithet "the god of Israel" (*'ĕlōhê yiśrā'ēl*, Exod 24:10; Num 16:9; 2 Sam 23:3; etc.), which follows a pattern commonly used in connection with the ancestral deity ("the *'ĕlōhîm* of PN"), is usually

---

[189]See below, *'Ĕlōhîm* in the Patriarchal Traditions of E.

[190]Alt, "God of the Fathers," 11-13; Schmidt, *THAT* 1:157-58; Cross, *CMHE*, 5.

[191]This passage will be discussed below; see E Beyond Genesis.

[192]Cf. Herbert G. May and Werner H. Schmidt, who consider this form of the expression with plural "fathers" to be a later (exilic and later) development of these archaic expressions, which they affirm to be genuine in the (preexilic) patriarchal narratives (May, "The God of My Father—A Study of Patriarchal Religion," *Journal of Bible and Religion* 9 [1941]: 155; Schmidt, *THAT* 1:157-58).

employed with reference to the national patron god. While this expression occurs with the implication of only one figure in that role, the epithet itself does not name a specific deity. Of course, in the dominant tradition in the Hebrew Bible, this title belongs exclusively to Yahweh (*yhwh 'ĕlōhê yiśrā'ēl*, Exod 5:1; Josh 7:13; Judg 4:6; etc.), but a vestige of another tradition is preserved in connection with the sanctuary at Shechem, in which the epithet is given to El: *'ēl 'ĕlōhê yiśrā'ēl* (Gen 33:20).[193]   Although the narrative context dictates understanding "Israel" in this instance as being in reference to the patriarch himself, remembering that the ancestral narratives portray the origins of the nation keeps this point in perspective. That is to say, a reference to an eponymous ancestor is never to be considered in isolation from the relevant population group and, in fact, always presupposes the latter. Thus, with respect to the epithet *'ĕlōhê yiśrā'ēl* in the etiology of the altar, one should not make too much of the distinction between the individual and the nation. In any case, the fact that we find the epithet accompanying the names of more than one deity is not to be minimized. The effect of this epithet being common to Yahweh and El is to ease the identification of the two[194] in the presentation of the biblical traditions concerning Israelite origins.[195] The title *'ĕlōhê yiśrā'ēl*, though, not only facilitates the identification of El with Yahweh but also gives expression to the idea necessitating such an identification, namely that there is only one "god of Israel."

---

[193]See Roland de Vaux, *Ancient Israel: Its Life and Institutions* (trans. J. McHugh; London: Darton, Longman, & Todd, 1961; repr. Grand Rapids, Mich.: Eerdmans, 1997), 294; Cross, *CMHE*, 49; W. Herrmann, "El אל‎," *DDD*, 277. In the biblical context, the name of El in this epithet is interpreted as a title of Yahweh, *'ēl* "God"; see Frank M. Cross, "אל‎ *'ēl*," *TDOT*, 255. The relationship of this passage to E is considered below, see *'Ĕlōhîm* in the Patriarchal Traditions of E.

[194]This identification was, to be sure, the result of a gradual and complex process; see Otto Eissfeldt, "El und Jahwe," in *Kleine Schriften* 3 (Tübingen: J. C. B. Mohr, 1966), 386-97; cf. Cross, *CMHE*, 44-75.

[195]See the linking of the two DNN by simple *'ĕlōhîm* in the proclamation repeated in Josh 22:22: *'ēl 'ĕlōhîm yhwh*.

Conclusions

A frequent usage of *'ĕlōhîm* as a common noun is in the identification of a patron deity, i.e., a god who is unique in his association with a particular social group, nation, or territory. The common form of reference to a patron deity follows the pattern "the *'ĕlōhîm* of PN/GN/*gntl.*" Two examples of this type of expression, the epithets "the god of the father" (in its various forms) and "the god of Israel," are noteworthy not only for their frequency of occurrence but also for their crucial roles in the formulation of ancient Israel's religious identity and tradition. *'Ĕlōhîm*, as featured in these titles and in other contexts, designates the god who stood in definitive relationship to Israel. The use of *'ĕlōhîm* with the contextual meaning patron deity will have great importance for the examination of grammatically absolute *'ĕlōhîm* as a title in the national religion.[196]

International Contexts

Another context in which appellative *'ĕlōhîm* figures prominently is in the depiction of international settings. An examination of *'ĕlōhîm*'s use in this context provides an occasion to observe its capacity for emphasizing religious commonality, as reflected in the literary traditions of the Hebrew Bible.

In the scenes of the Joseph story that are set in Egypt, the appropriate term in reference to the divine is *(hā)'ĕlōhîm*. Joseph rebuffs the advances of his master's wife—whose eventual false accusations of him play on a xenophobic suspicion of "the Hebrew"—by pointing out that adultery with her would be not only an offense against her husband but a sin "against *'ĕlōhîm*" (39:9). For the sake of religious commonality in this scenario, the general term *'ĕlōhîm* is preferable to any DN. The same applies to Joseph's speech to Egyptian officials (40:8), to Pharaoh (41:16, 25, 28, 32), to his brothers (who in these instances know him only as an Egyptian ruler, 42:18; 43:29), and in the etymologies of the names of Joseph's sons born by his Egyptian wife (41:51, 52). This emphasis on religious

---

[196]See below, Chapter 3. The Title *'ĕlōhîm* in Israelite Religion.

continuity through the use of 'ĕlōhîm is also made in the words of Pharaoh to Joseph (41:39) and in those of the brothers to (a yet unrecognized) Joseph (44:16). The use of 'ĕlōhîm among Israelites in this story is consistent with the fact that all of those instances are depicted in an international setting, in Egypt: in conversation among the brothers, 42:28; in the speech of Joseph to his brothers upon and after their reconciliation, 45:5, 7, 8, 9; 50:19, 20, 24; Joseph, to his father, 48:9; Israel, to Joseph, 48:11, 21.[197] The preference for 'ĕlōhîm as a designation of the divine in these narratives is inclusive, emphasizing common religious ground between parties of differing national or ethnic heritage.

An international context is key to the book of Jonah, which portrays the Ninevites' repentance and faithfulness, using only (hā)'ĕlōhîm in reference to God (3:5-10). Most noteworthy is that 'ĕlōhîm is deemed appropriate in this episode not only for the speech of the king of Nineveh (vv. 8-9) but also for that of the narrator (vv. 5, 10), who uses the DN Yahweh when the action is not set in Nineveh (1:1, 4, etc.).[198] The implication is that the appropriateness of 'ĕlōhîm's use in an international context is dependent not only on a foreigner's unfamiliarity with the name of the god of Israel but also on a sense of commonality conveyed by the term, a sense which accords well with the universalism expressed in Jonah.

In a passage already mentioned, "the god of Abraham and the god of Nahor" ('ĕlōhê 'abrāhām wĕ'lōhê nāhôr, Gen 31:53) are invoked in the agreement between Jacob and Laban.[199] The story of the treaty between Jacob and Laban qualifies as an "international" episode as it represents an ancestral precursor to Israelite-Aramean

---

[197]As pointed out by W. Rudolph, the particular divine designation used in the Joseph material corresponds to the given narrative context: Yahweh, in the narrator's comments; El-Shadday, in those of characters speaking in Palestine; and Elohim, in Egypt; see Paul Volz and Wilhelm Rudolph, *Der Elohist als Erzähler: Ein Irrweg der Pentateuchkritik?* (BZAW 63; Giessen: Alfred Töpelmann, 1933), 148-51, 180-83. However, some of this material, especially 48:8-22, is definitely (on other grounds) to be attributed to E, which characteristically prefers 'ĕlōhîm as the divine designation; see below, Preliminary Discussion of E.

[198]Cf., though, the use of (hā)'ĕlōhîm in 4:7-9 and 'ĕlōhê haššāmayim "the God of Heaven" in 1:9.

[199]See above, The Concept of the Patron Deity in the Hebrew Bible.

relations.[200] As explained above, the use of the form of expression "god of PN" in place of the respective DNN emphasizes both the ancestral connection between each man and his patron god and the role of the latter as a witnessing deity to the agreement. Perhaps less formal is Laban's assertion that *'ĕlōhîm* will oversee Jacob's compliance with the agreement (v. 50). Here, simple *'ĕlōhîm* (the relevant) "deity" is appropriate in language between parties having allegiances to different gods. The use of *'ĕlōhîm* in this context emphasizes religious continuity between Jacob and Laban, between Israelite and Aramean.

Qohelet, as is characteristic of wisdom literature, is international in its orientation and viewpoint. In contrast to the book of Proverbs, which regularly uses the DN Yahweh, Qohelet uses *'ĕlōhîm* in accordance with the wisdom tendency to refer to the divine as "the god (in question)."[201] In the reflection on universal questions concerning the divine, the use of *'ĕlōhîm* insures an inclusive frame of reference.

As the generic word for "god" in Biblical Hebrew, *'ĕlōhîm* is often used in an international setting to emphasize religious continuity between individuals or groups who do not worship the same god. In this context the generic sense of *'ĕlōhîm* makes it useful in place of a specific divine name.

Due in large part to its abstract nature, *'ĕlōhîm* was both generic in meaning and flexible in usage, as demonstrated in the broad range of its use with the sense "god," "deity," or "the divine." This semantic flexibility possessed by *'ĕlōhîm* is observed in its use in legal and religious technical expressions, which often rely on *'ĕlōhîm*'s generic meaning. At the same time, these technical expressions also convey a sense of particularity, by making reference to a specific though unnamed deity, "the god (in question)." Both in this technical

---

[200]Hence the separate Hebrew and Aramaic GNN explained by the etiology and the characterization of Laban as "the Aramaean" (Gen 31:20, 24).

[201]Choon Leong Seow, *Ecclesiastes: A New Translation with Introduction and Commentary* (AB 18c; New York: Doubleday, 1997), 146. On the preference for the generic term for god in wisdom literature, see Frankfort, *Ancient Egyptian Religion*, 67; Hornung, *The One and the Many*, 50-60; and the indefinite use of "the god" in *Ludlul bēl nēmeqi* and in "The Babylonian Theodicy" (both discussed above, First-Millennium Akkadian).

language and in connection with patron deities, '*ĕlōhîm* often occurs in place of a DN that would be known or that is known from context. In this way, we see how '*ĕlōhîm* naturally presented itself for use as a title.

Plural '*ĕlōhîm* as a Counterpart to Singular '*ĕlōhîm*

More International Contexts

The discussion of '*ĕlōhîm*'s appellative usage does not end with the consideration of its generic meaning. As discussed, the Hebrew Bible's depiction of speech concerning the divine in an international setting often favors the use of singular '*ĕlōhîm*. However, in a couple of these instances where one would expect the singular, '*ĕlōhîm* is clearly a plural.

Abraham, in conversation with Abimelech, mentions "when '*ĕlōhîm* caused me to wander from my father's house" (*ka'ăšer hit'û 'ōtî 'ĕlōhîm mibbêt 'ābî*, Gen 20:13). The pairing of '*ĕlōhîm* with a plural verb form is especially noteworthy in view of its use with singular verbs elsewhere in this passage, in the comments of the narrator (vv. 3, 6, 17). The treatment of otherwise singular '*ĕlōhîm* as a plural in speech to a non-Israelite is no doubt due to the polytheistic frame of reference of Abraham's interlocutor, Abraham himself (according to biblical tradition) being of polytheistic origins.[202]

In the narrative describing the battle at Ebenezer, Philistine soldiers acknowledge the presence of the ark among the Israelites with the following words:

---

[202]The expression "polytheistic" is used here, for lack of a better term, to describe the Hebrew Bible's portrayal of non-Israelites as being typically worshipers of numerous gods, in contrast with Israelites who, according to the dominant biblical view, properly and characteristically worship only one god.

bā'û 'ĕlōhîm 'el-hammaḥăne(h) . . .
mî yaṣṣîlēnû miyyad hā'ĕlōhîm hā'addîrîm hā'ēlle(h)
'ēlle(h) hēm hā'ĕlōhîm hammakkîm 'et-miṣrayim bĕkol-makkâ ûbĕmō-deber[203]

Gods have come into the camp! . . .
Who will deliver us from the hand of these mighty gods?
These are the gods who struck the Egyptians with every sort of plague and
with pestilence. (1 Sam 4:7-8)

It is clear from the coordination of *'ĕlōhîm* with a variety of plural
forms—finite verb form, attributive and demonstrative adjectives,
demonstrative and personal pronouns, and a participle—that, though it
is used in reference to Yahweh, *'ĕlōhîm* is a plural in this verse. That
the Philistines' refer to Yahweh as "gods" is not too surprising,
though, in light of the fact that they themselves worship more than one
god.

Why do these passages not use singular *'ĕlōhîm* as others do in
the depiction of international contexts?[204]   It hardly needs to be
argued that the polytheistic viewpoint made explicit in Gen 20:13 and
in 1 Sam 4:7-8 was characteristic of the religion of ancient Palestine-
Syria. In cultic and mythic texts from Late Bronze Age Ugarit, which
represent the religious heritage of Iron Age Canaan, deities are defined
by their relationships within the pantheon. Inscriptions produced by
ancient Israel's neighbors include not only references to various deities
but also mention of "the gods": Phoenician *'lnm* in Yehimilk (*KAI*
4.4-5, 7), Yehawmilk (*KAI* 10.10, 16), and Eshmunazor (*KAI* 14.9,
16, 18, 22) and *'lhn* at Deir 'Alla (I.1, 5), Zenjirli (*KAI* 214.2-3, 4,
12, 13), Sefire (*KAI* 222 C 15, 21; 223 C 13; 224.14, 17) and Tell
Fekherye (l. 14).[205] The use of plural *'ĕlōhîm* among the Philistines
and by Abraham in speech to Abimelech represents what would have

---

[203] *Bā'û* in v. 7, which is indicated by the LXX, is preferable to *bā'* in the MT, as
it corresponds to the other plural verb forms; see P. Kyle McCarter, Jr., *I Samuel: A
New Translation with Introduction, Notes and Commentary* (AB 8; New York:
Doubleday, 1980), 104. As McCarter points out, *ûbĕmō-deber* ("and with pestilence")
in v. 8, which is based on the consonantal reading reflected in the LXX, agrees with the
biblical tradition of the exodus, while the reading of the MT, *bmdbr* ("in the wilderness")
does not.

[204] See above, International Contexts.

[205] For more details on these references, see above, Deir 'Alla.

been the conventional religious language of the day when speaking of the divine. So it is not surprising to find the perception of the god of Israel and its ancestors expressed by plural *'ĕlōhîm* in a non-Israelite setting, and the question should be restated thus: Why does singular *'ĕlōhîm* appear in international contexts, as discussed above?

In the Hebrew Bible, the Israelites are presented as being properly and characteristically worshipers of only one god. Most noteworthy is the consistency with which the Hebrew Bible, in representing Israelite religious expressions, offers singular *'ĕlōhîm* as an alternative to the otherwise common notion of "the gods." An illustration is provided by the comparison of two different versions of the same oath formula, one spoken by foreigners and the other by Israelites. The imprecation invoked by Jezebel and by Ben-Hadad of Damascus, reads: *kō(h)-ya'ăśûn lî 'ĕlōhîm wĕkō(h) yôsīpûn*, "So may the gods do to me and more also . . ." (1 Kgs 19:2; 20:10), with *'ĕlōhîm* as the subject of a plural verb. The same oath as pronounced by an Israelite has *'ĕlōhîm* as a singular: *kō(h)-ya'ăśe(h) 'ĕlōhîm wĕkō(h) yôsīp*, "So may God do (to me/you) and more also . . ." (1 Sam 3:17; 14:44; cf. 20:13 and Ruth 1:17, which name Yahweh). In the Bible's portrayal of Israel as religiously monolatrous, singular *'ĕlōhîm* serves as a counterpart to the notion of "the gods," which was common among Israel's neighbors.

A more striking illustration of this point is found in a comparison of biblical and extrabiblical material. The parallels between biblical *'ĕlōhîm* and Deir 'Alla *'lhn* merit review:

1. *wy'tw 'lhn 'lwh blylh . . .*
wy'mrw lbl'm brb'r
Gods came to him in the night . . .
Then they said to Balaam, son of
Beor . . .
(Deir 'Alla I.1, 2)

1. *wayyābō' 'ĕlōhîm 'el-*
bil'ām laylā wayyō'mer lô
God came to Balaam at night and
said to him . . . (Num 22:20)

2. *wlkw r'w p'lt 'lhn*
Now come, see the deeds of the
gods! (Deir 'Alla I.5)

2. *lĕkû ûrĕ'û mip'ălôt 'ĕlōhîm*
Come and see the deeds of God!
(Ps 66:5)

In these comparisons, singular *'ĕlōhîm* corresponds to plural *'lhn*, a usage which, as noted in the discussion above (Deir 'Alla), has implications for the international setting of Deir 'Alla. In religious language deemed "orthodox" within the dominant view expressed in the Hebrew Bible, singular *'ĕlōhîm* is preferred as the Israelite counterpart to "the gods." Thus *'ĕlōhîm* is appropriate in international settings not only because of its generic meaning (see above) but also because of its direct correspondence to the expression "the gods" so prevalent in the religion of ancient Palestine-Syria.

Plural *'ĕlōhîm* in Israelite Contexts

The Hebrew Bible, in spite its portrayal of the Israelites as predominantly monolatrous, preserves traces of an Israelite belief in "the gods," signified by ostensibly plural *'ĕlōhîm*.

Central to the narrative of Sodom and Gomorrah are the three (and then two) divine beings whose visit precipitates the cities' cataclysmic demise (Gen 18-19). Though the Genesis narrative explicitly credits Yahweh with this act of divine retribution, the event is recalled elsewhere by the peculiar expression *kĕmahpēkat 'ĕlōhîm 'et-sĕdōm wĕ'et-'ămōrâ*, "as when *'ĕlōhîm* overthrew Sodom and Gomorrah" (Isa 13:19; Jer 50:40; Amos 4:11).[206] The use of *'ĕlōhîm* in this expression stands out from its context for three reasons: (1) *'ĕlōhîm* is not used in the relevant narrative in Genesis; (2) grammatically singular absolute *'ĕlōhîm* is not used in the prophetic books in reference to Yahweh; and (3) it is Israel's god who is speaking in all three occurrences of the phrase. We are perhaps dealing with a frozen expression that corresponds to a version of the story in which a group (or pair) of "gods" brings about the destruction

---

[206]Due the grammatical construction of this expression, the number of *'ĕlōhîm* here is ambiguous. On the value of this expression as an indication of the story's pre-Yahwistic origin, see Hermann Gunkel, *Genesis übersetzt und erklärt* (Handkommentar zum Alten Testament I.1; Göttingen: Vandenhoeck & Ruprecht, 1901), 196.

of the two cities, a mythological element that is retained in the Genesis narrative.[207]

In the etiology of Bethel related in Gen 28:10-22, the appearance of Yahweh and the revelation he delivers (vv. 13-16) are superfluous to the explanation of the place name, which is provided by v. 17—"How awesome is this place! This is none other than a house of gods (*bêt 'ĕlōhîm*), and this is the gate of heaven"—and by the portrayal of the site as a kind of threshold through which divine beings (*mal'ăkê 'ĕlōhîm*, v. 12) pass between heaven and earth. Thus, behind the Yahwistic and Elohistic (see Jacob's oath in vv. 20-22) elements of the present form of the story, Bethel's cultic origins are explained in polytheistic terms by its existence as a "house of gods."[208]

Another instance in which *'ĕlōhîm* is used in the portrayal of divine plurality is the etiology of the GN Mahanaim (Gen 32:2-3 [1-2]). The brief passage is as follows:

wĕya'ăqōb hālak lĕdarkô wayyipgĕ'û-bô mal'ăkê 'ĕlōhîm wayyō'mer
ya'ăqōb ka'ăšer rā'ām mahănē(h) 'ĕlōhîm ze(h) wayyiqrā'
šēm-hammāqôm hahû' mahănāyim

As Jacob went on his way, divine messengers (*mal'ăkê 'ĕlōhîm*, alternatively, "messengers of God") met him, and Jacob said when he saw them, "This is a camp of gods (*mahănē[h] 'ĕlōhîm*, alternatively, "the camp of God")." So he named that place Mahanaim.

While the expression *mahănē(h) 'ĕlōhîm* as retained in the biblical version of the tradition is reinterpreted to mean "camp of God," it is clear from the description of the band of divine beings encountered by Jacob that *'ĕlōhîm* in the folk etymology of the place name was originally understood as a plural. Here we have another example of

---

[207]The connection to the phrase in Isa 13:19, etc. and its implications for the originally polytheistic character of the story are discussed by Bernardus Dirks Eerdmans, *Die Komposition der Genesis* (Alttestamentliche Studien 1: Giessen: Alfred Töpelmann, 1908), 71. On Gen 18, see Gunkel, *Genesis*, 181.

[208]See Gunkel, *Genesis*, 288-91. For more discussion on the polytheistic implications of this passage, see below, Bethel Traditions of *'ĕlōhîm*. See above, The Abstract Nature of *'ĕlōhîm*, on the abstract meaning of *'ĕlōhîm* in construct expressions like *bêt 'ĕlōhîm*, though the portrayal of "gods" in this specific instance is clear. This also applies to Gen 32:2-3 [1-2], which is discussed in the following paragraph.

the use of plural *'ĕlōhîm* in a polytheistic tradition that has been preserved in the Bible with a reinterpretation oriented toward monolatry.

These early traditions imbedded in the biblical materials bear witness to the fact that the conception of divine plurality, as expressed by pl. *'ĕlōhîm*, was genuine to Israel's religious heritage.[209] The ease with which these traditions are reinterpreted to suit a monolatrous frame of reference is due in large part to the correspondence between pl. and sg. *'ĕlōhîm*.

Summary

Our lexical study of *'ĕlōhîm* has demonstrated the generic sense and abstract nature of the common noun—qualities which made the term useful as a substitution for a specific DN in the context of technical language, in the designation of patron deities, and in the portrayal of international settings. We have also observed that, in the Bible's portrayal of Israelite religion as monolatrous, sg. *'ĕlōhîm* serves as a counterpart to pl. *'ĕlōhîm* and its cognates in other Northwest Semitic languages. The importance of this correspondence for *'ĕlōhîm*'s place in Israelite religion will become clear in the following discussion of that topic.

---

[209]This is not to mention the portrayal of Yahweh as the enthroned sovereign of the divine assembly; see, e.g., 1 Kgs 22:19-23; Job 1:6-12; Pss 82:1; 103:19-21. Divine plurality in Israelite tradition receives further discussion below; see Divine Plurality in the Exodus Tradition.

CHAPTER 3

The Title *'ĕlōhîm* in Israelite Religion

As we have observed, Biblical Hebrew *'ĕlōhîm*, both by itself and in certain set expressions, is commonly used in the literary traditions preserved in the Bible as an alternative to the name of Israel's god. In this chapter, we will consider whether the divine title *'ĕlōhîm* was strictly a literary phenomenon or whether it actually had a place in Israel's worship during the period of its political independence. As the discussion unfolds, it will become apparent that the texts which are most suggestive of *'ĕlōhîm*'s role in Israelite religion have a northern, i.e., non-Judahite, frame of reference.[1]

THE TITLE *'ĕlōhîm* IN THE NATIONAL CULT

That the term *'ĕlōhîm* had a special significance in northern Israelite religion is suggested by the description of the national cultus established Jeroboam I, in which a worship credo featuring *'ĕlōhîm* is associated with a bull statue representing the deity (1 Kgs 12:28-29). Provided this cult formula was a genuine feature of the national religious establishment instituted by Jeroboam, we have a sound basis

---

[1]Under Jeroboam I (922-901 B.C.E.), the "northern" tribes of Israel—that is, all of the tribes except for Judah and Benjamin—seceded from the Davidic monarchy based in Jerusalem and existed as an independent kingdom, as "Israel" over against "Judah," until its destruction by the Assyrians in 722. To avoid the ambiguity of the term Israel, which is also used in reference to the United Monarchy under David and Solomon, the northern kingdom is often designated Samaria, after the capital established by Omri (876-869 B.C.E.), and Ephraim, in reference to the central hill country which comprised its heartland. The term northern will be used in reference to the kingdom of Israel during the Divided Monarchy and to the territory and populations encompassed by that state. For lack of a better term, "northern" (in quotes) will also be used, in a broader sense, to designate whatever is not characterized by a particularly southern or Judahite orientation, i.e., traditions belonging to a common-Israelite heritage.[2]

79

for concluding that *'ĕlōhîm* had a prominent role in the official cult of the northern kingdom. This prospect bears further investigation.

Jeroboam's Cult Formula

The liturgical slogan that is associated with Jeroboam is also featured, along with the bull image, in the account of Aaron's rebellion in Exod 32. In connection both with Aaron at the foot of Sinai and with Jeroboam in the establishment of his royal cultus at Bethel and Dan, the cult statue is introduced by the formula

> *'elle(h)* (cf. *hinnē(h)*) *'ĕlōhêkā yiśrā'ēl 'ăšer he'ĕlûkā mē'ereṣ miṣrāyim*
> These (cf. "Here") are your gods, O Israel, who brought you up from
> the land of Egypt. (Exod 32:4, 8; cf. 1 Kgs 12:28)

In light of the polemical intent of both passages, one must ask whether the slogan associated with the disparaged bull statue is an authentic cult formula and, if so, whether it is accurately represented.

The identification in 1 Kgs 12 both of Bethel as a leading sanctuary of the northern Israelite kingdom and of the bull image featured there as the principal national cult symbol is confirmed by the warning of Hosea 10:5 that "the inhabitants of Samaria (i.e., of the northern Israelite kingdom) will fear for the bull of Beth-aven (literally, "House of Iniquity," Hosea's disparaging substitution for Bethel).[2] The question of whether the exodus formula cited was a genuine cult formula featured in worship at Bethel is closely related to that of the significance of its use of apparently plural *'ĕlōhîm*.

Leaving aside for now the disapproval of the tauromorphic image as expressed in Exod 32 and 1 Kgs 12,[3] the use of plural

---

[2]Hos 4:15; 5:8; see also the pun of Amos 5:5 *bêt-'ēl yihye(h) lĕ'āwen*, "Bethel will become iniquity," alternatively, "Bethel will become adversity."

[3]Possible reasons for the disapproval of the bull image include that it was understood by its southern critics as an unacceptable symbol of Yahweh, either as an image (Otto Eissfeldt, "Lade und Stierbild," *Kleine Schriften* 2 [Tübingen: J. C. B. Mohr, 1964], 282-305, esp. 304-5; Morton Smith, *Palestinian Parties and Politics That Shaped the Old Testament* [London: SCM, 1971], 16) or as a pedestal for the deity (William F. Albright, *Yahweh and the Gods of Canaan* [London: Univ. of London, 1968; repr. Winona Lake, Ind.: Eisenbrauns, 1994], 197-98; Frank M. Cross, *Canaanite Myth and Hebrew Epic: Essays in the History of the Religion of Israel* [Cambridge, Mass.: Harvard Univ. Press, 1973], 73 n. 117); that it represented another deity, such as El (Nicolas Wyatt, "Of

'ĕlōhîm "gods" in the formula would have been objectionable to the biblical writers because it attributes the exodus event to a plurality of "gods," a notion that would seem to be at odds with the biblical portrayal both of the Israelites as monolatrous and of Yahweh and Yahweh alone as the God of the exodus.[4] However, as we have seen, the Bible preserves many traditions which retain evidence of polytheistic origins.[5] In any case, apart from its possibly "heterodox" character, the formula is peculiar in that it seems to identify a single cultic image by plural *'ĕlōhîm*.

Possible Explanations for the Plural Formula

Commentators on these passages have offered three possible explanations for the plural formulation of the exodus litany. According to the first, pl. *'ĕlōhîm* corresponds to the two bull images (one at Bethel and one at Dan) mentioned in the narrative of 1 Kgs 12, which narrative, according to this solution, is presupposed by the story in Exod 32.[6] The problem with this solution is that, in connection with the bull images of Jeroboam, the liturgical formula would have been recited in the presence of only one statue at a time, and so the discrepancy between the plural formula and a single cult image remains.

A second explanation is that *'ĕlōhîm* here is a singular and that the plural pronoun and verb forms are in acquiescence to the plural

---

Calves and Kings: the Canaanite Dimension in the Religion of Israel," *SJOT* 6 [1992]: 68-91; see Smith, *Palestinian Parties*, 162 n. 53), Baal (see Rainer Albertz, *A History of Israelite Religion in the Old Testament Period* [trans. J. S. Bowden; 2 vols.; OTL; Philadelphia: Westminster John Knox, 1994], 1:144-46 and nn. 46-51), or a moon god (Loyd R. Bailey, "The Golden Calf," *HUCA* 42 [1971]: 97-115); or even that the bull was an idolatrous representation of Moses (Jack M. Sasson, "Bovine Symbolism in the Exodus Narrative," *VT* 18 [1968]: 380-87). Bailey's review of the scholarly discussion on the relationship between these two passages, though slightly dated, provides a concise summary of what continue to be the significant points of this debate (p. 97 n. 2).

[4] See, e.g., Exod 20:2; Deut 5:6; Josh 24:5-7, 17; 1 Kgs 8:51, 53; 2 Kgs 17:7; Jer 2:6; Dan 9:15; Amos 2:10; Ps 81:6-7; Neh 9:9, 12.

[5] See above, Plural *'ĕlōhîm* in Israelite Contexts.

[6] John Gray, *I & II Kings: A Commentary* (OTL; Philadelphia: Westminster, 1963), 291; Martin Noth, *Exodus: A Commentary* (trans. J. S. Bowden; OTL; Philadelphia: Westminster, 1969), 246.

form of *'ĕlōhîm.*[7] An inclination toward morphological congruence can result in the occurrence of sg. *'ĕlōhîm* in coordination with plural substantive forms (i.e., those containing the masculine plural absolute substantive ending *-îm*): e.g., *'ĕlōhîm rā'îtî 'ōlîm min-hā'āreṣ,* "I see a god coming up from the ground" (1 Sam 28:13); *'ĕlōhîm qĕdōšîm hû',* "He is a holy god" (Josh 24:19); *'ĕlōhîm ḥayyîm,* "a living god" (Deut 5:23; 1 Sam 17:26, 36; Jerem 10:10; 23:36).[8] However, no instances involving finite verbs, pronouns, or any other forms besides nominal absolutes emerge to support this explanation of the plural formula.[9]

A third explanation offered is that the formula as related in these passages is a polemical distortion of a litany, which in its genuine form contained sg. *'ĕlōhîm* and other singular forms.[10] That is to say, the originally singular formula—"This is your god . . ."—was pluralized by a critic of Jeroboam's cult on the basis of the two bull images, so as to accentuate the appearance of idolatry.[11] Before evaluating this solution, it is appropriate to bring into the discussion another biblical passage in which pl. *'ĕlōhîm* occurs in association with Israel's god.

Another Instance of Plural *'ĕlōhîm*

In a passage mentioned above, 1 Sam 4:7-8, the Philistines' reaction to the arrival of the Israelite ark at Ebenezer includes the following

---

[7]Karel van der Toorn, *Family Religion in Babylonia, Syria, and Israel: Continuity and Change in the Forms of Religious Life* (Studies in the History and Culture of the Ancient Near East 7; Leiden: Brill, 1996), 279 n. 55; Wyatt, "Calves and Kings," 78 and n. 27.

[8]Cf. *'ĕlōhîm ḥay,* "a living god" (2 Kgs 19:4, 16; Isa 37:4, 17).

[9]Cf. GKC §145i; Paul Joüon and Takamitsu Muraoka, *A Grammar of Biblical Hebrew* (2 vols.; Subsidia biblica 14/1-2; Rome: Pontifical Biblical Institute, 1993), 2:§150; the instances of sg. *'ĕlōhîm* with a plural verb cited in these works are either textually suspect (Gen 35:7; 2 Sam 7:23), or are actually numerical plurals (Gen 31:53). *'Ădōnāyw yittēn* (Exod 21:4) and *bĕ'ālāyw yûmat* (v. 29), both cited in Joüon and Muraoka, are, like sg. *'ĕlōhîm,* examples of the concretized abstract plural (see above, Grammatical Issues).

[10]Cross, *CMHE,* 73-74 and n. 117; Harold Motzki, "Ein Beitrag zum Problem des Stierkultes in der Religionsgeschichte Israels," *VT* 25 (1975): 482-3, 485; Albert Šanda, *Die Bücher der Könige* (2 vols.; Münster: Aschendorf, 1911), 1:342-43.

[11]The singular version of the formula in Neh 9:18 represents an avoidance of the implication of polytheism.

exclamation:

> *bā'û 'ĕlōhîm 'el-hammaḥăne(h)* . . .
> *mî yaṣṣîlēnû miyyad hā'ĕlōhîm hā'addîrîm hā'ēlle(h)*

> Gods have come into the camp! . . .
> Who will deliver us from the hand of these mighty gods?[12]

The notion expressed here of an army's gods accompanying it into battle is in keeping with the cultic aspect of warfare in the ancient Near East, a topic which has received thorough treatment in scholarship.[13] Narratives within the Hebrew Bible illustrate the necessity of ritual consultation of the deity prior to military engagement.[14] The role of the ark as a battlefield cult symbol and emblem of the deity's presence is evident in this episode of 1 Samuel.[15] What alerts the Philistines to the presence of the ark is the raising of the ritual shout, the *tĕrû'â*, in the Israelite camp and the resulting divine panic shaking the earth (v. 5). Thus in the moments prior to battle, a time fraught with religious significance, it is fitting that the Philistines might be engaged in such a theological discussion.

What is striking, however, is the specific content of the Philistines' speech. As noted above, the use of pl. *'ĕlōhîm* by the Philistines, themselves worshipers of more than one deity, in reference to Israel's god is not surprising. However, the continuing speech of the Philistines suggests that there is more at work here than mere pagan misapprehension. The shaken Philistines are made to say further:

---

[12] See above, More International Contexts.

[13] See, e.g., Gerhard von Rad, *Der Heilige Krieg im alten Israel* (4th ed.; Göttingen: Vandenhoeck & Ruprecht, 1965), 14-33; Morton Cogan, *Imperialism and Religion: Assyria, Judah and Israel in the Eighth and Seventh Centuries B.C.E.* (Missoula, Mont.: Scholars Press, 1974); J. Nicholas Postgate, "The Land of Assur and the Yoke of Assur," *World Archaeology* 23 (1992): 247-63; Lawrence E. Toombs, "War, ideas of," *IDB* 4:796-801; Roland de Vaux, *Ancient Israel: Its Life and Institutions* (trans. J. McHugh; London: Darton, Longman, & Todd, 1961; repr. Grand Rapids, Mich.: Eerdmans, 1997), 258-61.

[14] E.g., Judg 7:9-14; 1 Sam 28:6; 30:7-8; 2 Sam 5:19, 23; 1 Kgs 22:5, 7-8.

[15] On this and the following comment, see de Vaux, *Ancient Israel*, 9, 254; P. Kyle McCarter, Jr., *I Samuel: A New Translation with Introduction and Commentary* (AB 8; New York: Doubleday, 1980), 106, 108-9.

'ēlle(h) hēm hā'ĕlōhîm hammakkîm 'et-miṣrayim bĕkol-makkâ ûbĕmō-deber[16]
These are the gods who struck the Egyptians with every sort of scourge
and with plague. (v. 8b)

It seems odd that the Philistines, though unaware that the Israelites
worship only one god, should be familiar with an aspect of the exodus
narrative, a religious tradition peculiar to that god.[7] Like the cultic
formula associated with the golden bull, this statement introduces a
central cult symbol of Israelite tradition (i.e., the ark) by reference to
an element of the exodus narrative and by use of plural *'ĕlōhîm*. These
similarities in content and context suggest that the affirmation placed
in the mouths of the Philistines is derived from a similar, perhaps
related, liturgical formula.

A comparison of the Philistines' recitation with the bull formula
reveals definite parallels in phraseology and sentence structure that are
most impressive.

(1) *'ēlle(h)* (2) *'ĕlōhĕkā yiśrā'ēl* (3) *'ăšer he'ĕlûkā mē'ereṣ miṣrāyim*
(1) *'ēlle(h) hēm* (2) *hā'ĕlōhîm* (3) *hammakkîm 'et-miṣrayim bĕkol-makkâ ûbĕmō-deber*

Each consists of a nominal clause (1) beginning with the demonstrative
pronoun (in one case, strengthened by the independent pronoun),[17] (2)
followed by a grammatically determined form of *'ĕlōhîm*, (3) followed
by a relative clause containing an element of the tradition of the
exodus. These similarities in content, vocabulary, and structure, along
with the cultic contexts, more specifically in connection with a central
cult object (the ark or the bull image) suggest not only the liturgical
character the affirmation ascribed to the Philistines but also a genetic
relationship between it and the formula associated with the bull. In
other words, the two liturgical quotations were likely derived from a
common source, namely, an extended cultic recitation of the events of
the exodus. We have, then, both in 1 Sam 4:8b and in Exod 32:4, 8
and 1 Kgs 12:28 the preserved fragments of a longer exodus litany, one
in which *'ĕlōhîm* serves repeatedly and exclusively as the designation
for the divine.

---

[16]On the reading *ûbĕmō-deber*, see McCarter, *I Samuel*, 104; see also above, More
International Contexts.

[17]See GKC §136d.

A New Frame of Reference for the Formula

The recognition of the extended exodus formula sheds new light on the use of *'ĕlōhîm* in the relevant passages. First, we resume our discussion of the formula's apparent treatment of *'ĕlōhîm* as a plural. The explanations given in connection with the bull image in Exod 32 and 1 Kgs 12 may now be considered in view of the other part of the exodus formula preserved in 1 Sam 4:8b. With the introduction of the latter passage into the discussion, the two explanations already rejected—i.e., plurality of cult images and morphological congruence—remain inadequate. The third possibility, that the plural formula is a polemical misrepresentation of the bull image, proves unsatisfactory, too, for the context of 1 Sam 4 has absolutely nothing to do with the bull image or any other aspect of Jeroboam's cult. Furthermore, the mockery of Jeroboam's cult, according to this explanation, would have consisted in the pluralization of the originally singular formula in correspondence to the two calves. It would not have occurred to an opponent of Jeroboam's cult to polemicize the latter by pluralizing a part of the formula and then placing it in the context of the Philistines before the ark. The implication is that the association of the formula with the single ark suggests that the plural formulation of the litany was genuine. Once the relationship of this passage to the bull formula has been understood, the supposition that the latter represents a polemical distortion based on Jeroboam's two bulls becomes untenable. A different explanation must be found for pl. *'ĕlōhîm* in the exodus formula, one that accounts for its citation in all of these passages.

A closer look at the formula's use in 1 Sam 4 provides new insight into its significance. That the reference in 1 Sam 4:8 to the plagues and pestilence afflicted on the Egyptians is integral to the narrative context is suggested by the fact that it alerts the reader to the exodus parallels that follow in the story.[18] Thus the quotation of the *'ĕlōhîm* formula was evidently original to the Ark Narrative, the

---

[18]McCarter, *I Samuel*, 106. On the importance of the exodus motif in the Ark Narrative see Antony F. Campbell, *The Ark Narrative (1 Sam 4-6; 2 Sam 6): A Form-Critical and Traditio-Historical Study* (SBLDS 16; Missoula, Mont.: Scholars Press, 1975). The exodus formula's significance for the Ark Narrative will receive further attention in the discussion to follow.

immediate literary context of the passage.[19] In contrast with the formula's association with the bull cult in Exod and 1 Kgs, its quotation in the speech of the Philistines does not necessarily have a pejorative connotation. While recitation by the uncircumcised in itself may not constitute a ringing endorsement of the formula as a legitimate expression of Israelite religion, both the content of the litany and its prescient character for the ensuing narrative do. Though one is thrown by the use of pl. *'ĕlōhîm*, the Philistines' acquaintance with the exodus tradition found elsewhere in the Hebrew Bible is accurate. That the captivity of the ark results in "plague" and "scourge" among the Philistines further legitimizes the Philistines' confession and its association with the ark. The connection of the formula with the ark and with the bull image will be explored below, but the matter of pl. *'ĕlōhîm* in the formula remains a problem.

Divine Plurality in the Exodus Tradition

The concept of a plurality of "gods" of the exodus is not as foreign to the tradition as it might seem initially. For traces of divine plurality are found throughout the biblical portrayal of the exodus. The narrative related in the book of Exodus depicts Yahweh working through supernatural agents, including "the destroyer" (*hammašḥît*, 12:23), who carries out the slaying of the first-born in Egypt[20] and both "the messenger of God/divine messenger" (*mal'ak hā'ĕlōhîm*, 14:19) and "the pillar-of-cloud by day and the pillar-of-fire by night" (*'ammûd he'ānān yômām wĕ'ammûd hā'ēš lāylâ*, 13:22; see also

---

[19]According to Leonhard Rost, the Ark Narrative, an originally independent literary account, comprised 1 Sam 4:1b-7:1 and 2 Sam 6 ("Die Überlieferung von der Thronnachfolge Davids," in *Das kleine Credo und andere Studien zum Alten Testament* [Heidelberg: Quelle & Meyer, 1965], 119-253, esp. 148-59; repr. of *Die Überlieferung von der Thronnachfolge Davids* [BWANT III, 6; Stuttgart: W. Kohlhammer, 1926]). On the basis of ancient Near Eastern parallels describing the spoliation and return of cult images, Patrick D. Miller, Jr., and J. J. M. Roberts demonstrated that 2 Sam 6, which relates David's bringing the ark to Jerusalem, would lie outside the thematic scope and compositional time frame of the original Ark Narrative and that portions of 1 Sam 2, which present Eli's wicked sons as the reason for the ark's capture, belong to the original literary work (*The Hand of the Lord: A Reassessment of the "Ark Narrative" of 1 Samuel* [JHNES; Baltimore: Johns Hopkins Univ. Press, 1977], esp. 61-75). Accordingly, Miller and Roberts redefine the extent of the Ark Narrative to 1 Sam 2:12-17, 22-25, 27-36; 4:1b-7:1; cf. McCarter, *I Samuel*, 26, 89-93, who excludes 2:27-36 as Deuteronomistic.

[20]See Samuel A. Meier, "Destroyer הׁשׁמַ," *DDD*, 241.

14:19), who lead the Israelites out of Egypt. Furthermore, Exod 15, the most archaic witness to the exodus tradition,[21] makes explicit reference to divine plurality in the context of the exodus:

> *mî-kāmōkâ bā'ēlîm yhwh*
> *mî kāmōkâ ne'dār baqqōdeš*
> *nôrā' tĕhillōt 'ōśē(h) pele'*

> Who is like you among the gods, Yahweh?
> Who is like you, majestic in holiness,
> awesome in praises, working wonders? (v. 11)

Ps 78:48-50 contains a remnant of tradition describing a number of minor deities who assist Israel's god in the deliverance from Egypt:

> *wayyasgēr labbārād bĕ'îrām ûmiqnêhem lārĕšāpîm*
> *yĕšallaḥ-bām ḥărôn appô 'ebrâ wāza'am wĕṣārâ mišlaḥat mal'ăkê rā'îm*
> *yĕpallēs nātîb lĕ'appô lō'-ḥāśak mimmāwet napšām wĕḥayyātām laddeber hisgîr*

> He gave over their cattle to Hail, and their herds to Pestilence.
> He sent against them the Burning of his Anger, Fury, Indignation, and Distress, a band of destructive messengers.
> He leveled a path for his Anger; he did not withhold their life's breath from Death; he gave over their life to Plague.

Although the monotheistic context of this Psalm requires that these attendants of Yahweh be domesticated into personified attributes of the deity and forces of nature, this passage preserves a tradition which portrays the deity in the company of his divine retinue, a common motif in the ancient Near East.[22] Here the deities Hail, Pestilence, Death, and Plague join Yahweh's personified attributes of wrath as members of his fighting forces.

Hail (*bārād*, v. 48), though thoroughly demythologized in the description of the plague in Exod 9:18, is related to *Baradu*, the divinized personification of that metereological phenomenon in texts

---

[21]McCarter, "Exodus," in *Harper's Bible Commentary* (ed. J. L. Mays; San Francisco: Harper & Row, 1988), 146.

[22]See Theodore Hiebert, *God of My Victory: The Ancient Hymn in Habakkuk 3* (HSM 38; Decatur, Ga.: Scholars Press, 1986), 93; J. J. M. Roberts, *Nahum, Habakkuk, and Zephaniah: A Commentary* (OTL; Louisville: Westminster John Knox, 1991), 154.

from third-millennium Ebla.[23]   In Isa 28:2, Hail is paralleled by Destruction (*qeteb*), another agent of Yahweh,[24] who in Deut 32:24 is also paired with Resheph: (Yahweh's people, as his enemy, shall be) "consumed by Pestilence and bitter Destruction" (*lĕḥūmê rešep wĕqeteb mĕrîrî*).   Reseph or, according to our translation, "Pestilence," who appears in Ps 78:48 in plural form (*hārĕšāpîm* "the Reshephs") is known in extrabiblical sources as an independent deity,[25] as are both Death and Plague (v. 49).[26]   In Hab 3:5, Plague appears with Pestilence as members of Yahweh's military entourage:[27]

> *lĕpānāyw yēlek dāber wĕyēṣē' rešep lĕraglāyw*
> Before him goes Plague, and Pestilence goes out at his feet.

The mention of Plague both in this passage and in Ps 78:50 provides a point of contact with the plural exodus formula, which mentions "the gods who struck the Egyptians . . . with plague (*bĕmô-deber*)" (1 Sam 4:8).   Although it is not clear that *deber* in this case designates the deity, the distinction between the god and his manifestation in the phenomenon of plague should not be drawn too sharply.   In any case, the parallel suggests the relevance of the exodus tradition's motif of divine plurality to the plural cult formula.

Yahweh's retinue as described in Ps 78:48-50 is composed also of his wrathful attributes—the Burning of his Anger (*ḥărôn appô*), Fury ('*ebrâ*), Indignation (*za'am*), and Distress (*ṣārâ*)—which are concretized and personified as *mišlaḥat mal'ăkê rā'îm*, "a band of destructive messengers" (v. 49).   The hypostatization of divine attributes[28] as Yahweh's agents in warfare is a motif that is found in

---

[23]Paolo Xella, "Barad ברד," *DDD*, 160-61.

[24]See Nicolas Wyatt, "Qeteb קטב," *DDD*, 673-74.

[25]See William J. Fulco, *The Canaanite God Rešep* (AOS Essay 8; New Haven: American Oriental Society, 1976).

[26]John F. Healey, "Mot מות," *DDD*, 598-603; Gregorio del Olmo Lete, "Deber דבר," *DDD*, 231-32.

[27]Roberts, *Habakkuk*, 135-36, 154.

[28]Hypostatization refers to the conceptualization of an abstract quality or an attribute of a deity as reified, or, as McCarter so aptly puts it, as having been "given substance (hypostasis)" (P. Kyle McCarter, Jr., "Aspects of the Religion of the Israelite Monarchy: Biblical and Epigraphic Data," in *Ancient Israelite Religion: Essays in Honor of Frank Moore Cross* [ed. P. D. Miller, P. D. Hanson, S. D. McBride; Philadelphia: Fortress, 1987], 147); see also Cross, *CMHE*, 153 n. 30.

Exod 15:6-7, 10:

yĕmînĕkā yhwh ne'dārî bakkōaḥ yĕmînĕkā yhwh tir'aṣ 'ōyēb
ûbĕrōb gĕ'ônĕkā tahărōs qāmêkā tĕšallaḥ ḥărōnĕkā yō'kĕlēmô kaqqaš
. . . .
nāšaptā bĕrûḥăkā kissāmô yam

Your Right Hand, Yahweh, was glorious in power; your Right Hand,
   Yahweh, shattered the enemy.
In the greatness of your majesty, you overthrew those who rose against
   you; you sent your Burning Anger, and it consumed them as chaff.
. . . .
You blew with your Breath, and the Sea covered them.

Here Yahweh's Right Hand (*yāmîn*), his Burning Anger (*ḥārōn*), and
his Breath (*rûaḥ*) are hypostatized and regarded as semi-independent
agents who fight on Yahweh's behalf to defeat the Egyptians.

In the mythic language of Ps 78, the "band of destructive
messengers" (*mišlaḥat mal'ăkê rā'îm*) enumerated are extensions of
Yahweh's identity, a divine army that fights on his behalf. His Anger
(*appô*), for whom, according to v. 50, a path was cleared, is described
in v. 31 as a punishing agent of Yahweh:

wĕ'ap 'ĕlōhîm 'ālâ bāhem wayyahărōg bĕmišmannêhem
The Anger of God[29] rose up against them and killed some of their
stoutest men.

The mention of another one of Yahweh's agents, *ḥārôn* "the *Burning*
of his Anger*," both in Ps 78:49 and in Exod 15:7, brings to mind
Horon, who is known, both from the biblical GN Beth-Horon ("House
of Horon") and from extrabiblical sources, as an independent deity.[30]
The subordinate deities and hypostatic forms mentioned in Ps 78
represent members of Yahweh's army, his divine host.

Inherent to the exodus tradition as preserved in the prose of the
book of Exodus and in the poetry of Exod 15 and Ps 78 is the
accompaniment of Yahweh by his military coterie. We have noted that
this motif is particularly salient in the older poetry found in Hab 3:5

---

[29] *'Ĕlōhîm* is the preferred designation for Yahweh in Pss 42-83, which are
commonly known as the Elohistic Psalter; see above, Introduction.

[30] Udo Rüterswörden, "Horon חרן," *DDD*, 425-26.

and in Deut 32:24. Indeed, the depiction of Yahweh as the Divine Warrior who leads his cosmic armies is one of the leading images of the deity in the Hebrew Bible,[31] as witnessed by one of the chief epithets of Israel's god, *yhwh ṣĕbā'ôt* "Yahweh of (divine) Armies."[32] In the vision of Micaiah ben Imlah, Yahweh is enthroned and surrounded by "the entire army of heaven" (*kol-ṣĕbā' haššāmayim*, 1 Kgs 22:19). The army of heaven includes the sun, moon, and stars (Deut 4:19; 17:3) and is equated with Yahweh's "angelic host" (Pss 103:20-21; 148:2-3).[33] In Judg 5, itself among the oldest poetry in the Bible,[34] the celestial army fights on Yahweh's behalf:

> *min-šāmayim nilḥāmû hakkôkābîm mimmĕsillôtām nilḥāmû 'im-sîsĕrā'*
> The stars fought from heaven, from their courses they fought against Sisera. (v. 20)

The presence of numerous adjutant deities of Yahweh is a motif befitting the martial aspect of the exodus tradition, which is conceived as the defeat of Egypt and its armies by Yahweh and his own armies. That this notion of divine forces under Yahweh's command survives in the preserved traditions of the exodus, in spite of its accommodation to the monotheistic viewpoint that prevails in the biblical material, indicates its prominence as an authentic element of the tradition.

The recognition of Yahweh's divine entourage in the cultic observance of the exodus is an emphasis that would have been most fitting in the Israelite national cult. For, during the period of the monarchy, Yahweh was regularly worshiped alongside one or more of his hypostatic forms, which, as embodiments of his cultic presence, were regarded as semi-independent deities.[35] The most prominent example of such a hypostatic figure that is mentioned in the Bible is Asherah, the personified "Trace (i.e., visible token)" of Yahweh's

---

[31]See, Patrick D. Miller, Jr., *The Divine Warrior in Early Israel* (HSM 5; Cambridge, Mass.: Harvard Univ. Press, 1973).

[32]Cf. Otto Eissfeldt, "Jahwe Zebaoth," in *Kleine Schriften* 3 (Tübingen: J. C. B. Mohr, 1966), 110-23.

[33]These references are supplied in this connection by Miller, *Divine Warrior*, 67.

[34]See David Noel Freedman, *Pottery, Poetry, and Prophecy: Studies in Early Hebrew Poetry* (Winona Lake, Ind.: Eisenbrauns, 1980), 77.

[35]See McCarter, "Religion of the Israelite Monarchy," 143-49.

presence, who at Kuntillet 'Ajrud is regarded as his consort.[36] In the form of Yahwism that survived into the fifth century at the Jewish military colony of Elephantine in Egypt, Yahweh was worshiped along with Bethel, the divinized persona of Yahweh's temple, and with his hypostatized attributes, which included *ḥrmbyt'l* ("the-Sacredness-of-the-Temple"), *'šmbyt'l* ("the-Name-of-the-Temple"), *'ntbyt'l* ("The-Sign-of-the-Temple"), and *'ntyhw* ("The-Sign-of-Yahu," as Yahweh was known at Elephantine).[37] That Yahweh's worship in the national cult of the northern kingdom included the representation of his divine entourage is intimated by the Deuteronomistic historian's condemnation of the cult's characteristic elements, which included "a molten image" (*massēkâ*), "an Asherah" (*'ăšērâ*), and the adoration of the "the entire army of heaven" (*kol-ṣĕbā' haššāmayim*; 2 Kgs 17:16). It seems that

---

[36]Early-eighth-century inscriptions discovered at 'Ajrud record blessings given in the name of "Yahweh of Samaria/Teman and his Asherah" (McCarter, "Religion of the Israelite Monarchy," 138-43). For this interpretation of Asherah, see McCarter, "Religion of the Israelite Monarchy," 149. McCarter's explanation remains valid, notwithstanding the comments of Mark S. Smith, *The Early History of God* (San Francisco: Harper & Row, 1990), 87-88, 109 n. 69. As Smith's insightful remarks on the verbal root ("stem") **'ṭr*—from which McCarter derives Asherah (*'ăšērâ*)—indicate, its basic meaning "to go/advance/proceed" is not inconsistent with the sense "place" that is associated with its nominal forms in Akkadian and Ugaritic, for a "place," "point," or "station" is that which is "left behind" after one has "proceeded"; consider the analogous relationship between the meanings of Biblical Hebrew *māqôm* "place" and the verbal root from which it is derived, *qwm* "to rise/stand." Smith's assertion that **'ṭr* (along with its derivatives) "does not mean 'trace' in any Northwest Semitic language" (p. 87) does not account for Biblical Hebrew **'ăšūr*, "step," "footprint" (note the passive vocalization, indicating that which has been "left behind"); Pss 17:5; 37:31; 40:3; 44:19; 73:2; and esp. Job 23:11, where the term is clearly used in reference to the path (observe the parallel with *derek* "way") "left behind" where one has walked; cf. **'aššūr*, Job 31:7. Although Smith's point that "name of Baal" and "face of Baal," respective epithets for the goddesses Astarte and Tannit, are not analogous to Asherah in the strictest sense is valid, these expressions do illustrate the perception of the those goddesses as hypostatic forms of other deities. Finally, Smith's criticism of the distinction McCarter makes between Israelite and Canaanite Asherah seems to reflect a misconstruing of his point. In explaining the former as an internal Israelite development, McCarter does not mean that the two are "unrelated"; cf. Smith's comments on p. 88 with McCarter's footnote 69.

[37]McCarter, "Religion of the Israelite Monarchy," 147; William F. Albright, *Archaeology and the Religion of Israel* (5th ed.; Garden City, N.Y.: Doubleday, 1969), 173-75; cf. Bezalel Porten (*Archives from Elephantine: the Life of an Ancient Jewish Military Colony* [Berkeley: Univ. of California Press, 1968], 173-79), who characterizes these forms as syncretistic, i.e., as representing a mixture of originally Israelite and non-Israelite elements.

the recognition of Yahweh's divine retinue as featured in the exodus tradition was an integral part of the state-sponsored worship that honored him.

In light of the notion of divine plurality proper to the exodus tradition, the meaning of pl. *'ĕlōhîm* in the formula becomes quite clear. "The gods who brought you up from the land of Egypt . . . the gods who struck the Egyptians" is an obvious reference to Yahweh and the divine forces under his command, which are composed of his own hypostatic forms and the minor deities standing in his service. In the cultic observance of the exodus, a genuinely Yahwistic tradition, the notion of divine plurality expressed by pl. *'ĕlōhîm* emphasized Yahweh's dominion both in the human and in the divine realm, an idea which is given expression in Exod 15:11: *mî-kāmōkâ bā'ēlīm yhwh,* "Who is like you among the gods, Yahweh?"

Summary

The worship formula cited in connection with Jeroboam's cult in 1 Kgs 12:28 and in connection with Aaron's rebellion in Exod 32:4, 8 is part of an extended cult recitation memorializing the exodus, another segment of which is attested in 1 Sam 4:8 in association with the ark. The only divine designation featured in the attested portions of the formula is pl. *'ĕlōhîm*, which refers to Yahweh and his divine entourage in the context of the deliverance of Israel from Egypt.

The *'ĕlōhîm* Formula's Associations with the Ark

The apparent connection between the ark and the exodus formula, as suggested by the Philistines' words in 1 Sam 4:8b, merits further consideration. Since the formula is not to be associated exclusively with Jeroboam or even with the bull image, it is no longer appropriate in our discussion to refer to it as "Jeroboam's formula" or as "the bull formula." Instead, we will call it simply the *'ĕlōhîm* exodus-formula or simply the *'ĕlōhîm* formula.

As noted, the ark's associations with the exodus tradition in the Ark Narrative, first signaled in this verse, is given expression in the rest of the narrative. Because the Philistines hold captive Yahweh's ark, he afflicts them with "plague" and "scourge," just as he had the Egyptians, who had held captive Yahweh's people. The release of the ark can be seen as a parallel to Yahweh's leading his people out of Egypt. Also suggestive of the ark's connection with the exodus in the Ark Narrative is the fact that Eli's sons, Hophni and Phinehas, whose sins are responsible for the ark's capture, have Egyptian names. All of this suggests that the quotation of the exodus formula in 1 Sam 4:8b was integral to the Ark Narrative's portrayal of Yahweh as the divine warrior who had been victorious over Egypt.[38]   Furthermore, it indicates that the Israelite authors of the Ark Narrative themselves associated the plural exodus formula with the ark.

This last consideration takes on great significance in light of the dating of the Ark Narrative's composition to a period well before the construction of the Jerusalem temple, perhaps prior to the monarchy.[39] In this early monarchic, perhaps premonarchic literary witness, the plural exodus formula is understood to belong not to a specific cult place but to the ark itself, the portable shrine of Yahweh and the central cult symbol of premonarchic Israel.

As discussed above, one source of confusion in the association of the plural formula with the bull symbol in Exod 32 and 1 Kgs 12—a matter to which we shall return below—is the discrepancy between the plural "gods" and the single cult image. By contrast, the ark, as we shall see, proves a most fitting cult symbol to be associated with the notion of divine plurality expressed by our exodus litany.

In the Ark Narrative, we observe that the ark is associated not only with the plural exodus formula but also with the divine title *yhwh ṣĕbā'ôt yōšēb hakkĕrūbîm*, "Yahweh-Sabaoth-Enthroned-upon-the-Cherubim (1 Sam 4:4)." As Eissfeldt explained, this is the expanded form of the liturgical name *yhwh ṣĕbā'ôt* that was associated with the

---

[38]Cf. Miller and Roberts, who note only that the mention of the exodus "calls to mind" this aspect of Yahweh's identity (*Hand of the Lord*, 35).

[39]According to Miller and Roberts, the Ark Narrative was composed some time after the battle at Ebenezer, which it describes, and before David's subduing of the Philistines and capture of their cult images (2 Sam 5:17-21), a turn of events which, in light of Near Eastern parallels, is conspicuously absent from the Ark Narrative (*Hand of the Lord*, 73-75); cf. the original explanation of the Ark Narrative formulated by Rost ("Thronnachfolge Davids") and followed by Campbell (*Ark Narrative*), which includes 2 Sam 6 (David's bringing the ark into Jerusalem) as the culminating episode and which attributes the work's composition to the Jerusalem priesthood who served either during David's reign or during the early part of Solomon's reign.

ark at Shiloh.[40] In the appellation *yhwh ṣĕbā'ôt*, the god represented by the ark is associated with divine armies.[41]

As the symbol of Yahweh's presence in battle, the ark was understood to be the dwelling of his hypostatized attributes.[42] The ark is associated with the manifestation of Yahweh's "Might" (*'ōz*). In Ps 132, we read

> *qûmâ yhwh limnûḥāteka 'attâ wa'ărôn 'uzzekā*
> Arise, Yahweh, to your resting place, you and the ark of your Might.
> (v. 8 = 2 Chr 6:41)

It is not by mere chance that, in the account of David's transfer of the ark (2 Sam 6), events to which this Psalm makes reference,[43] Uzzah (written both *'uzzā'* and *'uzzâ*) is the name of the attendant of the ark whom God strikes dead for touching the ark.[44] Psalm 78:61 makes

(like drone, like Uriah)

---

[40]Eissfeldt suggested that the expanded form of the epithet signified the combination of the ark with the Canaanite imagery of the cherub throne at Shiloh ("Jahwe Zebaoth," 120-21).

[41]Albright, following Haupt, interpreted the expression as a sentence name meaning "He-Who-Creates-the-Hosts (of Israel)" (Paul Haupt, "Der Name Yahweh," *OLZ* 12 [1909]: 211-14; William F. Albright, "Contributions to Biblical Archaeology and Philology: The Name *Yahweh*," *JBL* 43 [1924]: 370-78). This interpretation is followed by David Noel Freedman, "The Name of the God of Moses," *JBL* 79 (1960): 151-56 and Cross, *CMHE*, 60-75, who understands *ṣĕbā'ôt* to be in reference to the *divine* hosts. Compare Eissfeldt's interpretation of the epithet, which recognizes two different versions of the title in which *ṣĕbā'ôt* is understood as a substantivized abstract plural meaning "might": *yhwh ṣĕbā'ôt*, "Yahweh the Mighty," and *yhwh 'ĕlōhê ṣĕbā'ôt*, "Yahweh the Mighty God" ("Jahwe Zebaoth," 106, 110-13).

[42]As Eissfeldt recognized, the imagery of the cherub throne, which had an origin distinct from the ark, was first associated with the latter at Shiloh ("Jahwe Zebaoth," 120-21; cf. Roland de Vaux, "Les chérubins et l'arche d'alliance," *MUSJ* 37 [1960-1961]: 93-124).

[43]See P. Kyle McCarter, Jr., *II Samuel: A New Translation with Introduction and Commentary* (AB 9; New York: Doubleday, 1984), 176-78; cf. Cross, *CMHE*, 95-99; cf. Delbert H. Hillers, "Ritual Procession of the Ark and Ps 132," *CBQ* 30 (1968): 48-55.

[44]It is likely that the etiology of the GN *pereṣ 'uzzâ*, whose incorporation into the account of David's transfer of the ark is suggestive of the importance of the divine *'ōz* in its association with the ark, was originally of a different nature than the story as preserved. A clue to this is that the son of Abinadab designated as the keeper of the ark is introduced in 1 Sam 7:1 not as Uzzah but as Eleazar. As McCarter explains, an alternation between the elements *'ōz* and *'ezer* in the name of the same person is not unusual (*II Samuel*, 169). The shift in this case was apparently prompted by the presence of the divine *'ōz* as a prominent feature of the original form of the story.

mention of the captivity of the ark described in the Ark Narrative by reference both to *'uzzô* "his Might" and to *tip'artô* "his Glory":

> *wayyittēn laššĕbî 'uzzô wĕtip'artô bĕyad-ṣār*
> He gave up his Might to captivity and his Glory into the
> hand of the adversary. (Ps 78:61; cf. 96:6; 1 Chr 16:27)

In Ps 96:6, Might and Glory, along with other personified attributes, are described as Yahweh's attendants in the sanctuary:

> *hôd-wĕhādār lĕpānāyw 'ōz wĕtip'eret bĕmiqdāšô*
> Splendor and Majesty are before him; Might and Glory are
> in his sanctuary.

It is clear that, in the poetic language of the Psalms, these references to personified divine attributes are compatible with monotheism. Nonetheless, the intimate association of the pair *'ōz* and *tip'eret* with the ark suggests a special role in the manifestation of the Yahweh's presence.

This consideration is brought into sharper focus by reflection upon the ark's similarities with the pre-Islamic Arab *qubbâ*, a portable tent shrine which served as a battle palladium and which housed two sacred stones representing the male deity's divine consorts Al-Lat and Al-Uzza.[45] While the identity of the first of these consorts is obscure, the second is clearly the hypostatized "Might" of the deity primarily associated with the tent shrine. The parallel between Al-Uzza of the *qubbâ* and the *'ōz* so closely associated with the ark is striking. That Al-Uzza and Al-Lat are understood to have a military significance, a notion implied by their attachment to the *qubbâ*, is reinforced by descriptions of a custom, according to which two young women serving as attendants to the *qubbâ* would ride into battle on camelback for the apparent purpose of encouraging the troops, a custom which suggests an analogous role for the deity's consorts in association with the *qubbâ*.[46] Although Yahweh's *'ōz*, as represented in our sources,[47]

---

[45]Julian Morgenstern, "The Ark, the Ephod, and The 'Tent of Meeting,'" *HUCA* 17 (1942-1943): 153-266, esp. 207-23.

[46]Ibid., 212-13.

[47]That is, by the grammatically masculine form of the word; but cf. the feminine form in the GN *pereṣ 'uzzâ* in 2 Sam 6:8 and the PN *'uzzâ*, alternatively written *'uzzā'* in 2 Sam 6 and elsewhere.

cannot be said to be his consort, both its role in warfare and its pairing with another hypostatic form, *tip'eret*, in connection with the ark are aspects of divine plurality associated with the ark that find parallels in comparisons with the *qubbâ*.

The *qubbâ* also provides a reminder that the ark, in distinction to a Canaanite, Syrian, or Mesopotamian cult statue, was in no way perceived as a depiction of a particular deity[48] but as a portable shrine,[49] hence the two very different attitudes expressed in the biblical sources toward the ark and the bull image as divine symbols. From this aspect of the ark arise its associations not only with Yahweh but also with the divine host under his command, including at least his hypostatic forms. Thus the ark as a symbol of the divine presence is quite compatible with notion of divine plurality expressed in our exodus litany.

The theme of divine armies assisting Yahweh in battle against Egypt, which is implicit in the *'ĕlōhîm* formula of the exodus, is most fitting in connection with the ark, which represents his presence in war as "Yahweh Sabaoth." As the portable war shrine representing Yahweh and his hypostatic forms, the ark is a most fitting cult symbol in association with the idea of divine plurality expressed in the liturgical formula. Thus it is likely that the *'ĕlōhîm* exodus-formula—which, as the Ark Narrative attests, was associated with the ark in the cult of premonarchic Israel—was composed for recitation in relationship to the ark. In view of these considerations, it is reasonable to conclude that the formula was associated with the ark in the central cultus of premonarchic Israel at Shiloh, in the cultic observance of the exodus.

The *'ĕlōhîm* Formula's Associations with the Bull Image

As our analysis of the *'ĕlōhîm* exodus-formula indicates, Jeroboam's use of the formula in his national cult constituted not an innovation, as implied by the Deuteronomistic account in 1 Kgs 12, but a reliance on an established religious tradition of common-Israelite heritage. The appropriation of a liturgical formula that had figured prominently in the

---

[48]Eissfeldt, "Lade und Stierbild," 305.

[49]For the view of the ark as a portable sanctuary, see Herbert G. May, "The Ark—A Miniature Temple," *AJSL* 52 (1936): 215-34.

central worship of premonarchic Israel represented Jeroboam's effort to provide a state cult that equaled that of Jerusalem in terms of the legitimizing force of its archaizing forms of worship.[50]   Though Jeroboam could not offer the ark, he could offer the formula that had once accompanied it in worship at the central sanctuary of premonarchic Israel.   The appeal to common-Israelite identity expressed in the formula's commemoration of Israel's founding event served Jeroboam's need to unify the northern tribes.[51]

As we have seen, the association of the plural exodus-formula with the bull at Bethel is at first confusing, though not with respect to the identity of the god it represented.   The bull iconography was clearly understood as a legitimate and traditional Yahwistic symbol.[52] Jeroboam's interests would in no way have been served by the introduction of cultic innovations, let alone the ascription of the exodus to another god.[53]   Had this been the case, as Cross notes, the Deuteronomist would have attacked this measure vociferously.   Like the use of the *'ĕlōhîm* exodus-formula, the appropriation of the bull iconography as an alternative to the cherubim imagery of the ark was consistent with Jeroboam's use of archaizing expressions in his religious establishment.

The confusion posed by the formula's association with the bull statue is due to the fact that a single cult statue is inherently inconsistent with the notion of divine plurality articulated in the *'ĕlōhîm* formula.   Unlike the ark, which was a portable war shrine representing *yhwh ṣĕbā'ôt* along with the divine forces under his command, the bull image, understood as a depiction either of the deity or of his pedestal, represented the deity alone.   It is likely that the cult of Bethel and Dan included accompanying symbols of "the gods" of Yahweh's entourage, which would have compensated for the discrepancy to some degree. However, this possibility notwithstanding, the conflict in numeric expression is ultimately mitigated by the fact that, by the time of the

---

[50]On Jeroboam's need to appeal to conservative sentiment, see Eissfeldt, "Lade und Stierbild," 296-97; Cross, *CMHE*, 75; van der Toorn, *Family Religion*, 279.

[51]See van der Toorn's characterization of the exodus as "national charter myth" (*Family Religion*, 287-315).

[52]Eissfeldt, "Lade und Stierbild," 296-98.

[53]Cross, *CMHE*, 74-75; cf. J. Alberto Soggin, "Der offiziell geförderte Synkretismus in Israel während des 10. Jahrhunderts," *ZAW* 78 (1966): 179-204.

litany's attachment to the bull iconography, its plural formulation was frozen as the language of an established cult formula.

While these considerations seem consistent with the notion that the formula and the bull image at Bethel were combined for the first time under Jeroboam, one must remember that Jeroboam was no innovator. As Cross points out, Jeroboam's curious choice of two national cult centers is explained by the indication in the biblical traditions that, at the time of the northern secession, Dan and Bethel were the chief sanctuaries of two rival priestly houses.[54] Thus the royal sanction given Bethel and Dan was a measure to secure the support for the monarchy from these well established religious parties, and the elevation of those cult sites as national sanctuaries probably involved the endorsement of their existing expressions of worship. On this basis, it is reasonable to consider whether the association of the formula with the bull at Bethel was not inaugurated but inherited by Jeroboam.

Bethel Traditions of *'ĕlōhîm*

To account for this possibility, we refer to Judg 20:18-28, which relates the war of the premonarchic tribes against Benjamin. According to vv. 26-28, the ark was the focus of worship at Bethel during this period of the tribal confederacy. The likelihood of the *'ĕlōhîm* formula's composition in relationship to the ark takes on new significance in light of the ark's connection with Bethel.

In our discussion of the etiology of Bethel in Gen 28, we noted an apparently original element of the narrative, namely, the site's description as a *bêt 'ĕlōhîm*, where numerous divine beings appear after making the descent from the "gate of heaven."[55] The present form of the story includes the depiction of numerous divine beings in an established tradition that illustrates the etymology of Bethel by (pl.) *'ĕlōhîm*. This emphasis on divine plurality at Bethel has relevance for the mention in 1 Sam 10:3 of men "going up to *'ĕlōhîm* at Bethel." The phrase *'ālâ 'el hā'ĕlōhîm/yhwh* is a technical expression, meaning

---

[54]Cross, *CMHE*, 199.

[55]Hermann Gunkel, *Genesis übersetzt und erklärt* (Handkommentar zum Alten Testament; Göttingen: Vandenhoeck & Ruprecht, 1901), 288-91. See the discussion above, Plural *'ĕlōhîm* in Israelite Contexts.

"present oneself before God/Yahweh,"[56] in which *'ĕlōhîm* can occur as a substitute for the DN.[57] However, *'ĕlōhîm* in this instance is not necessarily to be understood either in its generic or its singular sense and could rather be the designation for a group of deities worshiped at Bethel.

This association of Bethel with a plurality of deities would seem to have relevance for the *'ĕlōhîm* formula of the exodus. As we have indicated, the compatibility between the ark—a portable war shrine of Yahweh and his hypostatic forms—as a cult symbol and the notion of divine plurality expressed in the exodus formula suggests that the formula was composed in association with the ark. The emphasis on divine plurality—an aspect of the exodus that is inherent to the tradition—in the formulation of the litany resonates favorably with the emphasis on the *'ĕlōhîm* at Bethel. Thus we would suggest that the composition of the exodus formula designating Yahweh and his subordinate deities as the *'ĕlōhîm* may have occurred at Bethel, while the ark was located there. This would explain why the formula, which continued to be associated with the ark, was retained at Bethel once the ark had been relocated to Shiloh.

The retention of the exodus formula at Bethel after the relocation of the ark would have necessitated the formula's association with an alternate cult symbol. It bears repeating that our exodus litany, which was perhaps composed at Bethel, had from its origin been connected with the ark. Thus the association of the formula with a different cult symbol would most certainly have required a justification, one establishing a connection that would have superseded the formula's association with the ark.

Exodus 32

An account of the formula's association with a cult symbol other than the ark can be found in Exod 32. The formula's association with the bull image, as portrayed in the passage, constitutes a departure from the proper worship of Israel's god and results in a "great sin" (v. 21). Aaron, who is credited with, or rather blamed for, introducing the

---

[56]See Exod 19:3, 24; 24:1, 12; 32:30; Deut 10:1; etc. the explanations and references cited here are provided by McCarter, *I Samuel*, 181.

[57]See above, Appellative *'ĕlōhîm* in Technical Language.

aberrant cultic innovation, creates a bull statue, which is venerated with the cry, "These are your gods, O Israel, who led you up from the land of Egypt" (vv. 4, 8).

As is clear from the focus on the bull image and the exodus formula, the story purports to present the dubious origins of the cult of Bethel as it is known in 1 Kgs 12. Also, the leading role played by Aaron in the cultus described in the story indicates that it prefigures that of Bethel. Bethel's connection with the Aaronid priesthood, though not mentioned in 1 Kgs 12, is noted in Judg 20:26-28, which reports the performance of priestly duties there by "Phinehas, son of Eleazer, son of Aaron." In Exod 32 we clearly have a tradition ascribing to Aaron the combination of the exodus formula and the bull statue as featured at Bethel.

Some have suggested that the present polemical form of the story was based ultimately on a cult legend about the origins of the bull cult at Bethel, in which the role played by Aaron was cast in a positive light.[58] As we have seen, the major elements of the cult described in the story—the bull symbol, its association with the *'ĕlōhîm* exodus-formula, and an Aaronic priestly identity—are all features associated with the Bethel cult. It can hardly be doubted that the priests of Bethel would have traced the origin of the cult they officiated to their priestly forebear Aaron. The possibility that the basis for the narrative in Exod 32 is a pro-Aaron cult legend will be considered further through a tradition-critical evaluation of the story.

The association of the exodus formula with the bull in Exod 32 is often attributed to the alleged dependence of this passage on the narrative of 1 Kgs 12.[59] However, Exod 32 bears indications of its autonomy from the latter. In addition to the points raised by others in this connection,[60] we make two important observations. First, as noted, the Aaronic identity of the Bethel priesthood, intimated in Judg 20:26-28 and given such importance in Exod 32, is conspicuously

---

[58]See, for instance, Eissfeldt, "Lade und Stierbild," 296.

[59]For citations of the secondary literature, see Bailey, "Golden Calf," 97 n. 2 and the discussion above, Jeroboam's Cult Formula.

[60]Ibid.

absent from 1 Kgs 12.[61] Second, the two passages report slightly but significantly differing versions of the same cult formula: *'ēlle(h) 'ĕlōhêkā* in Exod 32:4, 8 corresponds to *'ēlle(h) hēm hā'ĕlōhîm* in 1 Sam 4:8b, while *hinnē(h) 'ĕlōhêkā* in 1 Kgs 12:28 does not.[62] The more authentic rendering of the formula in Exod 32 establishes this passage's independence from 1 Kgs 12.

As Cross has explained, the story of Aaron's rebellion in Exod 32 belongs to the "stories of conflict in the wilderness," biblical traditions which reflect rivalries between Israel's early priestly houses.[63] Naturally, the postexilic Jerusalem priesthood, which claimed Aaronic descent, can be eliminated from consideration as the source of the story.[64] We will consider the suggestion by Cross that the Elohistic account is derived from a polemic directed against the bull cult of the Aaronid priesthood at Bethel by the rival northern priesthood at Shiloh, which supported the iconographic tradition represented by the ark.[65] It is Shiloh which, subsequent to the ark's maintenance at Bethel, had come to be the shrine associated with the ark. As we have seen, the Ark Narrative's association of the ark with the exodus formula is given expression in the description of the ark's arrival at Ebenezer from its cultic home in Shiloh (1 Sam 4:8), the implication being that the Ark Narrative's author knew the formula to have been connected with the ark at Shiloh.

In light of these considerations, the suggestion that the story in Exod 32 is based on a Shilonite critique of Bethel is quite reasonable. The offense at Sinai as portrayed by the narrative lies in the identification of the *'ĕlōhîm* of the exodus with the bull statue, an equation which constitutes idolatry. The effect of the idol's designation as "gods," which, as Cross says, "is weird,"[66] is explained by the fact that the polemic, like the Bethelite cult itself, cites a frozen formula. Here we can easily think of a Shilonite source. For, from

---

[61]This is not to say that the Deuteronomist was unaware of Aaron's association with the bull image, which is referenced, after all, in Deut 9:16-21, a passage which, though not mentioning the exodus formula, follows the exodus account in other respects.

[62]The Deuteronomist alters the formula so as to accentuate the hint of idolatry in his portrayal of Jeroboam's cult; see below, Back to 1 Kings 12:25-33.

[63]*CMHE*, 73-75, 198-99.

[64]Ibid., 198; Noth, *Exodus*, 245.

[65]*CMHE*, 198-99.

[66]Ibid., 74.

the viewpoint of the Shiloh priesthood—whose unique status as the custodians of Yahweh's ark would have been threatened by his association with an alternate cult symbol—the offense would lie both in the illegitimacy of the bull as a Yahwistic symbol and in its association with the exodus formula, which belonged with the ark at Shiloh.   The impropriety of this association would have been heightened by the discrepancy we have noted between the plural exodus formula and the single statue, an object which, unlike the ark, did not represent a shrine for Yahweh and his divine host. Whether the notion of a Canaanite cult statue as an unacceptable symbol for Yahweh was original to the Shiloh priesthood or, as implied by the representation of Yahweh by the ark, was authentic to earlier Yahwism, it would have served the interests of the Shiloh priesthood to protect its own unique status. Thus we can imagine that the charge of idolatry, which is a mockery of the use of a cult statue, would have been present in a Shilonite polemic against the bull cult of Bethel.

This critique would have played on the association of the formula with the statue at Bethel. The introduction of the bull by the slogan "These are your gods . . ." is portrayed as an identification constituting idolatry, an equation which is impossible in the formula's connection with the ark. Thus the citation of the exodus formula seems to have been original to the attack against the bull cult that is represented in our text, which itself was most likely derived from a Shilonite polemic.

Such a polemic would have been effective only if its description of the Bethel cultus and the claim of Aaron as its founder corresponded to Bethelite tradition.   This reinforces the likelihood of what we surmised prior to our tradition-historical assessment of Exod 32, namely, that the association of the formula with the bull image, a feature of the cult known from 1 Kgs 12:28, belonged to a tradition of the Bethel priesthood crediting Aaron as the founder of its cult. This tradition would have satisfied the need of the Bethel priesthood, described above, to justify the association of the exodus tradition as expressed in the 'ĕlōhîm formula, which was composed at Bethel in relationship to the ark, with an alternate cult object after the ark had been relocated to Shiloh. The claimed implication of such a story would have been that the authority of the ark at Shiloh, as a symbol of the exodus, was superseded by the bull image, which was introduced as a symbol of the tradition by Aaron at Sinai, before the ark had even been constructed.

To summarize our discussion of the *'ĕlōhîm* formula thus far, the ark was understood as a portable shrine for Yahweh and his divine armies. As such it was a fitting cult symbol to be associated with notion of divine plurality—an element authentic to the exodus tradition—expressed in the extended exodus formula cited in Exod 32:4, 8; 1 Sam 4:8; and 1 Kgs 12:28. This compatibility between the ark and the formula, along with the connection established between the two in the Ark Narrative, suggests that the formula was originally associated with the ark before the time of the monarchy. The indication in Judg 20:26-28 of the ark's location at Bethel during the period of the tribal league and the prominence of the *'ĕlōhîm* as an element of the mythic and cultic tradition of Bethel suggest that the exodus formula, which refers to Yahweh and his subordinates exclusively as the *'ĕlōhîm*, was formulated at Bethel under the influence of the traditions proper to that cult place. Upon the relocation of the ark, ultimately if not immediately, to Shiloh, the formula, by then established as a common-Israelite tradition in association with the league's central worship, continued to be associated with the ark in cultic practice. But, because it was indigenous to Bethel and because it expressed a genuine affinity with Bethel's traditions, the formula also continued in cultic use there, in association, of course, with an alternate cult symbol, the bull statue. The critique in Exod 32 of the representation of Yahweh by the bull image, as expressed in its association with the exodus formula, most likely had its ultimate origin in a cult legend of the Bethel priesthood that gave sanction to the bull iconography as a symbol authorized by its priestly forebear Aaron in connection with the exodus formula. Thus, by the time of Jeroboam, the *'ĕlōhîm* formula was an established Israelite tradition, both in its specific association with Bethel and as part of the common religious heritage of premonarchic Israel.

Back to 1 Kings 12:25-33

As indicated above, 1 Kgs 12:28—in which the cult formula begins *hinnē(h) 'ĕlōhêkā*, "Here are your gods" (cf. *'elle(h) 'ĕlōhêkā*, "These are your gods" in Exod 32:4, 8)—presents an altered form of the exodus litany. This emendation of the formula is to be understood in the context of the Deuteronomistic writer's portrayal of Jeroboam's religious establishment as idolatrous.   According to the account provided by the Deuteronomist, Jeroboam introduces the bull statues by quoting the exodus formula:

> *wayya'aś šěnê 'eglê zāhāb wayyō'mer 'ălěhem rab-lākem mě'ălôt yěrûšalayim hinnē(h) 'ělōhêkā yiśrā'ēl 'ăšer he'ělûkā mē'ereṣ miṣrāyim*
>
> (Jeroboam) made two bulls of gold and said to (the people), "For too long you have gone up to Jerusalem; *here* are your gods, O Israel, who brought you up from the land of Egypt." (1 Kgs 12:28)

One may speculate as to whether the Deuteronomist was aware of the original significance of pl. *'ělōhîm* in the formula.   It is clear that in this passage pl. *'ělōhîm*, which as we have seen originally denoted Yahweh and his divine entourage in battle, is understood in connection with the two statues erected by Jeroboam.   In the formula as represented here, *hinnē(h)* replaces *'ēlle(h)*, which was original to the formula, so as to indicate that Jeroboam is speaking the formula in the presence of the statues.[67]   The resulting effect is that the statues themselves are identified as "your gods," an equation which amounts to idolatry.   Both the emendation of the exodus formula and the misrepresentation of its use of pl. *'ělōhîm* serve the Deuteronomist's effort to accentuate the hint of idolatry in his portrayal Jeroboam's cult.

Despite this polemical reinterpretation, the association of the *'ělōhîm* formula with the bull image was the feature of Jeroboam's cultus which provided the basis for the Deuteronomist's attack.   As our analysis has indicated, this was an authentic feature of the cult at Bethel before the time of Jeroboam.   It is unclear whether the bull iconography and the *'ělōhîm* formula of the exodus were featured in the cult of Dan prior to its elevation as a national sanctuary.   What we can say is that the young bull, as an alternative cult symbol to the ark, and the exodus litany, as a cult formula of Israel's common worship prior to the monarchy, were traditional expressions of Yahwism that held enormous potential for the legitimation of Jeroboam's monarchy. Even if these cultic elements had not been featured at Dan prior to Jeroboam's rise to power, their authority as traditional symbols would

---

[67]On the sense of immediacy conveyed by the particle *hinnē(h)*, see GKC §105b; Joüon and Muraoka, *Grammar of Biblical Hebrew*, §105d.

have justified the prominence they receive in the national cult sponsored by Jeroboam at that site.

Our analysis of the *'ĕlōhîm* formula's own history of tradition confirms what scholars have assumed on the basis of Jeroboam's need to archaize, namely that Jeroboam was appropriating a well established cult formula.[68] By Jeroboam's time, the *'ĕlōhîm* formula had long been a set expression of Israelite religious heritage, one which had been prominent in the central worship of the premonarchic tribes and which continued in cultic use at Bethel if not at other sanctuaries.

From the time of the formula's recitation in the central worship of premonarchic Israel, its use of *'ĕlōhîm* exclusively as the divine designation would have certainly reinforced the term's importance among the northern tribes as a divine title. Whatever status the title *'ĕlōhîm* enjoyed before Jeroboam's time was certainly enhanced by the royal sanction granted to the *'ĕlōhîm* formula under Jeroboam. As we have seen, the quotation of the formula in 1 Kgs 12:28 and in Exod 32:4, 8 represents one segment of an extended formula.[69] Whether this was the only portion of the litany included in the bull cult at Bethel or, more likely, a partial quotation that stood for the longer formula, it indicates the prominence of *'ĕlōhîm* as a divine designation in the national religion of the northern kingdom.

Conclusions

The *'ĕlōhîm* cult-formula cited in Exod 32:4, 8; 1 Sam 4:8; and 1 Kgs 12:28 was a well established religious tradition of common-Israelite heritage, which had been featured in the central worship of premonarchic Israel. Its appropriation by Jeroboam I in the establishment of the national cultus of the northern kingdom perpetuated the influence of *'ĕlōhîm* as an important divine title. The exclusive role of *'ĕlōhîm* in this important Israelite tradition suggests that the term already enjoyed a certain status among the northern tribes as a divine designation, a status that would become authoritative in the national cultus.

---

[68]See above, The *'ĕlōhîm* Formula's Associations with the Bull Image.
[69]See above, Another Instance of Plural *'ĕlōhîm*.

'*Ĕlōhîm* IN LITERARY TRADITIONS OF NORTHERN ORIENTATION

Pentateuchal Traditions

The prominence of '*ĕlōhîm* in northern Israelite tradition is reflected in the northern (i.e., non-Judahite) orientation of the portions of the Pentateuch in which '*ĕlōhîm* is the preferred divine designation.[70] These materials show a keen interest in the cultic centers of Shechem (Gen 35:1-4), Bethel (Gen 28:20-21a, 22; 35:1-7), and Beersheba (Gen 21:14; 46:1-4);[71] by contrast, these traditions show no such interest in southern shrines, including Hebron and Jerusalem.   The preoccupation with the eponymous ancestors of the northern tribes, especially Reuben (30:14-15), in the Elohistic material in Genesis 30:1-24 indicates the significance of '*ĕlōhîm* in association with the northern kingdom; no Elohistic traditions of Judah are attested.[72] The northern associations of '*ĕlōhîm*, which are most evident in the thoroughly Elohistic tradition of the blessing of Ephraim and Manasseh (48:8-22), are concisely expressed in the benediction "May '*ĕlōhîm* make you like Ephraim and Manasseh!" (v. 22).

Other Elohistic traditions of the Pentateuch exhibit a geographic orientation that is best described as northern Israelite. The concerns expressed about the border between Israel and Aram-Damascus in the etiology of Galeed/Jegar-Sahadutha (Gen 31:44-54) are concerns relevant to the northern kingdom of Israel. In the Elohistic Balaam material in Num 22:1-21, 36-40 Israel is antagonized by Moab, whose northern boundary is given as the Arnon (v. 36). These details correspond to the historical background depicted in the inscription of Mesha, who claims, after a long period of oppression under the

---

[70]At this point in the discussion, it is sufficient to speak of "Elohistic traditions of the Pentateuch," i.e., those which exhibit a preference for '*ĕlōhîm* as a divine designation, and to reserve judgment, for the moment, on the matter of E as a continuous and unified narrative source, a matter which will be addressed below; see Preliminary Discussion of E.

[71]Regarding Beersheba's northern associations, see Amos 5:5, which implies that religious pilgrims from the northern kingdom frequently "crossed over" to travel to Beersheba, and 8:14, which associates Beersheba with cultic activity at Dan and Samaria; for discussion of the latter passage, see below, Amos.

[72]The use of the term '*ĕlōhîm* by the patriarch Judah in Gen 44:16 is in speech ostensibly addressed to a foreigner and is not necessarily due to an Elohistic preference; see above, International Contexts.

Israelite king Omri and under "his son," to have expanded his own dominion northward, beyond the Arnon, and to have taken territories formerly under Israelite control.[73] The emphasis on this territory and the appropriation of the Balaam tradition itself, which was at home in an area of the Transjordan that remained under Israelite control for much of the northern kingdom's history,[74] indicate the northern Israelite viewpoint of this Elohistic passage.

The importance of *'ĕlōhîm* as the preferred divine designation in these Pentateuchal traditions of northern Israelite orientation would seem to imply the divine title's prominence in the northern kingdom. This is in keeping with what we have argued regarding *'ĕlōhîm*'s role in the national cult authorized by Jeroboam, viz., that it both presupposed and further perpetuated *'ĕlōhîm*'s importance as a divine designation in northern Israelite religious tradition. Of course, one assumes here a continuity between pl. *'ĕlōhîm*, as expressed in the exodus formula, and unequivocally singular *'ĕlōhîm*, as featured in the Pentateuchal material. In order to account for such a continuity, we consider the use of *'ĕlōhîm* in other portions of the Bible having northern associations.

Prophets Addressing the Northern Kingdom

As stated, whatever status *'ĕlōhîm* possessed as a divine designation before the time of Jeroboam I was confirmed and perhaps enhanced by its use in the national cult of the northern kingdom of Israel. An examination of Amos and Hosea, two eighth-century prophetic books addressed to the northern kingdom, will seek to determine whether *'ĕlōhîm* continued to be a significant title in northern Israelite religion.

Amos

The book of Amos presents a Judean prophet's denunciation of an affluent and self-assured kingdom of Israel during the time of its unmatched prosperity under Jeroboam II (786-746 B.C.E.).[75] As

---

[73]*ANET*, 320-21.

[74]See above, Deir 'Alla.

[75]"Amos," as distinct from "the book of Amos," in this section is used in reference to the material in the book that is derived from the eighth-century prophet and his

commentators have noted, Amos refers to his god simply as Yahweh and never as *'ĕlōhîm* (including suffix forms meaning "my/your/his/their God").[76] Amos uses *'ĕlōhîm* in only one passage (Amos 8:14). In view of the avoidance of the term *'ĕlōhîm* by Amos, its use in this passage may give some insight into *'ĕlōhîm*'s significance as a divine designation in the northern kingdom.

In Amos 8:14, the prophet refers to those who patronize sanctuaries important for the northern kingdom as

> *hannišbā'îm bĕ'ašmat šōmĕrôn*
> *wĕ'āmĕrû hê 'ĕlōhêkā dān*
> *wĕhê drk bĕ'ēr-šāba'*

Those who swear by the Guilt of Samaria
and say, "As Your God lives, O Dan,"
and, "As the Way (alternatively, "Power") of Beer-sheba lives."[77]

These three references to oath-taking represent the full geographic extent of the cult places supported by the inhabitants of the northern

---

followers of the same era; in addition to this material, the book contains editorial insertions from the time of Josiah or later; see James L. Mays, *Amos: A Commentary* (OTL; Philadelphia: Westminster, 1969), 12-14; Hans Walter Wolff, *Joel and Amos: A Commentary on the Books of the Prophets Joel and Amos* (ed. S. D. McBride; trans. W. Janzen et al; Hermeneia; Philadelphia: Fortress, 1977), 106-13; cf. Shalom Paul, *Amos: A Commentary on the Book of Amos* (Hermeneia; Minneapolis: Fortress, 1991), 5-6.

[76]Mays, *Amos*, 7-8; Wolff, *Amos*, 101. As Wolff explains, references both to "Lord Yahweh" (*'ădōnay yhwh*) and to "[God of] [the] hosts" are "demonstrably later additions." The reference in 2:8 to *bêt 'ĕlōhêhem*, "the house of their god," belongs with the phrase *'ēṣel kol-mizbēaḥ*, "beside every altar," found earlier in the verse, as a secondary addition that is influenced by Hos 4:12-14 (see Wolff, *Amos*, 134 n. r, citing Marti, Duhm, and Alt; cf. Mays, *Amos*, 47). Furthermore, the use of *'ĕlōhîm* in 4:11-12 belongs to a series of later additions which relate Amos' references to Bethel (e.g., 4:4-5) to Josiah's destruction of the altar at Bethel, which is described in 3:14 (see Wolff, *Amos*, 111-12, 215-17; cf. Mays, *Amos*, 83-84). In 4:11, the term *'ĕlōhîm* occurs in the stereotyped phrase *kĕmahpēkat 'ĕlōhîm 'et-sĕdōm wĕ'et-'ămōrâ*, "as when *'ĕlōhîm* overthrew Sodom and Gomorrah," which also occurs in Isa 13:19 and Jer 50:40 (see above, Plural *'ĕlōhîm* in Israelite Contexts) and is invoked to describe the northern kingdom's destruction as an accomplished fact. The language of the expression *hikkôn liqra't-'ĕlōhêkā yiśrā'ēl*, "prepare to meet your god, Israel," in Amos 4:12 is reminiscent both of the Sinai pericope (Exod 19:15, 17) and of the Covenant Formula (Exod 20:2; Deut 5:6) (see Wolff, *Amos*, 222; Paul, *Amos*, 150, n. 115).

[77]See below on the interpretations of *drk* in this context.

kingdom.[78] While the context of this verse may not require that this
be an expression of disapproval of worship at those sites, the
disparaging phrase *'ašmat šōmĕrôn*, "The Guilt of Samaria," makes it
clear that the forms of worship denoted are regarded here with
disdain.[79]

The *'ĕlōhêkā* invoked in connection with Dan is unmistakably
recognized from the formula used at the royal sanctuaries there and at
Bethel, which begins *ēlle(h) 'ĕlōhêkā yiśrā'ēl*.[80] That the cultic oath
associated with Dan invokes the deity simply as *'ĕlōhêkā* attests to the
continuing importance both of the *'ĕlōhîm* exodus-formula and of the
divine designation *'ĕlōhîm* in the national cult of the northern kingdom
of Israel. While the disapproval for *'ĕlōhîm*'s use at Dan that is
expressed here may have to do only with the prophet's opposition to
the royal sanctuaries—as dramatized in Amos' confrontation with
Amaziah, priest of Bethel, in 7:10-17—the reference may indicate a
rejection of some aspect of the cult practiced there. A consideration
of the other oath formulae may shed light on this possibility.

---

[78]The geographic range represented here is obviously that "from Dan to Beersheba,"
i.e., the full length of Israelite territory. Verses 13-14 are a development of the image
described in v. 12: "They shall wander from sea to sea, from north to east; they shall run
about seeking the word of Yahweh, but they shall not find it" (Mays, *Amos*, 150).
Northern Israelite connections with Beersheba are also accentuated in 5:5, which suggests
that pilgrims regularly "cross over" from Samaria to worship at this shrine in the
southern Judean desert (Mays, *Amos*, 150; Wolff, *Amos*, 239).

[79]For the view that this verse expresses religious polemic, see Wolff, *Amos*, 321-44;
Hans M. Barstad, *The Religious Polemics of Amos: Studies in the Preaching of Am 2, 7B-
8; 4, 1-13; 5, 1-27; 6, 4-7; 8, 14* (VTSup 34; Leiden: Brill, 1984), 143-201; Paul, *Amos*,
268-72.

[80]See above, Jeroboam's Cult Formula. That this is an allusion to the cult at Dan,
as described in 1 Kgs 12:28-30, is considered possible by Wolff (*Amos*, 332) and likely
by Paul (*Amos*, 270-71 and n. 20); cf. Mays (*Amos*, 150), who does not mention 1 Kgs
12:28, and Barstad (*Religious Polemics*, 185-90), both of whom understand the
expression not as a title but an expression emphasizing the relationship of Dan to its local
god. A possible reflection of the enduring importance of *'ĕlōhîm* as the chief divine
designation at Dan is a bilingual (Greek and Aramaic) inscription recovered from Tel
Dan, which is dated to the late third- or early second-century B.C.E. and which reads "to
the god who is in Dan"; see Avraham Biran, "To the God who is in Dan," in *Temples
and High Places in Biblical Times Proceedings of the Colloquium in Honor of the
Centennial of Hebrew Union College-Jewish Institute of Religion, Jerusalem, 14-16
March 1977* (Jerusalem: Hebrew Union College-Jewish Institute of Religion, 1981), 142-
51.

The expression *'ašmat šōměrôn*, "The Guilt of Samaria," may be explained as a distortion either of *'ăšīmat šōměrôn*, "The Name of Samaria,"[81] or, more likely, of *'ăšērat šōměrôn*, "The Asherah of Samaria."[82] In either case, the reference is to the representation of Yahweh's cultic presence in the form of an hypostatized attribute, understood as his consort.[83] Likewise, *drk bě'ēr-šāba'*, understood either as "the Way of Beersheba"[84] or "the Power of Beersheba,"[85] represents a cultic manifestation of the deity by which he was invoked in worship at this particular sanctuary. Alongside these references, we may consider *'ĕlōhêkā*, which, in the frozen formula recited in the national cult, makes reference to Yahweh and his divine entourage.[86]

---

[81]According to this interpretation, *'ăšīmā is an Aramaic form of the common Semitic term for "name" with prosthetic *aleph*, used in reference to the deity's cultic presence (see Albright, *ARI*, 169-70; William J. Fulco, "Ashima [deity]," *ABD* 1:487); see, e.g., *šmbyt'l*, "The Name of the Temple," a hypostatic form of Yahweh worshiped as a semi-independent deity at fifth-century Elephantine (see Albright, *ARI*, 168-75; cf. Porten, *Archives*, 169 and appendix V); Ashima of Hamath (mentioned in 2 Kgs 17:30); and the mention of a goddess Ashima (*'šym'*) in an Aramaic inscription from Teima (see Morton Cogan, "Ashima אשׁי׳מא," *DDD*, 105-6). It is highly unlikely that our reference is to Ashima of Hamath, whose worship, according to 2 Kgs 17:30, was brought to Samaria only after its conquest and repopulation under the Assyrians.

[82]The mention of "Yahweh of Samaria and his/its Asherah" (*lyhwh. šmrn. wl'šrth*) at Kuntillet 'Ajrud weighs in favor of this solution (see McCarter, "Religion of the Israelite Monarchy," 154 n. 54).

[83]On the consort as a hypostasis of the deity's cultic presence, see McCarter, "Religion of the Israelite Monarchy," 147 and the discussion above, Divine Plurality in the Exodus Tradition.

[84]In view of Beersheba's location in the southern Judean desert and its notoriety as a favorite destination of religious pilgrims (see 5:5), it would not be surprising for the pilgrim route, the *derek* itself, to have had prominence in association with the shrine. Thus the *drk bě'ēr-šāba'* could have become so closely identified with the deity as to represent the deity himself, perhaps even in the cultic representation of the god, a possibility that is suggested by the parallels with *'ašmat šōměrôn* and *'ĕlōhêkā*; cf. Hans M. Barstad, "Way דרך," *DDD*, 895; cf. the personification and deification of the sanctuary as Bethel, Ḥerem-Bethel, etc. (see Albright, *ARI*, 168-75; McCarter, "Religion of the Israelite Monarchy," 147).

[85]See Phoenician *drk*, meaning "dominion," (Frank M. Cross, "A Recently Published Phoenician Inscription in the Persian Period from Byblos," *IEJ* 29 [1979]: 40-44) and Ugaritic epithet for Anat, *b'lt drkt* "Lady of Power" (RS 24.252, see Barstad, "Way," 896). For Biblical Hebrew *drk* with the possible meaning "power, dominion," see Jer 3:13; Hos 10:13; Pss 119:37; 138:5. The deity Derceto known from Hellenistic Ashkelon (see Barstad, "Way," 896) was likely derived from the hypostatized *drkt* of a major god.

[86]See above, The Title *'ĕlōhîm* in the National Cult.

The oath formula—read literally, "*living* (sg.) is Your God, O Dan" (*ḥê 'ĕlōhêkā dān*)—would suggest that *'ĕlōhîm* at Dan by the eighth century had come to be regarded as singular, despite the established form of the litany. In any case, the oath indicates that Yahweh was invoked at Dan by the title *'ĕlōhîm*.

Common to these oaths and to the cultic expressions that they represent is the invocation of Yahweh by reference to his various cultic forms, which in our passage are regarded as unacceptable expressions of Yahwism. In connection with vv. 11-12, the oaths represent vain attempts to seek Yahweh's word (*dibrê yhwh*, v. 11).[87] It is within this framework that we understand the disapproval expressed by our passage. For the perceived offense seems to consist not so much in the localization of Yahweh represented here[88] as in the obfuscation of his distinct identity in these cultic manifestations. The potential confusion is well illustrated by modern interpretations of this passage which recognize in it references to foreign deities.[89] The failure to hear Yahweh's words, described in v. 11 as the result of a "famine" sent by Yahweh, is due in part to the peoples' failure to address him appropriately and directly. As we have noted, it is in a most direct manner that Amos himself makes reference to the deity, calling him simply Yahweh and avoiding *'ĕlōhîm*. The title *'ĕlōhîm* and the corresponding representation of Yahweh in the national cult are counted by Amos among these expressions that obscure Yahweh's identity.

The fact that Amos, a Judean addressing a northern audience, declines to use *'ĕlōhîm* is not without significance. As we shall see, Hosea, himself a strident Yahwist, makes frequent use of *'ĕlōhîm*. Amos' disapproval of the northern Israelite use of *'ĕlōhîm* is not merely inferred from silence, for he speaks derisively of this convention in the passage discussed. The distinctly northern (again, non-Judahite) use of *'ĕlōhîm* as featured in the Ephraimite cult was apparently not recognized as legitimate by this prophet from Judah. It is possible that, for Amos, the northern use of the title *'ĕlōhîm* obscured the identity of Israel's god. Turning to Hosea, himself a northerner, we see a similar concern expressed differently.

---

[87]Mays, *Amos*, 150.

[88]So Wolff, *Amos*, 332.

[89]See, e.g., Barstad (*Religious Polemics*, 164-201), who determines that each oath represents a deity other than Yahweh.

Hosea

Like Amos, Hosea addresses the northern kingdom during the eighth century.[90]   At the center of Hosea's message is the claim that Israel is bound to Yahweh in an exclusive covenant relationship, according to which he is their god and they are his people (1:9; 2:25; 6:7; 8:1). Thus Hosea frequently uses *'ĕlōhîm* plus a pronominal suffix (i.e., meaning "my/your/his/their God"), but even more frequent is its use of the DN Yahweh.[91]   Hosea allows no room for ambiguity in understanding the identity of Israel's god.

According to Hosea, Israel's exclusive relationship to Yahweh is threatened by cultic infidelity. In the simplest form, this consists in the worship of other gods, including Canaanite Baal (2:15, 19; 9:10; 11:2; 13:1).[92]   Another aspect of the problem, as Hosea sees it, is the worship of Yahweh as "Baal" (2:18). In chs. 1-3, Yahweh's relationship with Israel is depicted metaphorically as a marriage. In a play on the word *ba'al* ("master," "husband"), Yahweh tells his people that a day will come when they will call him "my husband" (*'îšî*) and not "my master" (*ba'lî*, 2:18 [16]). The pun presupposes that Israelites called Yahweh by the title *ba'al* ("Master"), something which is indicated by biblical and extrabiblical evidence.[93]   The use of the title

---

[90]For a general introduction to Hosea, see James L. Mays, *Hosea: A Commentary* (OTL; Philadelphia: Westminster, 1969), 1-17; Hans Walter Wolff, *Hosea: A Commentary on the Book of the Prophet Hosea* (ed. P. D. Hanson; trans. G. Stansell; Hermeneia; Philadelphia: Fortress, 1974), xxi-xxii.

[91]By Wolff's count Yahweh occurs 45 times and *'ĕlōhîm*, 26 times "in genuine sayings" (*Hosea*, xxv).

[92]That the particular deity in question, at least in ch. 2, is Canaanite Baal is indicated by the emphasis on agricultural productivity (2:7, 10-15) and by the word-play on the term *ba'al* in 2:18. However, in Hosea 2:15, 19; 11:2, as elsewhere in the Hebrew Bible, the expression *habbĕ'ālîm* is used as a collective term in reference to various Canaanite male deities (see Judg 2:11; 8:33; 10:6, 10; 1 Sam 7:4; 12:10; Jer 2:23; 9:14; 2 Chr 17:3; 24:7). The use of "the Baals" as a blanket term was probably based on the existence of various local manifestations of Canaanite Baal, as well as on numerous local deities who were called by the title Baal, "Lord"; see Wolff, *Hosea*, 28-30; Mark S. Smith, *Early History of God*, 46-48. On the use of Baal as a title for Yahweh, see below.

[93]The evidence, recounted succinctly by Wolff (*Hosea*, 49-50), includes the names of sons of Saul and David (Eshbaal *'ešba'al* and Baaliada *bĕ'alyādā'*, respectively), the frequent use of Baal as a PN element in the eighth-century Samaria Ostraca, and the PN "Baaliah" *bĕ'alyâ* in 1 Chr 12:6.

in reference to Yahweh represents not a syncretistic "Baalization of Yahweh"[94] but a standard mode of representing Yahweh in myth and cult, in which he has taken the place of Baal and has taken on his roles and attributes.[95] To a certain extent, this same tendency is expressed in Hosea, where Yahweh is credited with providing the fertility of the land, a role that is characteristic of Baal (2:7, 10-11). However, for Hosea, the use of *ba'al* as a title for Yahweh obscures his distinct identity and thus is to be rejected in the interest of providing a clarification of the identity of Israel's god.[96]

Hosea emphasizes Yahweh's distinct identity by reference to the exodus from Egypt, the tradition which provides the primary justification for Yahweh's claim to Israel's undivided loyalty (2:17; 11:1; 12:14). In response to the self-assurance Israel finds in its own affluence (12:9), Yahweh says through Hosea:

> *wĕ'ānōkî yhwh 'ĕlōhêkā mē'ereṣ miṣrāyim*
> *'ōd 'ōšîbĕkā bā'ŏhālîm kîmê mô'ēd*

> But I, Yahweh, have been your god from the land of Egypt!
> I will make you live in tents again, as during the days of meeting.
> (12:10).[97]

In the proclamation of his name, Yahweh distinguishes himself from Baal, who is sought only for the prosperity he can provide.[98] Hosea's use of *'ĕlōhîm* here emphasizes that it is Yahweh alone who has been Israel's god since it left Egypt, and it is to Yahweh alone that Israel is

---

[94]So Wolff, *Hosea*, 16, 49.

[95]Mark S. Smith speaks of "the coalescence of various deities and/or some of their features into the figure of Yahweh," a phenomenon which he refers to as "convergence" (*Early History of God*, xxiii, 21-24). The portrayal of Yahweh by the appropriation of imagery regularly associated with Baal is not uncommon in the Hebrew Bible—e.g., Ps 29 (see Mark S. Smith, *Early History of God*, 49-55; Cross, *CMHE*, 151-77). On the portrayal of Yahweh as Baal in the Ark Narrative, see Choon Leong Seow, *Myth, Drama, and the Politics of David's Dance* (HSM 46; Atlanta: Scholars Press, 1989), 55-76.

[96]See Mark S. Smith's description of the processes of "convergence" and "differentiation" which characterize the development of Israelite religion vis-à-vis its Canaanite heritage (*Early History of God*, xxiii-xxv, 146, 154-57, 163).

[97]For the translation of *kîmê mô'ēd*, see the discussion of Wolff, *Hosea*, 215. The NJPS translation renders the expression in this context, "as in the days of old."

[98]Mays, *Hosea*, 167.

accountable. Nonetheless, as 13:1-2 continues, Ephraim has "incurred guilt through Baal," with whom Hosea associates the cultic use of images, including bulls (v. 2). Again Yahweh's distinctiveness from Baal is emphasized in the self-introductory formula:

> *wĕ'ānōkî yhwh 'ĕlōhêkā mē'ereṣ miṣrāyim*
> *wē'lōhîm zûlātî lō' tēdā' ûmôšîā' 'ayin biltî*

> But I, Yahweh, have been your god from the land of Egypt!
> You have not known a god except for me, and there is no deliverer
> besides me. (13:4)

Hosea's reference to Yahweh as Israel's *'ĕlōhîm* emphasizes his unique status as the nation's divine patron acting on its behalf. Hosea's repeated reference to Yahweh as Israel's god (*'ĕlōhîm*) is grounded in the claim of the exodus.

The formula of self-introduction which Hosea uses is reminiscent of the formula that prefaces the Decalogue in Exod 20:2 and Deut 5:6:

> *'ānōkî yhwh 'ĕlōhêkā 'ăšer hôṣē'tîkā mē'ereṣ miṣrāyim mibbêt 'ăbādîm*

> I am Yahweh, your god, who brought you out of the land of Egypt,
> out of the house of slavery.

One may note that both the covenant formula and the formula employed by Hosea in 12:10 and 13:4 bear a strong resemblance to the *'ĕlōhîm* exodus-formula that was featured in the central cult of the premonarchic league and then in the official cult of the northern kingdom:

> *'ēlle(h) 'ĕlōhêkā yiśrā'ēl 'ăšer he'ĕlûkā mē'ereṣ miṣrāyim*

> These are your gods, O Israel, who brought you up from the land
> of Egypt! (Exod 32:4, 8; cf. 1 Kgs 12:28)[99]

Though the relationships among these formulae may be difficult to establish with great precision, Joanne Wijngaards' analysis of

---

[99]See above, Jeroboam's Cult Formula.

references to the exodus offers some assistance.[100]   Wijngaards identified two distinct versions of the exodus formula, broadly considered: (1) one which uses the verb *'lh* ("go up," *hip'il* "bring up") and which presupposes the giving of the land and (2) one which uses the verb *yṣ'* ("go out," *hip'il* "bring out") and which originated in association with the tradition of the giving of the law at Sinai.[101] As Wijngaards points out, Hosea's reference to the exodus in 12:14, along with the formula attested in Exod 32 and 1 Kgs 12, represents the first category, while the Decalogue formula, which uses *yṣ'* belongs to the second.[102] Hosea also uses *'lh* in reference to the exodus in 2:17, but he never employs *yṣ'* in this connection.

Without being too dogmatic in applying Wijngaards' schema, it seems reasonable to suggest that Hosea was familiar with an exodus tradition not as stated in the Decalogue formula (using *yṣ'*) but one in which Israel "came up" (*'lh*) from Egypt. The formula of Yahweh's self-introduction in Exod 20:2 and Deut 5:6 seems, in light of the premonarchic origins which we have established for the *'ĕlōhîm* formula, to represent an adaptation of the old exodus formula in the development of the traditions of law-giving at Sinai.[103] Hosea would have known the old formula quite well from its prominence in the national cult at Dan and Bethel, and, based on the similarity of Hos 12:10 and 13:4 to the covenant formula preceding the Decalogue, he was familiar with an adaptation of the exodus formula in connection with the Sinai tradition.[104]   The variation on the exodus formula featured in 12:10 and 13:4, whether representing material borrowed by Hosea or his own modification of the old formula, reflects the importance of *'ĕlōhîm* as a title in the national religion. For Hosea, the deliverance from Egypt was accomplished not by *'ĕlōhêkā*, "your god," merely (as in Exod 32:4, 8; 1 Kgs 12:28) but by *yhwh 'ĕlōhêkā*,

---

[100]Joanne Wijngaards, "הוֹצִיא and הֶעֱלָה A Twofold Approach to the Exodus," *VT* 15 (1965): 91-102.

[101]Ibid., 101-2.

[102]Ibid., 92, 96, 100.

[103]Cf. Wijngaards (pp. 101-2), who suggests that the *'lh* formula was a later development of the *yṣ'* formula. On the distinct origins of the exodus and Sinai traditions, see Gerhard von Rad, "The Form-Critical Problem of the Hexateuch," in *The Problem of the Hexateuch and Other Essays* (trans. E. W. Trueman Dicken; New York: McGraw-Hill, 1966), 13.

[104]Also Hosea mentions *tôrâ* in connection with "covenant" (*bĕrît*) in 8:1; cf. 6:7.

"Yahweh your God." Like his objection to the use of *ba'al* as a title for Yahweh, Hosea's invocation of the exodus formula is motivated by a concern to clarify the identity of Israel's god.

To summarize, Hosea employs *'ĕlōhîm*, usually with a suffix-pronoun, to emphasize that, as Israel's god, Yahweh is entitled to the nation's exclusive loyalty. As an indirect, if not direct, citation of the *'ĕlōhîm* exodus-formula featured in the national cult, Hosea's language in 12:10 and 13:4 attests to *'ĕlōhîm*'s importance as a title for Israel's god in the traditions of the northern kingdom and to a concern that the identity of the *'ĕlōhîm* of Israel be made clear.

The Elijah Cycle

The need for clarification of the identity of Israel's god is a chief concern expressed by the Elijah traditions (1 Kgs 17-19; 21; 2 Kgs 1-2:18), in which the divine designation *'ĕlōhîm* has a special significance.[105]

First Kings 17-19 deals with the conflict between Yahweh and Phoenician Baal, who is called simply *habba'al* "(the) Baal" in the text (16:31-32; 18:19, 21, etc.; 19:18) and is most likely to be identified as Baalshamem.[106] The portrayal of Yahweh's control over rainfall (17:1, 7; 18:1, 5, 41-46) and his manifestation through meteorological phenomena (18:38; 19:11) make the point that Yahweh rules the domain of nature traditionally assigned to Baal, though Yahweh is not merely a storm god (19:11-12).[107] Of course, ch. 18 treats the

---

[105]The existence of these traditions as a pre-Deuteronomistic cycle of narratives is widely recognized; see in Cross, *CMHE*, 191-93; Judith A. Todd, "The Pre-Deuteronomistic Elijah Cycle," in *Elijah and Elisha in Socioliterary Perspective* (ed. Robert B. Coote; Semeia Studies; Atlanta: Scholars Press, 1992), 1-35; Marsha White, *The Elijah Legends and Jehu's Coup* (BJS 311; Atlanta: Scholars Press, 1997).

[106]There is some question about whether the Phoenician deity whose worship is introduced by Jezebel and sponsored by Ahab (16:31-32) is Melqart (so Albright, *YGC*, 243-44; de Vaux, *Ancient Israel*, 280) or Baalshamem, the two leading male deities of Jezebel's home city of Tyre. Another question is whether this god is the same Baal encountered in Elijah's contest at Carmel in ch. 18 (see Gray, *I & II Kings*, 350-52). Mark S. Smith notes a number of factors which point to Baalshamem in both cases, the chief among which is that, like the Baal of Carmel and of Jezebel, Phoenician Baalshamem is clearly represented as a storm god, while Melqart is not (see Smith, *Early History of God*, 41-44).

[107]Cross, *CMHE*, 194.

rivalry between Yahweh and Baal in direct and explicit terms, in the account of the contest between these two gods. The block of material in chs. 17-19 reveals an acute concern on the part of the pre-Deuteronomistic writers who assembled these narratives to establish Yahweh's unique status over against Phoenician Baal, who had received official sanction under Ahab and Jezebel (16:31-32). This is a concern that belongs to the time of Ahab's reign or shortly thereafter.[108]

Yahweh's preeminence over Baal is settled in the legend of the contest at Carmel (18:16-40). The central question addressed by the narrative is "Who is the *'ĕlōhîm* of Israel?" (vv. 21, 36-37). Elijah presents the people of Israel with a dilemma:

> *'ad-mātay 'attem pōsĕḥîm 'al-šĕtê hassĕ'ippîm*
> *'im-yhwh hā'ĕlōhîm lĕkû 'aḥărāyw wĕ'im-habba'al lĕkû 'aḥărāyw*

How long will you limp on two crutches?[109]
If Yahweh is the *'ĕlōhîm*, then follow him; but if Baal is, then follow him. (v. 21)

Loyalty to Yahweh and loyalty to Baal are presented as two mutually exclusive alternatives for Israel. There can be only one *'ĕlōhîm*. The presumption that the title *'ĕlōhîm* confers a unique status resonates with Hosea's use of the term to emphasize Israel's exclusive relationship to Yahweh (see above). For the Elijah narrative as well as for Hosea, this notion of exclusivity is related to *'ĕlōhîm*'s use in reference to the patron deity of the individual, group, or nation.[110]

The matter at Carmel is resolved with the climax of the story, the consumption of the altar by divine fire, which is set up by the prophet's plea:

---

[108]In a recent treatment of these materials, Marsha White characterizes the emphasis on prophetic authority and on anti-Baal polemic as later propaganda from the court of Jehu and as not actually deriving from prophetic parties during Ahab's time (*Elijah Legends and Jehu's Coup*, 1-43). However, such propaganda would have required the real influence of prophetic circles and a broad-based antagonism for Phoenician Baal to have been effective.

[109]For "crutches" as the meaning of *hassĕ'ippîm*, see *HAL* 3:719.

[110]See above, Patron Deities. Note references to Yahweh as Elijah's god: "my god" (*'ĕlōhay*), 17:20, 21; "your god" (*'ĕlōhêkā*), 17:12; 18:10.

yhwh 'ĕlōhê 'abrāhām yiṣḥāq wĕyiśrā'ēl hayyôm yiwwāda' kî-'attâ
'ĕlōhîm bĕyiśrā'ēl wa'ănî 'abdekā

O Yahweh, God of Abraham, Isaac, and Israel, let it be known today
that you are *'ĕlōhîm* in Israel and that I am your servant. (v. 36)

Upon the deity's favorable response, the story's question is answered
by those looking on:

yhwh hû' hā'ĕlōhîm yhwh hû' hā'ĕlōhîm
Yahweh indeed is the *'ĕlōhîm*; Yahweh indeed is the *'ĕlōhîm*! (v. 39)

Yahweh, as represented by Elijah, is Israel's god; that is to say, the
narrative renders a verdict in favor of the veneration of Yahweh alone
as the national god.

An important aspect of the story is that the sending of fire upon
the altar is not only a sign of Yahweh's power but of his
responsiveness. In contrast to Baal, who remains silent despite his
worshipers' exhaustion of all available means for eliciting a response
(vv. 26-29), Yahweh requires only the plea of his servant to respond
actively and decisively (vv. 36-38). Yahweh proves to be the *'ĕlōhîm*
by his efficacious response. A similar emphasis is made in connection
with the use of the term *'ĕlōhîm* elsewhere in the Elijah cycle. In 2
Kgs 1:1-8, when Ahaziah, the king of Samaria, falls ill, he sends
messengers to Baal-zebub,[111] the god of Ekron, to inquire whether he
will recover. At Yahweh's prompting, Elijah intercepts the
messengers, and asks:

hamibbĕlî 'ēn-'ĕlōhîm bĕyiśrā'ēl 'attem hōlĕkîm lidrōš bĕba'al zĕbûb
'ĕlōhê 'eqrôn

Is it because there is no *'ĕlōhîm* in Israel that you are going to inquire of
Baal-zebub, the *'ĕlōhîm* of Ekron? (v. 3; see also v. 6)

The question implies that an *'ĕlōhîm* is one who is responsive and
reliable at least for an answer if not for assistance. In this sense, the
term *'ĕlōhîm* emphasizes not only exclusive status but the deity's

---

[111]The element *zĕbûb* "flies" in this title is probably a mocking distortion of *zbl*
"Prince," an epithet of Baal Zaphon at Ugarit.

efficacious presence. As the *'ĕlōhîm* of Israel, Yahweh is active on behalf of his people and is thus entitled to their exclusive loyalty.

The Carmel narrative and the Elijah cycle in general give witness to a desire in the context of the northern kingdom during the late ninth century to remove all ambiguity from the identity of the *'ĕlōhîm*. This concern finds its starting point in the national religion's focus on the deity designated by that title. The emphasis on the title *'ĕlōhîm* in these narratives is that Yahweh as Israel's *'ĕlōhîm* is entitled to the nation's exclusive worship and allegiance.

Conclusions

Our examination of the formula featured in the national cult instituted by Jeroboam I revealed the existence of a longer cultic recitation commemorating the exodus, a recitation which had been featured in Israel's central worship prior to the time of the monarchy. The exclusive designation for Israel's god in the formula is pl. *'ĕlōhîm*, which originally denoted Yahweh and his divine entourage. Jeroboam's appropriation of this worship formula constituted both a recognition and a reinforcement of the prominence of *'ĕlōhîm* as a title for Israel's god. The comments of the prophets Hosea and Amos indicate that during the eighth century Yahweh was still worshiped in the northern kingdom as *'ĕlōhîm*. These prophets emphasized a need to clarify the identity of the national *'ĕlōhîm* as Yahweh. That this same concern had been alive among the Yahwistic prophetic circles of the ninth century is indicated by the central place given to this theme in the Elijah cycle. The association of the divine title *'ĕlōhîm* with northern localities and interests in certain traditions of the Pentateuch is in keeping with the picture that we have reconstructed, which indicates that *'ĕlōhîm*, owing to its prominence in Israel's premonarchic worship and later in the national cult of the northern kingdom, enjoyed a special significance in northern Israelite religion. The clear use of *'ĕlōhîm* as a singular in these texts associated with the northern kingdom indicates that pl. *'ĕlōhîm* in the frozen form of the old cult formula had been reanalyzed as singular *'ĕlōhîm*, "the (patron) deity" of Israel.

CHAPTER 4

The Significance of *'ĕlōhîm* in Pentateuchal E

The prominent use of *'ĕlōhîm* in the portions of the Pentateuch commonly identified as E makes the examination of this material an essential component of the study of biblical *'ĕlōhîm*. This chapter will address the role and meaning of *'ĕlōhîm* in Pentateuchal E. First, though, we will consider the current assessment of E in critical scholarship and establish a definition of E for the purposes of this study.

PRELIMINARY DISCUSSION OF E

Critical Problems Concerning E

For more than a century, the Documentary Hypothesis, which was given its definitive expression by Julius Wellhausen,[1] has provided the dominant scholarly paradigm for understanding the composition of the

---

[1]In his works "Composition des Hexateuchs" (*Jahrbücher für Deutsche Theologie* 21 [1876-1877]: 392-450; 536-602; repr. in *Die Composition des Hexateuchs und der historischen Bücher des Alten Testaments* [Berlin: G. Reimer, 1889], 1-210) and *Prolegomena zur Geschichte Israels* (2d ed.; Berlin: G. Reimer, 1883), Wellhausen made a persuasive case for the Documentary Hypothesis, the major elements of which had already been worked out by Karl H. Graf and Abraham Kuenen (Graf, *Die geschichtlichen Bücher des Alten Testaments* [Leipzig: T. O. Weigel, 1866]; Kuenen, *The Religion of Israel* [trans. A. H. May; London: Williams & Norgate, 1874-1875]; trans. of *De godsdienst van Israël* [Haarlem: A. C. Kruseman, 1869-1870]; idem., *An Historico-Critical Inquiry into the Origin and Composition of the Hexateuch [Pentateuch and Book of Joshua]* [trans. P. H. Wicksteed; London: Macmillan, 1886]). In its classic form, the Documentary Hypothesis proposed that the Pentateuch/Hexateuch was composed of four source documents, which came to be called J (the Yahwist), E (the Elohist), D (the Deuteronomist), and P (the Priestly source).

Pentateuch.[2] A basic element of the Documentary Hypothesis in its classic form is the identification within the biblical materials of a distinct and independent literary source of the Pentateuch labeled E, so called for its use of *'ĕlōhîm* in reference to Israel's god.[3] One of the principal modifications of the Documentary Hypothesis has been the tendency to view E not as a continuous and coherent narrative source but as redactional material dependent on J.[4]

---

[2]Though the Documentary Hypothesis has come under increasing attack in recent decades, it remains the leading model for the explanation of the Pentateuch's composition; see, e.g., Antony F. Campbell, *The Study Companion to Old Testament Literature: An Approach to the Writings of Pre-Exilic and Exilic Israel* (Collegeville, Minn.: Liturgical Press, 1992), 13-138; Bernhard W. Anderson and Katherine P. Darr, *Understanding the Old Testament* (4th abridged ed.; Englewood Cliffs, N.J.: Prentice-Hall, 1998). Recent challenges to the Documentary Hypothesis have come both from those remaining within a source-critical framework (e.g., John Van Seters, *Abraham in History and Tradition* [New Haven: Yale Univ. Press, 1975]; idem, *The Life of Moses: The Yahwist as Historian in Exodus-Numbers* [Louisville: Westminster, 1994]; idem, *Prologue to History: The Yahwist as Historian in Genesis* [Louisville: Westminster, 1992]; Hans Heinrich Schmid, *Der sogennante Jahwist: Untersuchungen zu den Berührungspunkten beider Literaturwerke* [ATANT 67; Zurich: Theologischer Verlag, 1981]) and from those who reject the notion of parallel sources of the Pentateuch (e.g., Rolf Rendtorff, *The Problem of the Process of Transmission in the Pentateuch* [trans. John J. Scullion; JSOTSup 89; Sheffield: JSOT Press, 1990], 11-42, 178-81; Erhard Blum, *Die Komposition der Vätergeschichte* [WMANT 57; Neukirchen: Neukirchener Verlag, 1984]; R. Norman Whybray, *The Making of the Pentateuch: A Methodological Study* [JSOTSup 53; Sheffield: JSOT, 1987], 20-131).

[3]The thesis of an E source independent from what is now known as P, was proposed by Karl David Ilgen, *Die Urkunden des Jerusalemischen Tempelarchivs* (Halle: Hemmerde und Schwetschke, 1798) and was argued persuasively by D. Hermann Hupfeld, *Die Quellen der Genesis und die Art ihrer Zusammensetzung* (Berlin: Wiegandt und Grieben, 1853). Martin Noth proposed that E and J were alternate recensions of a common source G (*Grundlage*) (*Überlieferungsgeschichte des Pentateuch* [Stuttgart: Kohlhammer, 1948]; trans. *A History of Pentateuchal Traditions* [Translated with an Introduction by B. W. Anderson; Englewood Cliffs, N.J.: Prentice-Hall, 1972], 38-41).

[4]For the view of E as a unified redaction, see Paul Volz and Wilhelm Rudolph, *Der Elohist als Erzähler: ein Irrweg der Pentateuchkritik* (BZAW 63; Giessen: Töpelmann, 1933), 23-24, 177-79; Sean E. McEvenue, "The Elohist at Work," *ZAW* 96 (1984): 315-32; Heinz-Josef Fabry, "Erste die Erstgeburt, dann der Segen: Eine Nachfrage zu Gen 27, 1-45," in *Vom Sinai zum Horeb: Stationen altestamentlicher Glaubensgeschichte* (ed. F. L. Hossfeld; Würzburg: Echter Verlag, 1989), 51-72; Jacques Vermeylen, "Les premières étapes littéraires de la formation du Pentateuque," in *Le Pentateuque en question* (ed. A. de Pury; Geneva: Labor et Fides, 1989), 149-97; Robert B. Coote, *In Defense of Revolution: The Elohist History* (Minneapolis: Fortress, 1991). Fred Winnett ("Re-Examining the Foundations," *JBL* [1965]: 1-19) and Claus Westermann (*Genesis 12-36* [Minneapolis: Augsburg, 1985], 571-72) deny the cohesiveness of E. Following his collaboration with Volz in *Der Elohist als Erzähler*, Rudolph denied the existence of

The main criticisms that have been raised against E as portrayed in classic source criticism are (1) that the divine designation *'ĕlōhîm* is not a reliable criterion for identifying a separate source, (2) that E is ill defined with respect to its themes and character, and (3) that E's representation in the text is sparse and fragmentary.[5] In light of the prevailing disagreement concerning the nature and extent of E, it would be advisable to begin this part of our study of biblical *'ĕlōhîm* with a clarification of our own understanding of the relevant biblical material.

We begin by considering the critical problems pertaining to E. The general objection regarding the alternation between *yhwh* and *'ĕlōhîm* as a criterion for identifying separate sources of the Pentateuch, though an old argument against the Documentary Hypothesis, has not endured with time, as witnessed by the continuing effort to explain the Elohistic portions of the Pentateuch. For implicit in this pursuit is the recognition that the preference for the divine designation *'ĕlōhîm* sets these materials apart.[6] The most notable critique of the use of the DNN to distinguish separate sources was

---

any independent E material and rather distributed it among J and its various editorial accretions (*Der 'Elohist' von Exodus bis Josua* [BZAW 68; Berlin: Alfred Töpelmann, 1938]). Doubt over E's existence as a complete source is voiced in the following: A. F. Campbell, *Study Companion*, 92-93; Antony F. Campbell and Mark A. O'Brien, *Sources of the Pentateuch: Texts, Introductions, Annotations* (Minneapolis: Fortress, 1993), 161-66; Damian J. Wynn-Williams, *The State of the Pentateuch: A comparison of the approaches of M. Noth and E. Blum* (BZAW 249; Berlin: Walter de Gruyter, 1997), 79-80. The defense of E as an independent source has been made by the following: Hans Walter Wolff, "Zur Thematik der elohistischen Fragmente im Pentateuch," *Evangelische Theologie* 29 (1969): 59-72; trans. "The Elohistic Fragments in the Pentateuch," trans. K. R. Crim, *Interpretation* 26 (1972): 158-73; repr. in *The Vitality of the Old Testament Traditions* (ed. W. Brueggemann and H. W. Wolff; 2d ed.; Atlanta: John Knox, 1982), 67-82, 154-56; Alan W. Jenks, *The Elohist and North Israelite Traditions* (SBLMS 22; Missoula, Mont.: Scholars Press, 1977); see also Karl Jaroš, *Die Stellung des Elohisten zur Kanaanäischen Religion* (OBO 4; Fribourg: Universitätsverlag, 1974), 18-22.

[5]See the next paragraph for citations of the secondary literature.

[6]A good example of such an effort is that of Winnett ("Re-Examining the Foundations"), who in his reluctance to "multiply sources" (p. 6) assigns the Elohistic materials of Genesis—which cannot be ascribed to the single J author he credits with the book's composition—to successive editions of J. For the rejection of the alternation of DNN as an indication of separate sources, see Volz and Rudolph, *Irrweg der Pentateuchkritik*, 36-37, 148-51, 180-83 (cf. 177); Rudolph, *Der "Elohist"*, 3, 11-12, 249. Objections to this criterion of source identification are answered by Noth, *Pentateuchal Traditions*, 23 and n. 69; cf. Van Seters (*Abraham*), who, though arguing against the criterion of DNN (pp. 126-27), still acknowledges its significance for source analysis (see, e.g., p. 173 n. 20).

made by Cassutto, who contended that the names, rather than indicating distinct sources, express different theological emphases: *yhwh*, for the portrayal of Israel's god in concrete terms and with an emphasis on nationalistic identity, and *'ĕlōhîm*, to stress God's abstract and transcendent character.[7] It has been recognized that Cassutto's explanation does not account for instances in which *'ĕlōhîm* is used in contexts where God is portrayed in concrete and anthropomorphic terms, such as Gen 32:31, where Jacob, after wrestling with God says, "I have seen *'ĕlōhîm* face to face."[8] The use of *'ĕlōhîm* in preference to *yhwh* continues, implicitly if not explicitly, to be recognized as a distinguishing feature of the texts that share this propensity.

The next question is whether any other common traits emerge to suggest a unity among the Elohistic materials, which brings us to a second objection concerning E, viz., that the texts assigned to E lack a coherence of style, viewpoint, or distinct emphases sufficient to grant their integrity as a single source.[9] Even opponents of E as an independent source have acknowledged a unity of style and viewpoint among at least some of the Elohistic materials of the Pentateuch.[10] These texts have included, at the bare minimum, the traditions concerning Abraham and Abimelech: Abraham and Sarah in Gerar (Gen 20:1-17) and Abraham's dispute and agreement with Abimelech

---

[7]Umberto Cassuto, *The Documentary Hypothesis and the Composition of the Pentateuch* (trans. I. Abrahams; Jerusalem: Magnes, 1961), 27-41. Cassutto is followed in this explanation by Ivan Engnell, *A Rigid Scrutiny: Critical Essays on the Old Testament* (trans. John T. Willis with the collaboration of Helmer Ringgren; Nashville: Vanderbilt Univ. Press, 1969), 55-56. According to Rudolph the variations in DNN in the Joseph material are determined by the scheme of a single author who uses Yahweh in his own comments, El-Shaddai in those of his characters when they are in Palestine and Elohim when they are in Egypt (in Volz and Rudolph, *Irrweg der Pentateuchkritik*, 148-51, 180-83); as Noth pointed out, this explanation accounts for the Joseph narratives only (*Pentateuchal Traditions*, 24).

[8]Helmer Ringgren, *TDOT* 1:284.

[9]Rudolph, *Der "Elohist,"* 255-63; Westermann, *Genesis 12-36*, 571-72. Winnett understands E material to be distributed among what he posits as successive revisions of J, which included materials that were of "a somewhat heterogeneous character and were manifestly drawn in part from different sources" ("Re-Examining the Foundations," 12). Campbell acknowledges the possibility that E "comprised a variety of different traditions supplementing J" (*Study Companion*, 93).

[10]According to Sigmund Mowinckel, E, as a literary deposit of a developing oral transmission of traditions, is not a continuous narrative and adds nothing substantially new to J but does have a distinctive vocabulary and theological outlook (*Erwägungen zur Pentateuch Quellenfrage* [Oslo: Universitetsforlaget, 1964], 111-12, 115).

at Beersheba (21:25-26, 28-31a), both of which, in terms of content, bear a close resemblance to stories in J (Gen 12[11] and 26:18-22, 26-33).[12] It is reasonable to include along with those Elohistic materials the dispute between Sarah and Hagar (21:9-21), which in the present text is grouped with those traditions and which also has a Yahwistic counterpart (Gen 16). These Elohistic texts, along with 31:2, 4-16, 24, 29; 35:1-4, 7, on the basis of their common interest and viewpoint, were assigned by Volz and Rudolph to a pious editor who had sought to correct potential moral difficulties in J's depiction of the patriarchs.[13]

The recognition of a common point of view among at least some of the Elohistic texts and the existence of doublets of corresponding material in Elohistic and Yahwistic texts would suggest that the Elohistic portions of the Pentateuch are the preserved fragments of an extended narrative source that resembled J in the scope of its content.[14] However, it is this sparse and fragmentary nature of the E material that poses a problem for such an identification of E.[15] Related to this third objection to E as an independent source is the criticism that E adds nothing of substance to J.[16] This recognition of coherence among E texts tempered by the paucity of Elohistic materials would seem to justify the characterization of E not as an extensive and independent source but as the deposit of editorial activity.

---

[11]There is, of course, also a Yahwistic variant of this tradition featuring Isaac and Rebekah (Gen 26:6-11).

[12]Van Seters (*Abraham*), who denies that the mere use of *'ĕlōhîm* is an adequate criterion for source analysis (p. 186), recognizes these Elohistic passages as a unified edition of earlier Yahwistic material (p. 313).

[13]Volz and Rudolph, *Irrweg der Pentateuchkritik*, 21-24, 34-36, 177-79; cf. Rudolph's subsequent work, *Der "Elohist"*, in which he sought to obliterate any notion of E, either as an author or as an editor. In this later effort, Rudolph relied heavily on the dismissal of *'ĕlōhîm*'s use as an indicator of distinct material. See Noth's response in *Pentateuchal Traditions*, 24.

[14]The presence of doublets has provided one of the leading arguments for viewing J and E as parallel narrative sources (see Noth, *Pentateuchal Traditions*, 22; Wolff, "Elohistic Fragments," 68).

[15]Campbell and O'Brien, *Sources of the Pentateuch*, 161-66; Wynn-Williams, *The State of the Pentateuch*, 79.

[16]Volz and Rudolph, *Irrweg der Pentateuchkritik*, 23-24; Mowinckel, *Erwägungen zur Pentateuch Quellenfrage*, 95-104. Campbell and O'Brien conclude that the one-sixth (by their estimation) of the E material that is unique over against J is an insignificant amount (*Sources of the Pentateuch*, 161-62).

The interpretation of E as an editorial correction of J on a grand scale was made most recently by Robert Coote.[17]   According to Coote, E resulted from an anti-Solomonic re-editing of the southern court history, which was carried out in the northern court of Jeroboam I.   Coote reads E as a kind of allegory in which three major thematically oriented divisions he recognizes in the editorial work—namely, (1) endangered sons, (2) Joseph, and (3) Horeb—represent concerns having significance for the life and reign of Jeroboam, respectively, (1) succession, (2) Jeroboam's exile in Egypt, and (3) the need for legal reform after the secession of the northern tribes. This line of reasoning is most unsatisfactory for the connection of E with the court of Jeroboam, as the very notion of such propagandistic allegory is not compelling, and the parallels Coote alleges often seem forced.[18]   Furthermore, Coote's schema for establishing unity among the E materials does not hold up to scrutiny. "Endangered sons" can hardly be considered a unique theme in the Bible.   The E material that Coote identifies in Exodus contains important themes that are not properly subsumed under the giving of the law, e.g., "fear of God" (Exod 1:17, 21), the revelation of the divine name (3:9-15), God's leading of the Israelites in the wilderness (13:17-22; 14:9).

Preliminary to his identification of this overarching thematic structure in E is Coote's presupposition of certain unifying characteristics attributed to E in traditional source criticism—its distinctive vocabulary, style, subject matter, and viewpoint.[19] Though Coote names these defining traits at the beginning of his study, he does so without reference either to biblical texts or to secondary sources, and he provides no detailed discussion at that point to justify his delineation of E.   In light of the objections that have been made to E's

---

[17]Coote, *In Defense of Revolution.*

[18]The supposed parallel between Joseph's coerced removal to Egypt and Jeroboam's exile in the court of Shishak, which seems to be a leading factor in Coote's association of E with Jeroboam (p. 87), is far from convincing, as are others—including the alleged parallels between the "endangered sons" of the patriarchs and the crisis of succession which Coote reconstructs for Jeroboam (p. 83), those between debt slavery (Gen 31) and corvée labor under Solomon (p. 74), and those between the announcement of the "rule of law" that Coote recognizes in the Sinai traditions of E and the legal reform he assumes for Jeroboam.

[19]Ibid., 10.

unity and cohesiveness, this is a point of methodology that one can scarcely afford to overlook.

As this discussion has shown, the existence of a unified tradition called E, either as an extended narrative source or as an editorial supplement to J, is not simply to be assumed. However, sufficient agreement over the unity of at least some of the Elohistic texts exists to allow one to speak of E, provided the relevant texts are identified and their assemblage is justified. It is appropriate to begin this part of our analysis of *'ĕlōhîm* with such a preliminary definition of E.

A Minimal Identification of E

Our delineation of E takes as its point of departure the limited group of Elohistic texts whose unity of viewpoint and interests is generally accepted:[20]

Gen	20:1-17	Abraham and Sarah in Gerar
	21:9-21	the expulsion of Hagar
	21:22-32	Abraham's covenant with Abimelech
	31:1-42	Jacob and Laban
	31:43-54	Jacob's covenant with Laban
	35:1-7	Jacob's journey from Shechem to Bethel.

An analysis of these texts is required to determine whether they share significant traits and emphases.

The characteristics that we will identify as being common to these texts are among those attributed to E in traditional source criticism.[21] While we do not make any new claims here, it is appropriate from a methodological standpoint to discuss these distinguishing traits of E with specific references to the texts and,

---

[20]These texts, which as noted above were, in their most minimal extent, regarded by Volz and Rudolph (*Irrweg der Pentateuchkritik*, 21-24, 34-36, 177-79) as a single edition, are included in E by Jenks (*The Elohist and North Israelite Traditions*, 67), Campbell and O'Brien (*Sources of the Pentateuch*, 167-74), and Coote (*In Defense of Revolution*, 141). Although Wolff ("Elohistic Fragments") does not list the texts he assigns to E, he refers to all of these except for the last two on our list.

[21]See, e.g., Georg Fohrer, *Introduction to the Old Testament* (trans. David Green; Nashville: Abingdon, 1968; reprint, London: S.P.C.K., 1976), 157-58; J. Alberto Soggin, *Introduction to the Old Testament* (trans. J. S. Bowden; revised ed.; OTL; Philadelphia: Westminster, 1980), 105.

thereby, to justify the unity that we ascribe to these materials by designating them as E.

Of course, the most striking feature that these texts have in common is their preference for *'ĕlōhîm* as the divine designation. While, on occasion, the deity is referred to as *hā'ēl* ("the god/God," as opposed to "El")[22] and frequently by one of the expressions for patriarchal deities ("the god of the fathers," *'ĕlōhê 'ăbî/-kā/-kem*, 31:5, 29, 42; "the god of Abraham," *'ĕlōhê 'abrāhām* 31:42, 53; etc.),[23] none of these designations is treated as a DN. The name Yahweh does not occur in these passages.[24] The use of sg. *'ĕlōhîm* either with or without the definite article is apparently random in these texts and has no semantic importance other than as an indication that the title *'ĕlōhîm*, "God," for Israel's deity is derived from an understanding of his status as *hā'ĕlōhîm*, "the God" (of the patriarchs, of the nation).[25] In these provisional E texts, *'ĕlōhîm* is used in the place of a DN.

Another unifying characteristic in these texts, which was mentioned above, is a pronounced ethical sensitivity. The scholarly discussion of this aspect of E is well known and need not be reviewed in full.[26] However, we may briefly mention the following: the rationalization of the claim by Abraham that Sarah is his sister (20:12); Abraham's concern over Sarah's harsh treatment of Hagar (21:11-12; cf. 16:6 = J); the attribution of Jacob's prosperity to divine providence rather than to his own cunning (31:59, 16, 36-42; cf. 30:37-43 = J). The expression of this concern for moral rectitude, though a

---

[22]Instead of *hā'ēl bêt-'ēl* in the MT of Gen 31:13, the reading represented by the LXX is *hā'ēl hannir'e(h) 'ēlêkā bammāqôm 'ăšer māšaḥtā šām maṣṣēbâ*, "the god who appeared to you in the place where you anointed a standing-stone," which is consistent with *lā'ēl hannir'e(h) 'ēlêkā bĕborḥăkā mippĕnê 'ēśāw 'āḥîkā*, "the god who appeared to you when you fled your brother, Esau," in 35:1 and *lā'ēl hā'ōne(h) 'ōtî bĕyôm ṣārātî*, "the god who answered me in the day of distress," in v. 3. In these references *hā'ēl* is clearly regarded as an appellative and not as a DN. See below, The Divine Designation *'ĕlōhîm*.

[23]See above, "The God of the Fathers," and below, The Divine Designation *'ĕlōhîm*.

[24]In place of *yhwh* in the MT of Gen 31:49, the LXX reads *ho theos*, which reflects the reading *(hā)'ĕlōhîm*.

[25]On the logic underlying the designation *(hā)'ĕlōhîm*, see GKC §125f.

[26]Volz and Rudolph, *Irrweg der Pentateuchkritik*, 177-79; Mowinckel, *Erwägungen zur Pentateuch Quellenfrage*, 111-12; Fohrer, *Introduction*, 157-58; Soggin, *Introduction*, 105.

distinguishing characteristic of E, is somewhat dependent on the contents of a given narrative, hence, the absence of this emphasis in 35:1-4, 7, which is concerned not with ethical but with cultic matters.

A third characteristic of these texts is that in their depiction of divine communication they emphasize the sublime remoteness of the deity. Revelations are delivered through heavenly messengers (21:17), through dreams and visions (20:6; 21:12, 14; 31:29), or through both (31:11). Although one may note that no dream or angel is mentioned in 35:1-4 and that in Yahwistic texts the deity *can* be represented by an angel (16:7) or communicate through a night vision (26:24), the emphasis on the supernal nature of the deity is uniquely and consistently accentuated in the Elohistic texts.

Another prominent aspect of these texts is their northern (i.e., non-Judahite) orientation.[27] In the discussion above, most of these passages, taken *separately*, were among those summoned as evidence of the northern Israelite associations of *'ĕlōhîm*.[28] This connection between *'ĕlōhîm* and the northern kingdom having been established, we may now consider whether the northern associations expressed in our Elohistic texts are indicative of a common literary origin.

The narrative of Abraham and Sarah's deception of Abimelech at Gerar (Gen 20), by its nature as a story of sojourning, has its setting outside of Israelite territory. Otherwise, the narratives show an appreciable interest in sites that were prominent in their associations with the northern kingdom: Beersheba[29] (21:9-21, 22-32); Bethel (31:2, 4-16; 35:1-7); and Shechem (35:1-4). By contrast, these texts make no mention of localities having a special cultic significance for the south, most notably Jerusalem and Hebron. As mentioned above,[30] northern Israelite interests are represented in the etiology of Galeed/Jegar-Sahadutha (Gen 31:44-54), which reflects a strong concern over the border between Israel and Aram-Damascus. The

---

[27]That E originated in the northern kingdom of Israel was argued most comprehensively by Otto Procksch, *Das Nordhebräische Sagenbuch: Die Elohimquelle* (Leipzig: J. C. Hinrichs, 1906); see also Jenks, *The Elohist and North Israelite Traditions*.

[28]See above, Pentateuchal Traditions.

[29]As noted above, Beersheba's northern associations are expressed in Amos 5:5 and 8:14.

[30]See above, Pentateuchal Traditions.

distinctly northern orientation of the Elohistic texts under discussion suggests their mutual coherence.

The texts that we have provisionally identified as E share a number of distinguishing characteristics: the exclusive use of *'ĕlōhîm* as a surrogate for the DN, a heightened ethical sensitivity, the depiction of visions and angels as the typical media of divine revelation, and a pronounced northern Israelite orientation. Though, in identifying the characteristic features of a particular literary work, one would not expect to find every element in every portion of the work, we witness a remarkable convergence of most or all of these leading traits in the E texts we have discussed. The clustering of these features establishes both the interrelatedness of these materials and their distinctiveness within the Pentateuch.

Other E Texts in Genesis

Having noted these traits within the passages identified as E material, we may consider whether they coalesce in other patriarchal materials commonly assigned to E. One such pericope is Gen 46:1-7, in which *'ĕlōhîm* is the chief divine designation.[31] The northern interests of the passage are expressed in connection with Beersheba, where Jacob offers cultic service "to the god of his father Isaac" (*lē'lōhê 'ābîw yiṣḥāq*, v. 1). Though one of E's characteristic emphases, namely, the concern for ethical issues, is not relevant to the scope of this passage, another one is: the mediation of divine communication, which this passage describes as being conveyed "in visions of the night" (*běmar'ōt hallaylâ*, v. 2). The convergence of these E traits in this passage commends its inclusion into our provisional delineation of E.

In Gen 46:1-7, the patriarch Jacob is called both by this name (vv. 2, 5, 6) and by his alternate name, Israel (vv. 1, 2, 5). In our inclusion of this passage into E, we set aside a characteristic of E as

---

[31]The narrator refers to Jacob's god most directly as *'ĕlōhîm* (v. 2). Both the statement that Jacob offered sacrifices "to the god of his father Isaac" (*lē'lōhê 'ābîw yiṣḥāq*, v. 1) and the deity's introduction of himself to Jacob as "the God, the God of Your Father" (*hā'ēl 'ĕlōhê 'ābîkā*, v. 3) indicate *'ĕlōhîm*'s status as Jacob's ancestral deity (see above, Patron Deities, and below, *'Ĕlōhîm* in the Patriarchal Narratives of E). The attachment of the definite article to *'ēl* suggests the intention that the term be understood as an appellative and not as the DN El; see 31:13 and the discussion above, A Minimal Identification of E.

identified by traditional source criticism, viz., the predilection for the PN Jacob rather than Israel.[32] The use of the name Israel in this story would seem to presuppose the assignment of this new name to Jacob, as related in the story of Jacob's wrestling in 32:24-32. This consideration might lead one to include the latter pericope into our collection of E texts, a measure that would seem to be supported by the passage's use of *'ĕlōhîm* to the exclusion of any other divine designation (vv. 29, 31). However, in the first instance of its use, in the phrase "with god and with man" (*'im-'ĕlōhîm wĕ'im-'ănāšîm*), *'ĕlōhîm* is hardly a clear reference to a specific deity. In the other instance, *'ĕlōhîm* is used in an etymology of the GN Penuel. While these facts do not automatically rule out the classification of this text as E, certain elements of the story are contrary to what we have observed in our E texts. E's portrayal of *'ĕlōhîm* in elevated terms, as a deity who communicates through dreams or through angels speaking from the heavens (21:17), would hardly accommodate this depiction of *'ĕlōhîm*'s messenger wrestling with Jacob in the dirt—and somewhat unsuccessfully at that. Furthermore, the depiction of Jacob, both in the action described and in the etymology of his name, as one who struggles "with god and man," as one who uses force to extort a blessing from a divine being, is inconsistent with E's portrayal of the patriarch's success as being the result of *'ĕlōhîm*'s favor (31:5-9, 36-42). Though it is possible that 32:24-32 belongs to E, its resemblance to our other E passages is not strong enough to warrant its inclusion into our preliminary demarcation of E.

The consideration of another text as belonging to our E material is prompted by allusions among those texts to *'ĕlōhîm*'s revelation to Jacob at Bethel (31:13; 35:1, 3, 7), allusions which point to the narrative in 28:10-22.[33] The references to this earlier episode include specific details found in the Bethel narrative of Gen 28: Jacob's flight from his brother Esau (35:1, 7); his anointing a standing stone (28:18; 31:13); his vow (28:20-22; 31:13); and his desire to return to his home (28:21; 31:13). The interest expressed by Gen 28 both in Beersheba, mentioned in v. 10, and in Bethel, the focus of the passage, is consistent with E's northern point of view. The prominence of divine

---

[32]See, e.g., Noth, *Pentateuchal Traditions*, 36 n. 136.

[33]On this and other narrative links among the E materials, see Wolff, "Elohistic Fragments," 76.

messengers (*mal'ăkê 'ĕlōhîm*, v. 12) in the theophany and its disclosure in a dream are in keeping with E's usual portrayal of divine communication. The Yahwistic block of material in vv. 13-16[34] and the rationalization of this Yahwistic insertion in v. 21b[35] are clearly intrusions into an Elohistic passage. Though one might argue that the preference for *'ĕlōhîm* in this context is motivated merely by the etiology of Bethel,[36] the convergence both of E elements and of the narrative links between this episode and other E texts make its inclusion in E fairly certain.

Two other Elohistic passages in which northern interests are given bold expression are the account of the births of Jacob's children in Gen 30:1-23 and the blessing of Ephraim and Manasseh in 48:8-22. Both of these passages are uniform in their use of *'ĕlōhîm* as the divine designation. The former passage is concerned with the eponymous ancestors of the northern tribes only and does not mention Judah. The other passage, in providing a rationalization for the preeminence of Ephraim before Manasseh, addresses matters of concern to the population groups of the north Israelite heartland. The northern frame of reference for this text is expressed most succinctly in the blessing quoted in v. 20: "May *'ĕlōhîm* make you like Ephraim and Manasseh!" It is clear that both of these passages are related to the other materials we have assembled and designated as E.

---

[34]The depiction of Yahweh as standing and speaking to Jacob either from beside him or from above "the ladder" (*wĕhinnē(h) yhwh niṣṣāb 'ālāyw*, v. 13) is inconsistent with the description in v. 12 of divine messengers traveling back and forth from heaven; see Wellhausen, *Composition des Hexateuchs*, 32. Also there is a disjunction between the content of Yahweh's speech to Jacob, which consists of promises of land and progeny found elsewhere in the Yahwistic materials (13:14-17), and Jacob's response to the revelation in his vow (vv. 20-21).

[35]In the formulation of the vow as it stands in the text, the first element of the apodosis, "then Yahweh will be my god" (*wĕhāyâ yhwh lî lē'lōhîm*), does not follow from the protasis, "If *'ĕlōhîm* will be with me . . ." Whereas, omitting this clause brings the protasis and the apodosis into agreement: "If *'ĕlōhîm* will be with me, . . . then this stone, which I have set up as a pillar, will be *bêt 'ĕlōhîm*" (vv. 20-22); see Noth, *Pentateuchal Traditions*, 35 n. 133.

[36]As does, e.g., Winnett, "Re-Examining the Foundations," 9.

Conclusions

The patriarchal narratives of Genesis contain a considerable amount of material which, in its distinctiveness and coherence, represents a single Elohistic contribution to the Pentateuch, which we will call E. For the time being, we will reserve judgment on whether the E texts are derived from a continuous source or from an editorial supplement to the material known as J. These texts include the following:

20:1-17	Abraham and Sarah in Gerar
21:9-21	the expulsion of Hagar
21:22-32	Abraham's covenant with Abimelech
28:10-12, 17-21a, 22	Jacob's dream at Bethel
31:1-42	Jacob and Laban
31:43-54	Jacob's covenant with Laban
35:1-7	Jacob's journey from Shechem to Bethel
46:1-7	Jacob's migration to Egypt
48:8-22	The blessing of Ephraim and Manasseh.

While other passages from Genesis may in fact belong to E, the occurrence of certain distinguishing traits in the texts listed is quite pronounced. Common to these texts is both the predominance of *'ĕlōhîm* as a substitute for the DN and a convergence of certain elements of style and viewpoint, including a northern Israelite orientation, an accentuated ethical sensitivity, and a portrayal of the deity as sublimely aloof in his interaction with the patriarchs. Rather than assuming these characteristics as typical E traits, we have begun with the texts themselves and have identified the distinguishing features that establish unity among these materials.

The strong northern "accent" of these materials—as articulated by the emphasis on the eponymous ancestors of the northern tribes to the exclusion of Judah; by the extensive attention given to sanctuaries located in or favored by the north while ignoring the leading Judahite sanctuaries; and by E's northern vantage point, including concerns over the boundary between Israel and Aram-Damascus (Gen 31:43-55)—betrays an origin for this collection of Elohistic material in the northern kingdom during the time of the divided monarchy. The task at hand now is to determine the significance of *'ĕlōhîm* in these northern patriarchal traditions.

'Ĕlōhîm IN THE PATRIARCHAL TRADITIONS OF E

As our discussion of *'ĕlōhîm*'s significance in northern Israelite religion has revealed, two leading issues for northern prophetic Yahwism during the ninth and eighth centuries were that the identity of the national *'ĕlōhîm* required clarification and that Yahweh, as Israel's *'ĕlōhîm*, merited the nation's undivided loyalty.[37] The notion of exclusive loyalty communicated by the use of *'ĕlōhîm* both in Hosea and in the Elijah cycle is related to *'ĕlōhîm*'s use in the context of patron deities.[38] In view of E's northern character, its virtually exclusive preference for the divine designation *'ĕlōhîm*,[39] and its portrayal of Israel's god as the patron deity of the nation's eponymous ancestors, one can hardly avoid considering whether similar emphases, viz., calls both for clarification of the identity of *'ĕlōhîm* and for exclusive loyalty, are at work in E. Our examination of *'ĕlōhîm*'s significance in the patriarchal traditions represented in E will take up these considerations.

The Divine Designation *'ĕlōhîm*

The designation for Israel's god in the E texts of Genesis is *'ĕlōhîm*, used clearly as a singular. In the comments of the narrator and of Israel's ancestors, *'ĕlōhîm* is used with singular grammatical forms. The only exception is 20:13, where *'ĕlōhîm* takes a plural verb in Abraham's speech to Abimelech, a foreigner:

> *wayhî ka'ăšer hit'û 'ōtî 'ĕlōhîm mibbêt 'ābî*
> When *'ĕlōhîm* caused me to wander from my father's house . . .

In this context *'ĕlōhîm* is understandably used as a plural.

The following examples illustrate E's regular treatment of *'ĕlōhîm* as a singular:

> *wayyitpallēl 'abrāhām 'el-hā'ĕlōhîm wayyirpā' 'ĕlōhîm 'et-'ăbîmelek*
> And Abraham prayed to *'ĕlōhîm* and *'ĕlōhîm* healed Abimelech. (20:17)

---

[37]See above, Chapter 3. The Title *'ĕlōhîm* in Israelite Religion.

[38]See above, Patron Deities.

[39]See the discussion of the expressions "the god of the father" (*'ĕlōhê 'ăbîkā*) and "the god/God" (*hā'ēl*) above, A Minimal Identification of E.

And *'ĕlōhîm* heard (*wayyišmaʻ*) the voice of the boy crying, and the messenger of *'ĕlōhîm* called to Hagar from heaven and said to her, "What is the matter with you, Hagar? Do not fear, for *'ĕlōhîm* has heard (*šāmaʻ*) the boy's voice where he is." (21:17)

Jacob made a vow saying, "If *'ĕlōhîm* will be with me (*'im yihye[h] 'ĕlōhîm 'immādî*) . . ." (28:20)

wĕlō'-nĕtānô 'ĕlōhîm lĕhāraʻ 'immādî
'Ĕlōhîm did not allow him to harm me. (31:7)

'Ĕlōhîm came (*wayyābō'*) to Laban the Aramaean in a dream of the night and said (*wayyō'mer*) to him . . . (31:24)

'Ĕlōhîm said (*wayyō'mer*) to Jacob . . . (35:1)

And *'ĕlōhîm* spoke (*wayyō'mer*) to Israel in visions of the night . . . (46:2)

And Joseph said to his father, "Those are my sons, whom *'ĕlōhîm* has given me (*bānay hēm 'ăšer-nātan-lî 'ĕlōhîm*)." (48:9)

Israel said to Joseph, "I did not expect to see your face again, and here *'ĕlōhîm* has let me see your offspring as well (*wĕhinnē(h) her'â 'ōtî 'ĕlōhîm gam 'et-zarʻekā*)." (48:11)

In this respect, E's use of *'ĕlōhîm* corresponds to that of Hosea and, perhaps, to the one instance in which Amos cites the divine title *'ĕlōhêkā* (8:14).[40] As is the case in Hosea, it is eminently clear in E that *'ĕlōhîm* refers to a single deity.

Also apparent in these passages is that, in contrast to its use with possessive pronominal suffixes (*'ĕlōhêkā*, etc.) once in the exodus formula and in the eighth-century prophetic books, *'ĕlōhîm* is used in E in the absolute state. This is the way the title is used in the ninth-century Elijah cycle, particularly in 1 Kgs 18, where *hā'ĕlōhîm*, "the Deity," is understood to refer to the national deity of Israel (*'ĕlōhîm bĕyiśrā'ēl*, v. 36; 2 Kgs 1:3, 5). In the same manner, the significance of the title *'ĕlōhîm* in E seems to be determined by the particular context, which is concerned with the patron deity of Israel's eponymous ancestors. E uses *'ĕlōhîm* in reference to the same god that is designated by the epithets "the god of the father" (*'ĕlōhê 'ābî/-ka/-kem*, 31:5, 29, 42), "the god of Abraham" (*'ĕlōhê 'abrāhām*, 31:42,

---

[40]See above, Prophets Addressing the Northern Kingdom.

53), and "the god of his father Isaac" (*'ĕlōhê 'ābîw yiṣḥāq*, 46:1). Note, especially *'ĕlōhîm*'s alternation with *'ĕlōhê 'ābî*, "the god of my father," in 31:5, 7, 9, 11, 16; with *'ĕlōhê 'ābî 'ĕlōhê 'abrāhām ûpaḥad yiṣḥāq*, "the god of my father, the god of Abraham, the 'fear' of Isaac,"[41] in 31:42; and with *'ĕlōhê 'ābîw yiṣḥāq*, "the god of his father Isaac," in 46:1, 2. The god portrayed in E is also referred to by the title *paḥad yiṣḥāq*, "the 'fear' of Isaac" (Gen 31:42, 53), another epithet for the ancestral god,[42] and by the designation *hā'ēl* "(the) God," which E uses both as a common noun and in a manner similar to *(hā)'ĕlōhîm*, that is, as a title and not as a DN ("El").[43] Thus, while simple *'ĕlōhîm* is not actually an abbreviation for "the god of the father" (*'ĕlōhê 'ābî/-ka/-kem* or *'ĕlōhê* PN), it almost functions in this way. For in the portrayal of the ancestral deity, who is called by these various titles, grammatically absolute *'ĕlōhîm* is understood to denote the *'ĕlōhîm*, the (patron) deity, of the patriarchs.

As we observed in our discussion above, the conception of the national patron deity which is operative in the Elijah material assumes that only one deity can stand in special relationship to the nation.[44] A similar understanding of exclusivity applies to the patron god of the ancestors as portrayed in E. Each ancestor is depicted in close relationship with a particular deity, his *'ĕlōhîm*. Furthermore, the

---

[41]On the "fear of Isaac," see below.

[42]So Emile Puech ("Fear of Isaac," *ABD* 2:779-80), who upholds the traditional interpretation of *paḥad yiṣḥāq* as "fear of Isaac"; see also Albrecht Alt, "The God of the Fathers," in *Essays on the Old Testament History and Religion* (trans. R. A. Wilson; Oxford: Basil Blackwell, 1966), 25-30; cf. William F. Albright, *From the Stone Age to Christianity* (2d ed.; Garden City, N.Y.: Doubleday, 1957), 248; cf. Delbert R. Hillers, "Pahad Yiṣḥāq," *JBL* 91 (1972): 90-92.

[43]That E retains this term (modified by the definite article) strictly as a title that is similar in meaning to *'ĕlōhîm* is clear in its use: *hā'ēl hannir'e(h) 'ēlêkā bammāqôm 'ăšer māšaḥtā šām maṣṣēbâ*, "the god who appeared to you in the place where you anointed a standing stone" (Gen 31:13, LXX); *lā'ēl hannir'e(h) 'ēlêkā bĕborḥăkā mippĕnê 'ēśāw 'āḥîkā*, "to the god who appeared to you when you fled your brother, Esau" (35:1); *lā'ēl hā'ōne(h) 'ōtî bĕyôm ṣārātî*, "the god who answered me in the day of distress" (v. 3); and *'ānōkî hā'ēl 'ĕlōhê 'ābîkā*, "God, the god of your father" (46:3). The addition of the definite article was certainly present in E and not the result of later editing. For, even if one overlooks the relative clauses in 31:13 and 35:1, the sporadic use of a DN in a unified work which otherwise confines itself to the title *'ĕlōhîm* would be quite surprising. E's use of *hā'ēl* receives further discussion below, The Identity of *'ĕlōhîm*.

[44]See above, The Elijah Cycle.

same god is presented as the divine patron of each of the patriarchs, a situation which corresponds to the common practice by which devotion to the family deity was passed from one generation to the next.[45] Thus E presents *'ĕlōhîm* as the patron deity of the ancestors in successive generations, beginning with Abraham (20:1-17; 21:9-32), then Isaac (21:10-12; 46:1), then Jacob (28:10-12, 17-21a, 22; 31:1-54; 35:1-7; 46:1-7), and finally Joseph and his sons, Ephraim and Manasseh, in Egypt (48:8-22). This notion of intergenerational continuity in the veneration of the deity is expressed in the amassing of patronymics in divine titles both in E (e.g., *'ĕlōhê 'ābî 'ĕlōhê 'abrāhām ûpaḥad yiṣḥāq*, "the god of my father, the god of Abraham, the fear of Isaac," 31:42) and in J (e.g., *'ĕlōhê 'ābî 'abrāhām wĕ'lōhê 'ābî yiṣḥāq yhwh*, "the god of my father Abraham, the god of my father Isaac, Yahweh," Gen 32:10). E's preference for simple *'ĕlōhîm* as the divine title facilitates the depiction of continuity and cohesion within Israel's ancestral religious heritage. Stated in other words, E's use of absolute singular *'ĕlōhîm* serves its portrayal of the patriarchs' exclusive devotion to one and the same god over many generations.

'Ĕlōhîm as the Ancestral Patron Deity

E's depiction of *'ĕlōhîm* in Genesis emphasizes the god's character as the personal deity of Israel's ancestors. The relationship between the patriarch and *'ĕlōhîm* is one of mutual devotion, characterized by obedience on the part of the patriarch and guidance and protection on the part of *'ĕlōhîm*.[46] Whenever *'ĕlōhîm* directs the patriarch to move, the latter responds faithfully. This is especially well illustrated in the case of Jacob, whom *'ĕlōhîm* instructs while he is with Laban, "Arise, and leave this land; return the land of your birth," (31:13), or later on, while he is at Shechem, "Arise, and go up to Bethel; dwell there, and make an altar there" (35:1). Near the end of Jacob's life, *'ĕlōhîm* tells him, "Do not be afraid to go down to Egypt, for I will make you a great nation there" (46:3). *'Ĕlōhîm*'s direction of the patriarchs is accompanied by his providential care, a point which is observed also in the deity's interaction with Abraham, to whom

---

[45]See above, "The God of the Fathers."

[46]Wolff discusses rewarded obedience as a major theme of E ("Elohistic Fragments," 70-75).

'ĕlōhîm offers both encouragement and instruction when Sarah demands that he expel Hagar and Ishmael from the household:

> Do not be distressed concerning the boy and concerning your servant woman; listen to all that Sarah says to you, for by Isaac shall your descendants be named. And I shall make the servant woman's son into a nation, too, for he is your descendant. (21:12-13)

Though the deity's providence for the ancestors has implications of international proportions, E's portrayal of *'ĕlōhîm* emphasizes his involvement in the personal concerns of the patriarchs.

The guidance provided by the ancestral deity is described colorfully and succinctly in a poetic section of the blessing of Ephraim and Manasseh. In 48:15-16a, Israel[47] refers to his deity as

> *hā'ĕlōhîm 'ăšer hithallĕkû 'ăbōtay lĕpānāyw 'abrāhām wĕyiṣḥāq*
> *hā'ĕlōhîm hārō'e(h) 'ōtî mē'ôdî 'ad-hayyôm hazze(h)*
> *hammal'āk haggō'ēl 'ōtî mikkol-rā'*

> The god before whom my fathers Abraham and Isaac walked,
> the god who has been my shepherd all my life until this day,
> the (divine) messenger who has redeemed me from all harm.

This description of the patron god is in keeping with E's portrayal of *'ĕlōhîm* as a constant companion and guardian to Israel's ancestors.

'Ĕlōhîm assuages Jacob's fears about going to Egypt with the reassurance, "I will go down to Egypt with you (*'immĕkā*), and I will surely bring you back up" (46:4), a divine promise which the patriarch passes on to his descendants: "*'ĕlōhîm* will be with you (*'immākem*) and will bring you back to the land of your fathers" (48:21). These words of promise spoken both *to* Jacob and *by* him in his old age echo the vow that he made as a young man: "If *'ĕlōhîm* will be with me (*'immādî*) and keep me on this journey that I am taking and provide me with bread to eat and clothing to wear and I return to the house of my father . . ." (28:20-21a). The theme of the ancestral god being "with" (*'im/'immād-*) the individual, though present in a few instances in

---

[47] As noted above, we acknowledge E's use of the name Israel for Jacob; see Other E Texts in Genesis.

Yahwistic material,[48] occurs as a connecting theme in almost every pericope that we have assigned to E.[49]

Abimelech and Phicol recognize Abraham's prosperity with the assertion, "*'ĕlōhîm* is with you (*'immĕkā*) in all that you do" (21:22). Likewise, Jacob, in explaining his unlikely success under Laban to his wives, says, "The god of my father has been with me" (*wĕ'lōhîm 'ābî hāyâ 'immādî*, 31:5). As the patron deity, *'ĕlōhîm* is "with" the patriarchs for more than just moral support; they not only survive under his protection but flourish. This theme which permeates the E material of Genesis gives emphasis to *'ĕlōhîm*'s efficacious presence as the patron deity of Israel's ancestors.

The Identity of *'ĕlōhîm*

As noted, a chief concern of northern prophetic Yahwism during the ninth and eighth centuries was the clarification of the identity of the deity designated in the national cult as the *'ĕlōhîm* of Israel.[50] It is most curious that in the E materials of Genesis, which share with those prophetic circles a northern orientation and a concern for the exclusive worship of one deity, the name of the patron deity is never revealed; he remains simply *'ĕlōhîm*, "the (patron) deity." However, E seems to preserve traditions that were associated with particular cult centers associated with specific deities.

E's use of *hā'ēl*, "(the) God," which represents the conversion of *'ēl* from a DN to a common noun (and perhaps a title) by the addition of the definite article, is often in connection with Bethel.[51] The relevant passages are as follows:

---

[48]26:3, 28; 28:15; 31:3.

[49]21:22; 28:20; 31:5; 35:3; 46:4; 48:21; cf. "*'ĕlōhîm* shall be with (*'ēt*) the lad" (21:20); "had the god of my father . . . not been *for* me (*lî*)" (31:42). Coote notes the significance of this theme in E (*In Defense of Revolution*, 10, 104 and n. 2).

[50]See above, Chapter 3. The Title *'ĕlōhîm* in Israelite Religion.

[51]On the clear use of *hā'ēl* as a title and not a DN name in E, see above, The Divine Designation *'ĕlōhîm*; cf. the interpretation by Coote, *In Defense of Revolution*, 104.

hā'ēl hannir'e(h) 'ēlêkā bammāqôm 'ăšer māšaḥtā šām
maṣṣēbâ wa'ăšer nādartā lî šām
the god who appeared to you in the place where you anointed a
standing stone and where you made a vow to me (Gen 31:13 LXX)

la'ēl hannir'e(h) 'ēlêkā bĕborḥăkā mippĕnê 'ēśāw 'āḥîkā
to the god who appeared to you when you fled your brother Esau (35:1)

la'ēl hā'ōne(h) 'ōtî bĕyôm ṣārātî
the god who answered me in the day of my distress. (v. 3)

As noted above,[52] the references to the anointing of a standing stone
and the vow are obvious allusions to the account of Jacob's dream in
28:10-12, 17-21a, 22, as are the details of Jacob's distress during his
flight from his brother mentioned in 35:1, 3. The obvious implication
of the persistent use of *hā'ēl* in connection with Bethel is that E
preserves traditions that were originally associated with El of Bethel.
In each of these references, including the etymology of Bethel (28:20-
21a, 22), the deity at that cult place is subsumed under the persona of
E's *'ĕlōhîm*. E's recognition of the tithe (28:22) and the altar (35:1-7)
of Bethel constitute an endorsement of these aspects its cult.

    However, one feature of the Bethel cultus that we have discussed
above is conspicuously absent, namely, the image of the bull.[53] In
fact, when Jacob prepares the members of his household for his return
to Bethel to build the altar there, one of the necessary preparations is
the removal of their divine images and their earrings, items which
might otherwise be used in the construction of a cult statue (35:2).
The collection of jewelry for the construction of a cult image is a
salient motif in other texts, namely, the story of Gideon (Judg 8:22-27)
and the account of Aaron's construction of the golden bull (Exod 32:2-
4), the latter of which we have seen to be a polemic against the cult of
Bethel.[54] The resemblance of the latter passage to Gen 35:2-4
includes the use of the same language in the description of the
jewelry—*nizmê hazzāhāb 'ăšer bĕ'oznêhem*, "the rings of gold which
were in their ears" (Exod 32:2); *hannĕzāmîm 'ăšer bĕ'oznêhem*, "the
rings which were in their ears" (Gen 35:4). This similarity in language
use implies that, in Gen 35, E anticipates not only the establishment of

---

[52]See Other E Texts in Genesis.

[53]See above, The Title *'ĕlōhîm* in the National Cult.

[54]See above, Exodus 32.

the bull iconography of Bethel but the very account of this event that is given in Exod 32.

The tradition of Jacob's founding of the altar at Bethel, as preserved in E, expresses an indirect but prescient censure of the bull statue at Bethel. While recognizing the legitimacy of the tithe and of the altar at Bethel, E objects to the presence of the bull image (or, for that matter, any other divine statue) in its cult. E's inclusion of Bethel material involves a distinction among its traditions, which provides both a basic endorsement of the sanctuary and a clarification of the identity of *'ĕlōhîm*. That is to say, the Bethel traditions that, according to E, are legitimately associated with the *'ĕlōhîm*, i.e., those in reference to which he is to be defined, include the traditions of Jacob's founding the sanctuary of Bethel but not those related to the bull image.

E's description of Jacob's preparation for the journey to Bethel to erect the altar there is set at or near Shechem, which had a long history as a sacred site.[55] The burying of cult images and jewelry "under the oak which was near Shechem" is understood as a memory of an old cultic practice derived from Shechem's days as the central sanctuary of the premonarchic tribes, a practice whose secondary association with Bethel reflects the prominence of the latter at the time of the account in Gen 35.[56] That Shechem retained a certain prominence as a sacred place during the time of the monarchy is indicated by that fact it was there that Solomon's successor Rehoboam was crowned and that, soon thereafter, Jeroboam I was made king of the seceding northern tribes (1 Kgs 12:1-20). Later, according to v. 25, Jeroboam "built," that is, rebuilt or fortified Shechem. For E, Shechem and its religious traditions are legitimately associated with the patriarchal deity E presents as *'ĕlōhîm*. These traditions would seem to include the epithet by which Jacob names the altar he builds near Shechem: *'ēl 'ĕlōhê yiśrā'ēl*, "God (originally, "El"), the god of

---

[55] In the biblical traditions, Shechem has strong associations with the idea of divine covenant, in the covenant with the Israelite tribes under Joshua (Joshua 24), in Moses' prescription of blessings and curses to be pronounced at Ebal and Gerizim (Deut 27-28), and in Judg 9, where the god of the pre-Israelite inhabitants of Shechem is identified as "El, lord of the Covenant" (*'ēl ba'al bĕrît*, vv. 4, 46); see Theodore J. Lewis, "The Identity and Function of El/Baal Berith," *JBL* 115 (1996): 401-23.

[56] So Albrecht Alt, "Die Wallfahrt von Sichem nach Bethel," in *Kleine Schriften zur Geschichte des Volkes Israel* 1 (Munich: C. H. Beck: 1953), 79-88.

Israel" (Gen 33:20). Since *'ēl* appears here without the definite article that is usually attached by E, one might be reluctant to include this passage in E. However, E—though reinterpreting the DN as a common noun or title—clearly acknowledges the connection of El with Shechem, for the god who appears to Jacob at Shechem in 35:1 calls himself *hā'ēl*, "the god" ("who appeared to you when you fled your brother Esau"). Again, E reinterprets the DN *'ēl* as an appellative or as a title (46:3, see below). Thus E defines the *'ĕlōhîm* in relationship to the traditions of El at Shechem.

While E's use of the title *hā'ēl* is usually in direct association with Bethel or Shechem, it is used once in connection with Beersheba. In Gen 46:3, when Jacob is offering sacrifices there to "the god of his father Isaac," *'ĕlōhîm* introduces himself to Jacob as *hā'ēl 'ĕlōhê 'ābîkā*, "God, the god of your father" (46:3). The mention of Beersheba in connection with Isaac and Abraham in ch. 21 made no reference to its cultic associations, unless one counts the oath sworn by Abraham and Abimelech in vv. 22-32. Nonetheless, the importance of Beersheba is emphasized in those narratives and the presence of a sanctuary is assumed in 46:1. We have discussed the importance of Beersheba as a cult site frequented by northern worshipers in connection with Amos 5:5 and 8:14.[57] According to E, the deity it presents as *'ĕlōhîm* is properly identified with the god known in association with Beersheba. While it is possible that the god of Beersheba was known as El, there is no indication of this outside of this passage. Thus E's use of *hā'ēl* in connection with its sanctuary is probably a carry-over from earlier stories of Jacob at Bethel and Shechem.

In E the designation *hā'ēl* functions not as a DN but as an appellative or as a title similar in meaning to *'ĕlōhîm* though superseded by the latter. While E declines to give the name of the deity it designates *'ĕlōhîm*, it does specify certain traditions according to which this god is understood. For E, *'ĕlōhîm* is the god associated with patriarchal traditions of Shechem, Bethel, and Beersheba. While he is the god honored at the sanctuaries at those sites, he is not to be represented by a cult statue, such as the bull at Bethel. E's inclusion of certain local traditions constitutes an endorsement of those traditions in the identification of the *'ĕlōhîm*.

---

[57]See above, Amos.

Internal Structure of E

As noted, a number of factors indicate a significant internal coherence within E. The theme of *'ĕlōhîm* being "with" the patriarch[58] can be added to the unifying attributes we have identified for E already—viz., its preference for *'ĕlōhîm*, its northern character, its ethical sensitivity, and its emphasis on the deity's transcendence in the depiction of divine communication.[59] Internal narrative links that we have noted among the E materials of Genesis are the recurring allusions both to the theophany to Jacob at Bethel (28:10-22; 31:13; 35:1, 3, 7)[60] and to Jacob's return to his ancestral homeland in Canaan (28:21; 46:3; 48:21). E's portrayal of the ancestral god follows a progression which presents *'ĕlōhîm*'s dealings with the patriarchs in successive generations, first with Abraham (20:1-17; 21:9-32) and then Isaac (21:10-12; 46:1)[61] at Beersheba; then with Jacob at Bethel, in the country of Laban, and at Shechem (28:10-12, 17-21a, 22; 31:1-54; 35:1-7; 46:1-7); and finally with Joseph and his sons, Ephraim and Manasseh, in Egypt (48:8-22). However, E's story cannot end in Egypt, for the promises, both that Jacob and his descendants will return from Egypt to the land of their forebears and that *'ĕlōhîm* will make a great nation of Abraham's line (21:12-13; 46:3; 48:19) point forward and imply that E does not end with the patriarchal narratives of Genesis.

Conclusions

The patriarchal narratives that we have assigned to E represent an account of Israel's ancestors living in close relationship to a single patron deity who guides them in their migrations, protects them, and causes them to prosper. What is more, E's portrayal of the ancestral deity looks ahead both by the indication that Jacob's descendants will

---

[58] See above, *'Ĕlōhîm* as the Ancestral Patron Deity.

[59] See above, Preliminary Discussion of E.

[60] See above, Other E Texts in Genesis.

[61] That the material in our E texts that deals with Isaac is somewhat slim is consistent with the sparseness of Isaac material in Genesis overall. The most substantial treatment of Isaac in the Elohistic material of Genesis is in the offering of Isaac in ch. 22, a passage that, from a source-critical viewpoint, is too complicated to include in our provisional delineation of E.

return from Egypt and by showing his providence to be part of his grand design to make Abraham and his descendants into a "great nation." Though E includes particular traditions which it regards as legitimate in association with the patriarchal god, the deity in question is referred to throughout E simply as *'ĕlōhîm*, a divine title which we have seen to be of special significance in the northern kingdom. That this unified presentation of patriarchal narratives, which lays so much emphasis on the exclusive relationship between the ancestors and their patron god, would not at some point indicate the god's identity would seem unlikely. E's persistent references to the promises both of nationhood for Abraham's descendants and of their return from Egypt imply that the narrative represented by E continues past the patriarchal stories of Genesis. Thus we look ahead, beyond the Genesis material we have identified as E, for the resumption of E and for a clarification of the identity of E's *'ĕlōhîm*.

E Beyond Genesis

That E material persists into the book of Exodus is suggested by 1:15-22, in which *'ĕlōhîm* serves as the divine designation (vv. 20, 21) and a heightened ethical sensitivity is displayed in the Hebrew midwives' courageous defiance of the Pharaoh's orders. Our consideration of whether E material is present outside of Genesis will begin with Exod 3:13-15, which presents something we expect to find in E, namely, the clarification of *'ĕlōhîm*'s identity.

The Disclosure of the Divine Name in Exodus 3

The disclosure of the DN Yahweh in these verses has been regarded by scholars as an element of the call of Moses that is unique to E.[62] A closer examination of this passage is necessary to confirm whether it belongs with the texts we have identified as E.

In support of the identification of J and E sources in Exod 3:1-15, Noth pointed out the striking alternation between *yhwh* and *'ĕlōhîm* and the apparent variants in this passage. Noth divides the material thus: J = 1-4a, 5, 7, 8; E = 1bβ, 4b, 6, 9-13, 15.[63] For the

---

[62]Alt, "God of the Fathers," 11-13; Noth, *Exodus*, 41-45; Childs, *Exodus*, 68-70.
[63]Noth, *Exodus*, 38-45.

purposes of our analysis of E, it is appropriate to inquire whether the material in Exod 3 designated as E exhibits the qualities that are present in the texts from Genesis that we have identified as E. The use of *'ĕlōhîm* in these verses is in keeping with what we have seen in E; it is a clear absolute singular form and stands in place of a DN. The distance between the divine and the human, as portrayed in E, is accentuated in v. 6 in Moses' fear of even turning his face toward *'ĕlōhîm*. In v. 12, *'ĕlōhîm* answers Moses' concern that he is inadequate for the task laid before him with the reassurance, "I will be with you" (*kî-'ehye(h) 'immāk*), another motif that we have seen to be prominent in our E texts. The preference for the divine designation *'ĕlōhîm* and the occurrence of distinguishing motifs of E suggest that the material represented in these verses belongs with the texts in Genesis that we have designated E. Before making any conclusions, though, it would be advisable to consider whether the revelation of the name in vv. 13-15 corresponds to the presentation of *'ĕlōhîm* in the patriarchal stories.

As we have observed, in the E narratives of Genesis, the name of the god of Israel's ancestors remains unknown; he is called simply *'ĕlōhîm*. So, too, in the material that we have isolated in Exod 3, the god's identity is withheld both from Moses and from the reader. The narrator refers to the deity as *'ĕlōhîm* (vv. 4a, 6, 11, 13, 14), and the latter does not volunteer his name to the servant whom he is about to commission but introduces himself as "the god of your father, the god of Abraham, the god of Isaac, and the god of Jacob" (*'ĕlōhê 'ābîkā 'ĕlōhê 'abrāhām 'ĕlōhê yiṣḥāq wē'lōhê ya'ăqōb*, v. 6). After learning of the deity's plans for him, Moses says to *'ĕlōhîm*:

> I am about to go to the Israelites and say to them, "The god of your fathers has sent me to you." And they will say to me, "What is his name?" What shall I say to them?

In the formulation of Moses' question to *'ĕlōhîm* in v. 13, the knowledge of the deity's name is tied closely to a validation of Moses' mission. In light of this fact, some commentators on this passage have inferred that the knowledge of the god's name by the Israelites in Egypt is presumed and either (1) that Moses requests the name in order to

convince others who know it of his own legitimacy[64] or (2) that
Moses' question, which is posed very indirectly, is an inquiry into a
deeper significance of the name.[65]

Against the second interpretation, one might remember that
Moses does not know the name of the god who is speaking to him.
The indirectness of Moses' speech has everything to do with the status
of his conversation partner. It would be quite surprising for Moses,
who is terrified even to look at the deity (v. 6), to ask directly, "What
is your name?" The aim of Moses' question, deferential though it may
be, is to learn the god's name.

The first interpretation mentioned, that the Israelites already
know the name Yahweh and will expect Moses to know it as a
validation of his claim, seems satisfactory at first glance. Accordingly,
Moses, who has been reared in the Egyptian court, is unaware of the
deity's name and must ask for his own information. Against this
interpretation, one might point out that Moses seems already to have
some acquaintance with the god of the Israelites' ancestors. For
initially Moses is drawn by curiosity, and he answers the supernatural
voice without hesitation; it is only when the deity introduces himself to
Moses as "the god of *your* father, the god of Abraham, the god Isaac,
and the god of Jacob" that Moses is overcome with reverential awe (v.
6). Moses himself knows enough about the ancestral deity to recognize
the reference to "the god of Abraham, the god Isaac, and the god of
Jacob." If the name of that deity had already been made known among
the Israelites, then Moses presumably would not have needed to ask
what it was. In addition, the deity could have simply introduced
himself to Moses as Yahweh, and Moses' question would have been
unnecessary.

If, as this interpretation suggests, the Israelites do know the name
Yahweh and Moses does not, Yahweh could have answered Moses'
question by saying, "Just tell them Yahweh sent you." That is more
or less the answer given in v. 15:

> kō(h)-tō'mar 'el-běnê yiśrā'ēl yhwh 'ĕlōhê 'ăbōtêkem 'ĕlōhê 'abrāhām 'ĕlōhê
> yiṣḥāq wĕ'lōhê ya'ăqōb šĕlāḥanî 'ălêkem ze(h)-šěmî lĕ'ōlām wĕze(h) zikrî lĕdōr
> dōr

---

[64]This is suggested by Campbell and O'Brien, *Sources of the Pentateuch*, 185 n. 51.
[65]Those expressing this view are cited in Childs, *Exodus*, 61-62.

Thus you shall say to the Israelites, "Yahweh, the god of your fathers, the god of Abraham, the god of Isaac, and the god of Jacob, has sent me to you." This is my name forever, and this is my memorial from generation to generation.

However, the matter is not so simple, for this is the second of two answers to Moses' question preserved in our text. The first answer is given in v. 14:

wayyō'mer 'ĕlōhîm 'el-mōše(h) 'ehye(h) 'ăšer 'ehye(h)
wayyō'mer kō(h) tō'mar libnê yiśrā'ēl 'ehye(h) šĕlāḥanî 'ălêkem

And '*ĕlōhîm* said to Moses, "I am the one who is," and he said, "Thus you shall say to the Israelites: ''*ehye(h)* (the one who is)[66] has sent me to you.'"

Though it is clear that the name *yhwh* is explained here by reference to the Biblical Hebrew verb *hyh*, "to be," the precise significance of this mysterious etymology is probably beyond our reach.[67] The simpler answer given in v. 15 appears to be a secondary clarification of the original but more abstruse answer given in v. 14.[68]

The deity does not simply relate the name to Moses, as though the Israelites would understand its significance upon hearing it. The provision of an etiology for the name assumes that it required a rationalization, an explanation, as though it were being heard for the first time. In other words, the manner in which the DN's disclosure

---

[66]Here we follow David Noel Freedman ("The Name of the God of Moses," *JBL* 79 [1960]: 151-56) in understanding '*ehye(h)* (literally, "I am") as the second member of an *idem per idem* expression; '*ehye(h)* is spoken from '*ĕlōhîm*'s perspective and thus is in the first person but means, "the-One-Who-Is." Once Moses repeats the name as given to him in indirect speech, it will come out *yihye(h)*, the third person form, which in the original version of the story probably approximated the form of the DN *yhwh* even more closely. Freedman, following Albright ("Contributions to Biblical Archaeology and Philology: The Name *Yahweh*," *JBL* 43 [1924]: 370-78) and ultimately Paul Haupt ("Der Name Yahweh," *OLZ* 12 [1909]: 211-14), understands both *yhwh* and its etymology in this passage to be based on the *hip'il* form of the verb to be; Cross also follows this interpretation of the DN and of this passage (*CMHE*, 68).

[67]Noth, *Exodus*, 43-45; Bertil Albrektson, "On the Syntax of אהיה אשר אהיה in Exodus 3:14," in *Words and Meanings: Essays Presented to David Winton Thomas* (ed. P. R. Ackroyd and B. Lindars; Cambridge: Univ. Press, 1968), 15-28; cf. Freedman, "The Name of the God of Moses," 152-54.

[68]So Campbell and O'Brien, *Sources of the Pentateuch*, 184-85 and n. 51; cf. Noth, *Exodus*, 43; Childs, *Exodus*, 69-70.

is offered as new information in v. 14 seems to presuppose that the name is unknown in the preceding narrative—unknown to Moses, to the Israelites, and to the reader.

On the other hand, if the Israelites do not know the name of the god of their ancestors, why does Moses expect them to ask him the god's name? Childs puts us on the right track by considering Moses' call in terms of a prophetic commission.[69] In a sense, Moses will go to the Israelites as a prophet, as one sent by the deity to speak and act on his behalf. It should not be too much to expect that one who claims to be the deity's representative would have sufficient acquaintance with the god to know his name.[70] Stated otherwise, in order for the individual to claim the deity's authority, he must at least know the name of the deity.

The disclosure of the DN in Exod 3 is just that, and, as such, it presupposes that the name is being revealed in the narrative for the first time. If the responses to arguments to the contrary seem overly subtle, this only underlines the fact that attempts to explain away the significance of the name's disclosure are in themselves, at best, overly subtle. Furthermore, these objections overlook the fact that, if the DN is already known within the narrative, as it is in J,[71] then this revelation is completely superfluous both to the account of Moses' call[72] and to the broader narrative. The disclosure of the name Yahweh in Exod 3 implies a narrative context in which the deity whose name is revealed has until that point been called 'ĕlōhîm (vv. 4b, 6, 11, 12, 13, 14) and "the god of the father" (vv. 6, 13). Thus the Elohistic passage identified here, which exhibits some of the same traits that characterize our E texts in Genesis, appears to be integral to the latter as a crucial part of the framework of an extended narrative. This larger narrative framework implied in Exod 3, in which 'ĕlōhîm plays

---

[69]However, we disagree with Childs' conclusion that this passage is motivated by the criterion of prophetic authority that one speak only in the name of Yahweh, as reflected in Deut 13:1-3 and 18:20. One would expect an issue this specific to be addressed more directly in the text. According to Childs this is done in v. 15, which we regard as a secondary (*Exodus*, 68-70). See the discussion above.

[70]See Noth, *Exodus*, 42.

[71]In J, people begin to "call on the name of Yahweh" in primordial times (Gen 4:26; see also 12:8; 13:4, 18; 26:25).

[72]As it is for J; so Alt, "God of the Fathers," 11-12.

a central role, suggests what proponents of classic source criticism have recognized, namely, that E existed as an extensive narrative source.

The disclosure of the name of the *'ĕlōhîm* in Exod 3:13-14 completes the portrayal of the patriarchal deity in Genesis. The god whom Israel's ancestors called *'ĕlōhîm* is Yahweh, the god of Moses. As Alt recognized, the equation of the two marks both continuity and dissonance in the extended narrative of E; for, in linking the traditions of Israel's patriarchs with the worship of Yahweh, a distinction between the two is acknowledged.[73] In E the epochs of patriarchal religion and of Mosaic Yahwism are linked by recourse to the divine designation *'ĕlōhîm*. Within this framework, *'ĕlōhîm* accommodates both the assimilation of distinct patriarchal traditions into the figure of a single god and the equation of this ancestral deity with Yahweh, the god of the exodus and the national deity of Israel.

By contrast, in J no such disjunction is apparent between the epochs of the patriarchal god and of Yahweh the god of the exodus, and the DN Yahweh is used freely throughout J's narrative. If the entire narrative spanning the patriarchal period and the exodus could be dealt with evenly without the use of a cover term like *'ĕlōhîm*, as it is in J, then why does E resort to the use of this designation?

E's employment of *'ĕlōhîm* in this capacity suggests that the author defers to this term on the basis of some significance it possessed outside of the narrative. As we have seen, *'ĕlōhîm* is significant in the context of patron deities[74] and as the chief designation of the national deity in the northern kingdom.[75] E's use of *'ĕlōhîm*, first of all, presupposes its status as a title for Israel's god in the national cult, but E, like the northern prophetic circles of the ninth and eighth centuries, accentuates *'ĕlōhîm*'s implications for exclusive loyalty to the patron deity, with an emphasis on the precise identity of the *'ĕlōhîm*. In the portrayal of patriarchal traditions and in the exodus narrative, including the disclosure of the DN to Moses, E answers the same question addressed by the Elijah cycle in the contest on Carmel: Who is the *'ĕlōhîm*? The answer for E, as for 1 Kgs 18, is clearly and decisively that Yahweh is the *'ĕlōhîm*. The resemblance between the concerns of E and of northern prophet circles regarding *'ĕlōhîm* suggests a

---

[73]"God of the Fathers," 11.

[74]See above, Patron Deities.

[75]See above, The Title *'ĕlōhîm* in the National Cult.

connection between the two, which is something that has been surmised on other grounds.[76]

As a surrogate for the DN in the patriarchal stories and in the narrative leading up to the name's disclosure, *'ĕlōhîm*, the title by which Yahweh was known in the national religion, reinforces the continuity between Yahweh and the deity of Israel's eponymous ancestors. In the portrayal of the *'ĕlōhîm* as the personal deity of the patriarchs, E fleshes out the notion of intimate and exclusive loyalty implied by the term *'ĕlōhîm* in the context of patron deities. The narrative of E in Genesis and continuing in Exodus addresses a concern of northern prophetic circles by providing a decisive clarification of the identity of the national *'ĕlōhîm* of Israel.

The Use of *'ĕlōhîm* after the Disclosure of the Divine Name

A problem for E scholarship has been the persistence of the title *'ĕlōhîm* beyond the disclosure of the name Yahweh.[77] If *'ĕlōhîm* functioned in E only as a surrogate for the DN, then its use after Exod 3 would be superfluous to the theological and narrative scheme of E. On the other hand, if the expression possessed a significance that was independent of the narrative and that was addressed by the narrative, as we have seen that it did, then the appearance of *'ĕlōhîm* in E after the revelation to Moses rather than posing a problem is completely consistent with the aims of the narrative. For E is concerned to demonstrate both that the *'ĕlōhîm* is Yahweh and that Yahweh is the *'ĕlōhîm*, that is, that Yahweh is the deity with whom Israel has an exclusive relationship as the national patron god. While the narrative is explicit in identifying Yahweh as the god denoted by the title *'ĕlōhîm*, E at the same time makes the point that Yahweh is not merely

---

[76]See Jenks, *The Elohist and North Israelite Traditions*.

[77]Kuenen, *Inquiry*, 56-57; Robert H. Pfeiffer, *Introduction to the Old Testament* (New York: Harper & Brothers, 1948), 168; Procksch, *Elohimquelle*, 197-98; Wellhausen, "Composition des Hexateuchs," 72; Hellmuth Zimmermann, *Elohim: Eine Studie zur israelitischen Religions- und Litteraturgeschichte nebst Beitrag zur Religionsphilosophie und einer Pentateuchtabelle* (Berlin: Mayer & Müller, 1900), 29. The relevant passages are Exod 13:17, 18, 19; 14:19; 18:1, 12, 15, 19; 20:1, 19-21; 24:11; Num 21:5; 22:9, 10, 12, 20, 22, 38; 23:4, 27; Josh 24:1. The heightened emphasis on exclusivity in the use of *'ĕlōhîm* in Deut 4:32, 35 anticipates the emergence of monotheism during the exile.

one deity among many to be worshiped by Israel; he is rather the *'ĕlōhîm*, the one god in relationship to whom the nation's identity is to be defined.

Summary

Our examination of Pentateuchal E has shown that, beyond serving merely as a substitute for Yahweh in anticipation of the disclosure of the DN, the title *'ĕlōhîm* persists in the narrative after the name has been introduced, implying that *'ĕlōhîm* had a significance that was independent of the narrative. In view of E's northern orientation, it is likely that this significance is derived from *'ĕlōhîm*'s status as a divine title in the national cult of the northern kingdom of Israel. The title is used in E in the portrayal of a single patron deity to whom the nation, like its ancestors, owed its exclusive devotion. The designation *'ĕlōhîm* is integral to the plan of E in demonstrating that the sole patron god of Israel and of its forebears is Yahweh. Results of our investigation which confirm the conclusions of others regarding E's composition, date, and provenance are that the theological scheme of E, in which *'ĕlōhîm* plays a crucial role, is suggestive of an extensive narrative and that E's emphases in its use of *'ĕlōhîm*, on clarifying the identity of the *'ĕlōhîm* and on exclusive loyalty to Yahweh, are indicative of ties with northern prophetic circles.

SUMMARY OF CONCLUSIONS

The singular noun *'ĕlōhîm* is an example of the concretized abstract plural, a Canaanite grammatical usage, and has the generic meaning "deity" or "god." The word's generic meaning makes it useful as a substitute for a DN in the portrayal of international settings, in technical language, and in the context of patron deities. Singular *'ĕlōhîm* comes to prominence in the religion of the northern kingdom of Israel as a reinterpretation of plural *'ĕlōhîm* in an archaic liturgical formula featured in the national cult. Northern proponents of the exclusive worship of Yahweh, including prophetic circles of the ninth and eighth centuries and the author(s) of Pentateuchal E, though concerned to clarify the identity of the *'ĕlōhîm*, seized upon the title as a reinforcement of the demand for undivided allegiance to Yahweh as the national deity.   Thus *'ĕlōhîm*, which had a fixed place in the national religion of the northern kingdom, played an important role in the development of exclusive Yahwism.

WORKS CITED

Abou-Assaf, Ali, Pierre Bordreuil, and Alan R. Millard, eds. *La statue de Tell Fekherye et son inscription bilingue assyro-araméenne*. Paris: Editions recherche sur les civilisations, 1982.

Albertz, Rainer. *A History of Israelite Religion in the Old Testament Period*. Translated by J. Bowden. 2 vols. Old Testament Library. Philadelphia: Westminster John Knox, 1994.

———. *Persönliche Frömmigkeit und offizielle Religion: Religionsinterner Pluralismus in Israel und Babylon*. Calwer theologische Monographien 9. Stuttgart: Calwer, 1978.

Albrektson, Bertil. "On the Syntax of אהיה אשר אהיה in Exodus 3:14." Pages 15-29 in *Words and Meanings: Essays Presented to David Winton Thomas*. Edited by P. R. Ackroyd and B. Lindars. Cambridge: Cambridge Univ. Press, 1968.

Albright, William Foxwell. *Archaeology and the Religion of Israel*. 5th ed. Garden City, N.Y.: Doubleday, 1969.

———. "Contributions to Biblical Archaeology and Philology: The Name Yahweh." *Journal of Biblical Literature* 43 (1924): 370-78.

———. *From the Stone Age to Christianity*. 2d. ed. Garden City, N.Y.: Doubleday, 1957.

———. *Yahweh and the Gods of Canaan*. London: Univ. of London, 1968. Repr. Winona Lake, Ind.: Eisenbrauns, 1994.

Alt, Albrecht. "The God of the Fathers." Pages 1-77 in *Essays on the Old Testament History and Religion*. Translated by R. A. Wilson. Oxford: Basil Blackwell, 1966.

———. "Settlement of the Israelites in Palestine." Pages 175-221 in *Essays on Old Testament History and Religion*. Translated by R. A. Wilson. Garden City, N.Y.: Doubleday, 1968.

———. "Die Wallfahrt von Sichem nach Bethel." Pages 79-88 in vol. 1 of *Kleine Schriften zur Geschichte des Volkes Israel*. Munich: C. H. Beck: 1953.

Anderson, Bernhard W. "God, Names of." Pages 407-17 in vol. 2 of *The Interpreter's Dictionary of the Bible*. Edited by G. A. Buttrick. 4 vols. Nashville: Abingdon, 1962.

Anderson, Bernhard W. and Katheryn Phisterer Darr. *Understanding the Old Testament*. Abridged 4th ed. Englewood Cliffs, N.J.: Prentice-Hall, 1998.

Assmann, Jan. *Egyptian Solar Religion in the New Kingdom: Re, Amun, and the Crisis of Polytheism*. Translated by A. Alcock. London: Kegan Paul, 1995.

Bailey, Lloyd R. "The Golden Calf." *Hebrew Union College Annual* 42 (1971): 97-115.

Barré, Michael. "'Fear of God' and the World View of Wisdom." *Biblical Theology Bulletin* 11 (1981): 41-43.

Barstad, Hans M. *The Religious Polemics of Amos: Studies in the Preaching of Am 2, 7B-8; 4, 1-13; 5, 1-27; 6, 4-7; 8, 14*. Vetus Testamentum Supplements 34. Leiden: Brill, 1984.

———. "Way דרך." Pages 895-97 in *Dictionary of Deities and Demons in the Bible*. Edited by K. van der Toorn, B. Becking, and P. W. van der Horst. 2d ed. Leiden: Brill, 1999.

Baumgärtel, Friedrich. *Elohim ausserhalb des Pentateuch: Grundlegung zu einer Untersuchung über die Gottesnamen im Pentateuch*. Leipzig: J. C. Hinrichs, 1914.

Behrens, Emil. *Assyrisch-Babylonische Briefe Kultischen Inhalts aus der Sargonidenzeit*. Leipziger semitische Studien 2. Leipzig: J. C. Hinrichs, 1906.

Berthier, André and René Charlier. *Le sanctuaire punique d'El-Hofra à Constantine*. Paris: 1952.

Biran, Avraham. "To the God who is in Dan." Pages 142-51 in *Temples and High Places in Biblical Times: Proceedings of the Colloquium in Honor of the Centennial of Hebrew Union College-Jewish Institute of Religion. Jerusalem, 14-16 March 1977*. Jerusalem: Hebrew Union College, 1981.

Blum, Erhard. *Die Komposition der Vätergeschichte*. Wissentschaftliche Monographien zum Alten und Neuen Testament 57. Neukirchen: Neukirchener Verlag, 1984.

———. *Studien zur Komposition des Pentateuch*. Beihefte zur Zeitschrift für die alttestamentliche Wissenschaft 189. Berlin: Walter de Gruyter, 1990.

Böhl, Franz M. Th. *Der Sprache der Amarnabriefe*. Leipziger semitistische Studien V/2 Leipzig: J. C. Hinrichs, 1909.

Boling, Robert. "Synonymous Parallelism in the Psalms." *Journal of Semitic Studies* (1960): 221-57.

Borger, Riekele. *Die Inschriften Asarhaddons Königs von Assyrien.* Archive für Orientforschung. Supplement 9. Graz, 1956.

Bottéro, Jean. "Les inventaires de Qatna." *Revue d'assyriologie et d'archéologie orientale* 43 (1949): 1-41, 137-216.

Botterweck, G. Johannes, Helmer Ringgren, and Heinz-Josef Fabry, eds. *Theological Dictionary of the Old Testament.* Translated by J. T. Willis, G. W. Bromiley, and D. E. Green. 11 vols. Grand Rapids, Mich: Eerdmans, 1974-.

Branden, Albertus van den. "Les inscriptions phéniciennes de Karatepe." *Melto* I (1965): 25-84.

Brichto, Herbert Chanan. *The Names of God: Poetic Readings in Biblical Beginnings.* Oxford: Oxford Univ. Press, 1998.

Brockelmann, Carl. *Grundriss der vergleichenden Grammatik der semitischen Sprachen.* Vol. 2. Berlin: Reuther & Reichard, 1913.

———. *Hebräische Syntax.* Neukirchen: Erziehungsvereins, 1956.

Brown, Francis. *The New Brown-Driver-Briggs-Gesenius Hebrew and English Lexicon with an Appendix Containing the Biblical Aramaic.* Peabody, Mass.: Hendrickson, 1979. Reprint of F. Brown, S. R. Driver, and C. A. Briggs. *A Hebrew Lexicon of the Old Testament.* Oxford: Clarendon, 1907.

Buccellati, Giorgio. "The Case Against the Alleged Akkadian Plural Morpheme *-ĀNŪ.*" *Afroasiatic Linguistics* 3 (1976): 28-30.

Buss, Martin J. "The Psalms of Asaph and Korah." *Journal of Biblical Literature* 82 (1963): 382-92.

Buttrick, George Arthur, ed. *The Interpreter's Dictionary of the Bible.* 4 vols. Nashville: Abingdon, 1962.

Campbell, Antony F. *The Ark Narrative (1 Sam 4-6; 2 Sam 6): A Form-Critical and Traditio-Historical Study.* Society of Biblical Literature Dissertation Series 16. Missoula, Mont.: Scholars Press, 1975.

———. *The Study Companion to Old Testament Literature: An Approach to the Writings of Pre-Exilic and Exilic Israel.* Collegeville, Minn.: Liturgical Press, 1992.

Campbell, Antony F. and Mark A. O'Brien. *Sources of the Pentateuch: Texts, Introductions, Annotations.* Minneapolis: Fortress, 1993.

156 A Reassessment of Biblical Elohim

Caplice, Richard. "Languages: Akkadian." Pages 170-73 in vol. 4 of *The Anchor Bible Dictionary*. Edited by D. N. Freedman. 6 vols. New York: Doubleday, 1992.

Caquot, André and André Lemaire. "Les textes Araméens de Deir 'Alla." *Syria* 54 (1977): 189-208.

Cassuto, Umberto. "אֱלֹהִים." Pages 297-321 in vol. 1 of *Entsiqlopēdiā Miqrā'it-Encyclopaedia Biblica* [= *Entsiklopedyah mikra'it*]. Edited by M. David. 9 vols. Jerusalem: Bialik Institute, 1950.

———. *The Documentary Hypothesis and the Composition of the Pentateuch*. Translated by I. Abrahams. Jerusalem: Magnes, 1961.

Cazelles, Henri. "Der persönliche Gott Abrahams und der Gott des Volkes Israel." Pages 46-61 in *Der Weg zum Menschen: Zur philologischen und theologischen Anthropologie für Alfons Deissler*. Edited by R. Mosis and L. Ruppert. Freiburg: Herder, 1988.

Cogan, Morton. "Ashima אֲשִׁימָא." Pages 105-6 in *Dictionary of Deities and Demons in the Bible*. Edited by K. van der Toorn, B. Becking, and P. W. van der Horst. 2d ed. Leiden: Brill, 1999.

———. *Imperialism and Religion: Assyria, Judah and Israel in the Eighth and Seventh Centuries B.C.E.* Missoula, Mont.: Scholars Press, 1974.

Coogan, Michael David. *West Semitic Personal Names in the Murašû Documents*. Harvard Semitic Monographs 7. Missoula, Mont.: Scholars Press, 1976.

Cooke, George Albert. *A Text-Book of North-Semitic Inscriptions*. Oxford: Clarendon, 1903.

Coote, Robert B., ed. *Elijah and Elisha in Socioliterary Perspective*. Semeia Studies. Atlanta: Scholars Press, 1992.

———. *In Defense of Revolution: The Elohist History*. Minneapolis: Fortress, 1991.

Cowley, Arthur Ernest, ed. *Aramaic Papyri of the Fifth Century B.C.* Oxford: Clarendon, 1923.

Crenshaw, James L. *Old Testament Wisdom: An Introduction*. Atlanta: John Knox, 1981.

Cross, Frank M. *Canaanite Myth and Hebrew Epic: Essays in the History of the Religion of Israel*. Cambridge, Mass.: Harvard Univ. Press, 1973.

———. "Notes on the Ammonite Inscription from Tell Sirān." *Bulletin of the American Schools of Oriental Research* 212 (1973): 12-15.

————. "A Recently Published Phoenician Inscription in the Persian Period from Byblos." *Israel Exploration Journal* 29 (1979): 40-44.

Cross, Frank M. and David Noel Freedman. *Early Hebrew Orthography: A Study of the Epigraphic Evidence*. American Oriental Series 36. New Haven: American Oriental Society, 1952.

Degen, Rainer. *Altaramäische Grammatik der Inschriften des 10-8 Jh. v. Chr.* Wiesbaden: F. Steiner, 1969.

Dietrich, Franz Eduard. *Abhandlungen zur hebräischen Grammatik*. Leipzig: Vogel, 1846.

Dion, Paul E. "Aramaean Tribes and Nations of First-Millennium Western Asia." Pages 1287-92 in vol. 2 of *Civilizations of the Ancient Near East*. Edited by Jack M. Sasson. 4 vols. New York: Scribners, 1995.

Donner, Herbert and Wolfgang Röllig. *Kanaanäische und aramäische Inschriften*. 3 vols. 2d ed. Wiesbaden: Otto Harrassowitz, 1966-1969.

Dossin, Georges. "Une lettre de Iarîm-Lim, roi d'Alep, à Iašûb-Iaḫad, roi de Dîr." *Syria* 33 (1956): 63-69.

Draffkorn, Anne E. "Ilāni/Elohim." *Journal of Biblical Literature* 76 (1957): 216-24.

Driver, Godfrey Rolles. *Aramaic Documents of the Fifth Century*. Oxford: Clarendon, 1957.

Driver, Samuel Rolles. *An Introduction to the Literature of the Old Testament*. Edinburgh: T & T Clark, 1891. Repr., New York: Meridian, 1956.

Ebeling, Erich, ed. *Die Akkadische Gebetsserie "Handerhebung."* Deutsche Akademie der Wissenschaften zu Berlin, Institut für Orientforschung 20. Berlin: Akademie-Verlag, 1953.

Edelman, Diana V., ed. *The Triumph of Elohim: From Yahwisms to Judaisms*. Grand Rapids, Mich.: Eerdmans, 1995.

Eerdmans, Bernardus Dirks. *Die Komposition der Genesis*. Alttestamentliche Studien 1. Giessen: Alfred Töpelmann, 1908.

Eichrodt, Walther. *Theology of the Old Testament*. Translated by J. A. Baker. Old Testament Library. Philadelphia: Westminster, 1961.

Eilers, Wilhelm. "Neue aramäische Urkunden aus Ägypten." *Archiv für Orientforschung* 17 (1956): 321-35.

Eissfeldt, Otto. "El und Jahwe." Pages 386-97 in vol. 3 of *Kleine Schriften*. Tübingen: J. C. B. Mohr, 1966.

———. "Jahwe Zebaoth." Pages 128-50 in *Miscellanea Academica Berolinensia*. Berlin: Akademie-Verlag, 1950. Reprinted, pages 103-23 in vol. 3 of *Kleine Schriften*. Tübingen: J. C. B. Mohr, 1966.

———. "Lade und Stierbild." *Zeitschrift für die alttestamentliche Wissenschaft* 58 (1940-1941): 190-215; reprinted, pages 282-305 in vol. 2 of *Kleine Schriften*. Tübingen: J. C. B. Mohr, 1964.

Ember, Aaron. "The Pluralis Intensivus in Hebrew." *American Journal of Semitic Languages and Literature* 21 (1905): 195-231.

Engnell, Ivan. *A Rigid Scrutiny: Critical Essays on the Old Testament*. Translated by J. T. Willis and H. Ringgren. Nashville: Vanderbilt Univ. Press, 1969.

Ewald, Heinrich. *The Psalms Chronologically Arranged*. London: Macmillan, 1867.

Fabry, Heinz-Josef. "Erste die Erstgeburt, dann der Segen: Eine Nachfrage zu Gen 27, 1-45." Pages 51-72 in *Vom Sinai zum Horeb: Stationen alttestamentlicher Glaubensgeschichte*. Edited by F. L. Hossfeld. Würzburg: Echter Verlag, 1989.

Finkelstein, Israel. *The Archaeology of the Israelite Settlement*. Jerusalem: Israel Exploration Society, 1988.

Fitzmyer, Joseph A. "The Phases of the Aramaic Language." Pages 57-84 in *A Wandering Aramean: Collected Aramaic Essays*. Chico, Calif.: Scholars Press, 1979.

Fohrer, Georg. *Introduction to the Old Testament*. Translated by David Green. Nashville: Abingdon, 1968. Reprint, London: S.P.C.K., 1976.

Foster, Benjamin. *Before the Muses: An Anthology of Akkadian Literature*. 2d ed. Bethesda, Md.: CDL Press, 1996.

Franken, Hendricus Jacobus. "Deir 'Alla re-visited." Pages 3-15 in *The Balaam Text from Deir 'Alla Re-evaluated: Proceedings of the International Symposium held at Leiden, 21-24 August 1989*. Edited by J. Hoftijzer and G. van der Kooij. Leiden: Brill, 1991.

———. "Deir 'All, Tell. Archaeology." Pages 126-29 in vol. 2 of *The Anchor Bible Dictionary*. Edited by D. N. Freedman. 6 vols. New York: Doubleday, 1992.

Frankfort, Henri. *Ancient Egyptian Religion: An Interpretation*. New York: Harper & Row, 1967.

Freedman, David Noel, ed. *The Anchor Bible Dictionary*. 6 vols. New York: Doubleday, 1992.

———. "The Name of the God of Moses." *Journal of Biblical Literature* 79 (1960): 151-56.

———. *Pottery, Poetry, and Prophecy: Studies in Early Hebrew Poetry*. Winona Lake, Ind.: Eisenbrauns, 1980.

Fulco, William J. "Ashima (deity)." Page 487 in vol. 1 of *The Anchor Bible Dictionary*. Edited by D. N. Freedman. 6 vols. New York: Doubleday, 1992.

———. *The Canaanite God Rešep*. American Oriental Series Essay 8. New Haven: American Oriental Society, 1976.

Garr, W. Randall. *Dialect Geography of Syria-Palestine, 1000-586 B.C.E.* Philadelphia: Univ. of Pennsylvania Press, 1985.

Gibson, John C. L. *Textbook of Syrian Semitic Inscriptions*. 3 vols. Oxford: Clarendon Press, 1971-1982.

Ginsberg, Harold Louis. "Aramaic Dialect Problems." *American Journal of Semitic Languages and Literature* 50 (1933): 1-9; 52 (1936): 95-103.

Gnuse, Robert K. "Redefining the Elohist?" *Journal of Biblical Literature* 119 (2000): 201-20.

Goetze, Albrecht. "The Akkadian Masculine Plural in *-ānū/ī* and its Semitic Background." *Language* 22 (1946): 121-30.

Gordon, Cyrus H. "אלהים in its Reputed Meaning of Rulers, Judges." *Journal of Biblical Literature* 54 (1935): 139-44.

Goulder, Michael. *The Psalms of the Sons of Korah*. Journal for the Study of the Old Testament: Supplement Series 20. Sheffield: Sheffield Academic Press, 1982.

———. *The Psalms of Asaph and the Pentateuch: Studies in the Psalter, III*. Journal for the Study of the Old Testament: Supplement Series 233. Sheffield: Sheffield Academic Press, 1996.

Graf, Karl H. *Die geschichtlichen Bücher des Alten Testaments*. Leipzig: T. O. Weigel, 1866.

Grave, Celia. "On the Use of an Egyptian Idiom in an Amarna Letter from Tyre and in a Hymn to the Aten." *Oriens antiquus* 19 (1980): 205-18.

Gray, John. *I & II Kings: A Commentary*. 2 vols. Old Testament Library. Philadelphia: Westminster, 1963.

Grelot, Pierre. "Les proverbes Araméens d'Aḥiqar." *Revue biblique* 68 (1961): 178-94.

Gunkel, Hermann. *Genesis übersetzt und erklärt*. Handkommentar zum Alten Testament. Göttingen: Vandenhoeck & Ruprecht, 1901.

Hackett, Jo Ann. *The Balaam Text From Deir 'Allā*. Harvard Semitic Monographs 31. Chico, Calif.: Scholars Press, 1980.

———. "Deir 'Alla, Tell. Texts." Pages 129-30 in vol. 2 of *The Anchor Bible Dictionary*. Edited by D. N. Freedman. 6 vols. New York: Doubleday, 1992.

Harper, Robert Francis. *Assyrian and Babylonian Letters Belonging to the Kouyunjik Collections of the British Museum*. 14 vols. Chicago: Univ. of Chicago Press, 1892-1914.

Harris, Zellig. *Development of the Canaanite Dialects: An Investigation in Linguistic History*. American Oriental Series 16. New Haven: American Oriental Society, 1939.

———. *A Grammar of the Phoenician Language*. American Oriental Series 8. New Haven: American Oriental Society, 1936.

Hartmann, Benedikt. "Elōhīm als Singular." *Mélanges de l'Université Saint-Joseph* 48 (1972-1973): 67-76.

Haupt, Paul. "Der Name Yahweh." *Orientalistische Literaturzeitung* 12 (1909): 211-14.

Healey, John F. "Mot מ ת." Pages 598-603 in *Dictionary of Deities and Demons in the Bible*. Edited by K. van der Toorn, B. Becking, and P. W. van der Horst. 2d ed. Leiden: Brill, 1999.

Hehn, Johannes. *Die biblische und die babylonische Gottesidee: die israelitische Gottesauffassung im Lichte der altorientalischen Religionsgeschichte*. Leipzig: J. C. Hinrichs, 1913.

Herrmann, Wolfgang. "El אל." Pages 274-80 in *Dictionary of Deities and Demons in the Bible*. Edited by K. van der Toorn, B. Becking, and P. W. van der Horst. 2d ed. Leiden: Brill, 1999.

Hiebert, Theodore. *God of My Victory: The Ancient Hymn in Habakkuk 3*. Harvard Semitic Monographs 38. Decatur, Ga.: Scholars Press, 1986.

Hillers, Delbert R. "*Paḥad Yiṣḥāq*." *Journal of Biblical Literature* 91 (1972): 90-92.

————. "Palmyrene Aramaic Inscriptions and the Bible." *Zeitschrift für Althebräistik* 11 (1998): 32-49.

————. "Ritual Procession of the Ark and Ps 132." *Catholic Biblical Quarterly* 30 (1968): 48-55.

Hoftijzer, Jacob and G. van der Kooij, eds. *Aramaic Texts from Deir 'Alla.* Documenta et monumenta Orientis antiqui 19. Leiden: Brill, 1976.

Holladay, William L. "Psalms from the North." Pages 26-36 in *The Psalms through Three Thousand Years: Prayerbook of a Cloud of Witnesses.* Minneapolis: Fortress, 1993.

Honeyman, A. M. "Larnax tēs Lapēthou: A Third Phoenician Inscription." *Le Muséon* 51 (1938): 285-98.

Hornung, Erik. *Conceptions of God in Ancient Egypt: The One and the Many.* Translated by J. Baines. Ithaca, N.Y.: Cornell Univ. Press, 1982.

Hrozný, Friedrich. "Keilschrifttexte aus Ta'annek." Pages 113-22 in *Tell Ta'annek.* Denkschriften der kaiserlichen Akademie der Wissenschaften in Wien, Philosophisch-Historische Klasse, vol. 50, no. IV. Edited by Ernst Sellin. Vienna: Kaiserliche Akademie der Wissenschaft, 1904.

Huehnergard, John. *The Akkadian of Ugarit.* Harvard Semitic Studies 34. Atlanta: Scholars Press, 1989.

————. *A Grammar of Akkadian.* Harvard Semitic Studies 45. Atlanta: Scholars Press, 1997.

Hupfeld, D. Hermann. *Die Quellen der Genesis und die Art ihrer Zusammensetzung.* Berlin: Wiegandt und Grieben, 1853.

Ilgen, Karl David. *Die Urkunden des ersten Buchs von Moses in ihrer Urgestalt: zum bessern Verständniss und richtigem Gebrauch derselben: in ihrer gegenwärtigen Form aus dem Hebräischen mit kritischen Anmerkungen und Nachweisungen auch einer Abhandlung über die Trennung der Urkunden.* Halle: Hemmerde und Schwetschke, 1798.

Izre'el, Shlomo. "Early Northwest Semitic 3rd pl m Prefix: The Evidence of the Amarna Letters." *Ugarit-Forschungen* 19 (1987): 77-90.

————. Review of J. Huehnergard, *Akkadian of Ugarit. Bibliotheca orientalis* 49 (1992): 168-80.

Izre'el, Shlomo and Itamar Singer. *The General's Letter from Ugarit: A Linguistic and Historical Reevaluation of RS 20.33 (Ugaritica V, No. 20)*. Tel Aviv: Tel Aviv Univ., 1990.

Janzen, Waldemar. "Land." Pages 143-54 in vol. 4 of *The Anchor Bible Dictionary*. Edited by D. N. Freedman. 6 vols. New York: Doubleday, 1992.

Jaroš, Karl. *Die Stellung des Elohisten zur Kanaanäischen Religion*. Orbis biblicus et orientalis 4. Fribourg: Universitätsverlag, 1974.

Jenks, Alan W. *The Elohist and North Israelite Traditions*. Society of Biblical Literature Monograph Series 22. Missoula, Mont.: Scholars Press, 1977.

Jenni, Ernst and Claus Westermann, eds. *Theologisches Handwörterbuch zum Alten Testament*. 2 vols. Munich: Chr. Kaiser, 1971-1976.

Jirku, Anton. *Altorientalischer Kommentar zum Alten Testament*. Leipzig: Deichert, 1923.

―――. "Elohim als Bezeichnung einer Gottheit." Page 358 in vol. 2 of *Reallexikon der Assyriologie*. Edited by E. Ebeling and B. Meissner. Berlin: Walter de Gruyter, 1938.

Jouön, Paul. "Notes grammaticales, lexicographiques et philologiques sur les papyrus araméens d'Égypte." *Mélanges de l'Université Saint-Joseph* 18 (1934): 1-100.

Joüon, Paul and Takamitsu Muraoka. *A Grammar of Biblical Hebrew*. Subsidia biblica 14/1-2. Rome: Pontifical Biblical Institute, 1993.

Kaiser, Otto. *Texte aus der Umwelt des Alten Testaments*. Gütersloh: G. Mohn, 1982-.

Kaufmann, Stephen A. "Languages (Aramaic)." Pages 173-78 in vol. 4 of *The Anchor Bible Dictionary*. Edited by D. N. Freedman. 6 vols. New York: Doubleday, 1992.

Kaufmann, Yehezkel. *The Religion of Israel*. Translated by M. Greenberg. Chicago: Univ. of Chicago Press, 1960.

Kautzsch, Emil, ed. *Gesenius' Hebrew Grammar*. Translated by A. E. Cowley. Oxford: Clarendon, 1910.

Knudtzon, Jorgen Alexander, ed. *Die el-Amarna-Tafeln*. Vorderasiatische Bibliothek 2. Leipzig, 1908-1915. Reprint, Aalen: Otto Zeller, 1964.

Koehler, Ludwig, Walter Baumgartner, and J. J. Stamm. *Hebräisches und Aramäisches Lexikon zum Alten Testament*. 5 vols. Leiden: Brill, 1967-1995.

Kraeling, Emil Gottlieb. *The Brooklyn Museum Aramaic Papyri: New Documents of the Fifth Century B.C. from the Jewish Colony at Elephantine*. New Haven: Yale Univ. Press, 1953.

Kuenen, Abraham. *The Religion of Israel*. Translated by A. H. May. London: Williams & Norgate, 1874-1875. Translation of *De godsdienst van Israël*. Haarlem: A. C. Kruseman: 1869-1870.

———. *An Historico-Critical Inquiry into the Origin and Composition of the Hexateuch (Pentateuch and Book of Joshua)*. Translated by P. H. Wicksteed. London: Macmillan, 1886.

Lambert, Wilfred G. *Babylonian Wisdom Literature*. Oxford: Clarendon, 1960.

———. "The Gula Hymn of Bullutsa-rabi (Tab. VIII-XXIII)." *Orientalia* (NS) 36 (1967): 105-32.

Lang, Bernhard. *Monotheism and the Prophetic Minority*. The Social World of Biblical Antiquity Series 1. Sheffield: Almond, 1983.

Langdon, Stephen. "A Phoenician Treaty of Assarhaddon: Collation of K. 3500." *Revue d'assyriologie et d'archéologie orientale* 26 (1929): 189-94.

———, ed. *Die Neubabylonischen Königsinschriften*. Vorderasiatische Bibliothek 4. Leipzig: J. C. Hinrichs, 1912.

Leander, Pontius. *Laut- und Formenlehre des Ägyptisch-Aramäischen*. Hildesheim: Georg Olms, 1966.

Lewis, Theodore J. "The Identity and Function of El/Baal Berith." *Journal of Biblical Literature* 115 (1996): 401-23.

Lindenberger, James M. "Ahiqar (Seventh to Sixth Century B.C.): A New Translation and Introduction." Pages 479-507 in vol. 2 of *The Old Testament Pseudepigrapha*. Edited by J. H. Charlesworth. 2 vols. New York: Doubleday, 1985.

———. *The Aramaic Proverbs of Ahiqar*. Johns Hopkins Near Eastern Studies. Baltimore: Johns Hopkins Univ. Press, 1983.

May, Herbert Gordon. "The Ark—A Miniature Temple." *American Journal of Semitic Languages and Literature* 52 (1936): 215-34.

———. "The God of My Father—A Study of Patriarchal Religion." *Journal of Bible and Religion* 9 (1941): 155-58.

Mayer, Werner. *Untersuchungen zur Formensprache der Babylonischen "Gebetsbeschwörungen."* Studia Pohl: Series Maior 5. Rome: Pontifical Biblical Institute, 1976.

Mays, James Luther. *Amos: A Commentary.* Old Testament Library. Philadelphia: Westminster, 1969.

———. *Hosea: A Commentary.* Old Testament Library. Philadelphia: Westminster, 1969.

Mazar, Amihai. "In the Shadow of Egyptian Domination: The Late Bronze Age (ca. 1550-1200 B.C.E.)." Pages 232-94 in *Archaeology of the Land of the Bible 10,000-586 B.C.E.* Anchor Bible Reference Library. New York: Doubleday, 1992.

McCarter, P. Kyle, Jr., "Aspects of the Religion of the Israelite Monarchy: Biblical and Epigraphic Data." Pages 137-55 in *Ancient Israelite Religion: Essays in Honor of Frank Moore Cross.* Edited by P. D. Miller, P. D. Hanson, and S. D. McBride. Philadelphia: Fortress, 1987.

———. "The Balaam Texts from Deir 'Allā: The First Collation." *Bulletin of the American Schools of Oriental Research* 239 (1980): 49-60.

———. "The dialect of the Deir 'Alla texts." Pages 87-99 in *The Balaam Text from Deir 'Alla Re-evaluated: Proceedings of the International Symposium held at Leiden, 21-24 August 1989.* Edited by J. Hoftijzer and H. van der Kooij. Leiden: Brill, 1991.

———. "Exodus." Pages 129-56 in *Harper's Bible Commentary.* Edited by J. L. Mays. San Francisco: Harper & Row, 1988.

———. *I Samuel: A New Translation with Introduction and Commentary.* Anchor Bible 8. New York: Doubleday, 1980.

———. *II Samuel: A New Translation with Introduction and Commentary.* Anchor Bible 9. New York: Doubleday, 1984.

McEvenue, Sean E. "The Elohist at Work." *Zeitschrift für die alttestamentliche Wissenschaft* 96 (1984): 315-32.

Meier, Samuel A. "Destroyer משחית." Pages 240-44 in *Dictionary of Deities and Demons in the Bible.* Edited by K. van der Toorn, B. Becking, and P. W. van der Horst. 2d ed. Leiden: Brill, 1999.

Merrilees, Robert S. "Political Conditions in the Eastern Mediterranean during the Late Bronze Age." *Biblical Archaeologist* 49 (1986): 42-50.

Meyer, Eduard. *Die Israeliten und ihre Nachbarstämme.* Halle: Niemeyer, 1906.

Milgrom, Jacob. "Priestly ('P') Source." Pages 454-61 in vol. 5 of *The Anchor Bible Dictionary*. Edited by D. N. Freedman. 6 vols. New York: Doubleday, 1992.

Miller, Patrick D., Jr. *The Divine Warrior in Early Israel*. Harvard Semitic Monographs 5. Cambridge, Mass.: Harvard Univ. Press, 1973.

Miller, Patrick D., Jr., and J. J. M. Roberts. *The Hand of the Lord: A Reassessment of the "Ark Narrative" of 1 Samuel*. Johns Hopkins Near Eastern Studies. Baltimore: Johns Hopkins Univ. Press, 1977.

Mitchell, Edward C. and Emil Kautzsch, eds. *Gesenius' Hebrew Grammar*. Translated by B. Davies. Andober: Warren F. Draper, 1884.

Moran, William L., ed. and trans. *The Amarna Letters*. Baltimore: Johns Hopkins Univ. Press, 1992.

———. "Early Canaanite *yaqtula*." *Orientalia* (NS) 29 (1960): 1-19.

———. "The Hebrew Language in its Northwest Semitic Background." Pages 54-72 in *The Bible and the Ancient Near East: Essays in Honor of William Foxwell Albright*. Edited by G. Ernest Wright. Garden City, N.Y.: Doubleday, 1961.

———. "New Evidence on Canaanite *taqtulū(na)*." *Journal of Cuneiform Studies* 5 (1951): 33-35.

Morgenstern, Julian. "The Ark, the Ephod, and The 'Tent of Meeting.'" *Hebrew Union College Annual* 17 (1942-1943): 153-266.

Motzki, Harold. "Ein Beitrag zum Problem des Stierkultes in der Religionsgeschichte Israels." *Vetus Testamentum* 25 (1975): 470-85.

Mowinckel, Sigmund. *Erwägungen zur Pentateuch Quellenfrage*. Oslo: Universitetsforlaget, 1964.

Müller, Hans-Peter. "Die aramäische Inschrift von Deir 'Allā und die älteren Bileamsprüche." *Zeitschrift für die alttestamentliche Wissenschaft* 94 (1982): 214-44.

Muraoka, Takamitsu and Bezalel Porten. *A Grammar of Egyptian Aramaic*. Handbuch der Orientalistik 32. Leiden: Brill, 1990.

Na'aman, Nadav. "On Gods and Scribal Traditions in the Amarna Letters." *Ugarit Forschungen* 22 (1990): 247-55.

Naveh, Joseph. "The Date of the Deir 'Allā Inscription in Aramaic Script." *Israel Exploration Journal* 17 (1967): 256-58.

Niehr, Herbert. *Der höchste Gott: Alttestamentlicher JHWH-Glaube im Kontext syrisch-kanaanäischer Religion des 1. Jahrtausends v. Chr.* Beihefte zur Zeitschrift für die alttestamentliche Wissenschaft 190. Berlin: Walter de Gruyter, 1990.

Noth, Martin. *Exodus: A Commentary.* Translated by J. S. Bowden. Old Testament Library. Philadelphia: Westminster, 1969.

————. *A History of Pentateuchal Traditions.* Translated with an Introduction by B. W. Anderson. Englewood Cliffs, N.J.: Prentice-Hall, 1972. Translation of *Überlieferungsgeschichte des Pentateuch.* Stuttgart: W. Kohlhammer, 1948.

Nougayrol, Jean. *Ugaritica V.* Paris: Librairie orientaliste Paul Geuthner, 1968.

————. "Textes et documents figurés." *Revue d'assyriologie et d'archéologie orientale* 41 (1947): 38-41.

Olmo Lete, Gregorio del. "Deber רבד." Pages 231-32 in *Dictionary of Deities and Demons in the Bible.* Edited by K. van der Toorn, B. Becking, and P. W. van der Horst. 2d ed. Leiden: Brill, 1999.

Pardee, Dennis. "The linguistic classification of the Deir 'Alla text written on plaster." Pages 100-105 in *The Balaam Text from Deir 'Alla Re-evaluated: Proceedings of the International Symposium held at Leiden, 21-24 August 1989.* Edited by J. Hoftijzer and H. van der Kooij. Leiden: Brill, 1991.

Parpola, Simo. "The Assyrian Tree of Life." *Journal of Near Eastern Studies* 52 (1993): 161-208.

————, ed. *Letters from Assyrian and Babylonian Scholars.* State Archives of Assyria 10. Helsinki: Helsinki Univ. Press, 1993.

————, ed. *Neo-Assyrian Treaties and Loyalty Oaths.* State Archives of Assyria 2. Helsinki: Helsinki Univ. Press, 1988.

Paul, Shalom M. *Amos: A Commentary on the Book of Amos.* Hermeneia. Minneapolis: Fortress, 1991.

Perles, Felix. "Zu Sachaus 'Aramäischen Papyrus und Ostraka.'" *Orientalistische Literaturzeitung* 14 (1911): 497-503.

Pfeiffer, Robert H. *Introduction to the Old Testament.* New York: Harper & Brothers, 1948.

————. *State Letters of Assyria.* American Oriental Series 6. New Haven: American Oriental Society, 1935.

————. "Three Assyriological Footnotes to the Old Testament." *Journal of Biblical Literature* 47 (1928): 184-87.

Porten, Bezalel. *Archives From Elephantine: The Life of an Ancient Jewish Military Colony.* Berkeley: Univ. of California Press, 1968.

Porten, Bezalel and Ada Yardeni, eds. *Textbook of Aramaic Documents from Ancient Egypt: Newly Copied, Edited and Translated into Hebrew and English. Vol. 3, Literature, Accounts, Lists.* Winona Lake, Ind.: Eisenbrauns, 1993.

Postgate, J. Nicholas. "The Land of Assur and the Yoke of Assur." *World Archaeology* 23 (1992): 247-63.

Pritchard, James B., ed. *Ancient Near Eastern Texts Relating to the Old Testament.* 3d ed. with Supplement. Princeton, N.J.: Princeton Univ. Press, 1969.

Procksch, Otto. *Das Nordhebräische Sagenbuch: Die Elohimquelle.* Leipzig: J. C. Hinrichs, 1906.

Puech, Emile. "Fear of Isaac." Pages 779-80 in vol. 2 of *The Anchor Bible Dictionary.* Edited by D. N. Freedman. 6 vols. New York: Doubleday, 1992.

Quirke, Stephen. *Ancient Egyptian Religion.* London: British Museum Press, 1992.

Rad, Gerhard von. *Der Heilige Krieg im alten Israel.* 4th ed. Göttingen: Vandenhoeck & Ruprecht, 1965.

————. *The Problem of the Hexateuch and other essays.* Translated E. W. Trueman Dicken. New York: McGraw-Hill, 1966.

Rainey, Anson F. *Canaanite in the Amarna Tablets: A Linguistic Analysis of the Mixed Dialect Used by the Scribes from Canaan.* 4 vols. Handbuch der Orientalistik 25. Leiden: Brill, 1996.

————. *El-Amarna Tablets 359-379: Supplement to J. A. Knudtzon,* Die El-Amarna Tafeln. 2d revised edition. Alter Orient und Altes Testament 8. Kevelaer: Butzon & Bercker, 1970.

Raphael, C. Nicholas. "Geography and the Bible (Palestine)." Pages 964-77 in vol. 2 of *The Anchor Bible Dictionary.* Edited by D. N. Freedman. 6 vols. New York: Doubleday, 1992.

Rendsburg, Gary. *Linguistic Evidence for the Northern Origin of Selected Psalms.* Society of Biblical Literature Monograph Series 4. Atlanta: Scholars Press, 1990.

Rendtorff, Rolf. *The Problem of the Process of Transmission in the Pentateuch.* Translated by John J. Scullion. Journal for the Study of the Old Testament: Supplement Series 89. Sheffield: JSOT Press, 1990.

Roberts, J. J. M. *The Earliest Semitic Pantheon: A Study of the Semitic Deities Attested in Mesopotamia Before Ur III.* Johns Hopkins Near Eastern Studies. Baltimore: Johns Hopkins Univ. Press, 1972.

————. *Nahum, Habakkuk, and Zephaniah: A Commentary.* Old Testament Library. Louisville: Westminster John Knox, 1991.

Röllig, Wolfgang. "El als Gottesbezeichnung im Phönizischen." Pages 403-16 in *Festschrift Johannes Friedrich.* Edited by R. von Kienle et al. Heidelberg: Universitätsverlag, 1959.

Rose, Martin. "Names of God in the OT." Pages 1001-11 in vol. 4 of *The Anchor Bible Dictionary.* Edited by D. N. Freedman. 6 vols. New York: Doubleday, 1992.

Rost, Leonhard. "Die Überlieferung von der Thronnachfolge Davids." Pages 119-253 in *Das kleine Credo und andere Studien zum Alten Testament.* Heidelberg: Quelle & Meyer, 1965. Reprint of *Die Überlieferung von der Thronnachfolge Davids.* Beiträge zur Wissenschaft vom Alten und Neuen Testament III, 6. Stuttgart: W. Kohlhammer, 1926.

Rudolph, Wilhelm. *Der 'Elohist' von Exodus bis Josua.* Beiheft zur Zeitschrift für die alttestamentliche Wissenschaft 68. Berlin: Alfred Töpelmann, 1938.

Rüterswörden, Udo. "Horon חורן." Pages 425-26 in *Dictionary of Deities and Demons in the Bible.* Edited by K. van der Toorn et al. 2d ed. Leiden: Brill, 1999.

Šanda, Albert. *Die Bücher der Könige.* 2 vols. Münster: Aschendorf, 1911.

Sasson, Jack M. "Bovine Symbolism in the Exodus Narrative." *Vetus Testamentum* 18 (1968): 380-87.

————, ed. *Civilizations of the Ancient Near East.* 4 Vols. New York: Scribners, 1995.

Schmid, Hans Heinrich. *Der sogennante Jahwist: Untersuchungen zu den Berührungspunkten beider Literaturwerke.* Abhandlungen zur Theologie des Alten und Neuen Testaments 67. Zurich: Theologischer Verlag, 1981.

Schroeder, Otto. *Keilschrifttexte aus Assur historischen Inhalts.* Leipzig: J. C. Hinrichs, 1922.

Segert, Stanislav. *Altaramäische Grammatik.* Leipzig: VEB Verlag Enzyklopädie, 1983.

————. *A Grammar of Phoenician and Punic.* Munich: C. H. Beck, 1976.

Seow, Choon Leong. *Ecclesiastes: A New Translation with Introduction and Commentary*. Anchor Bible 18c. New York: Doubleday, 1997.

————. *Myth, Drama, and the Politics of David's Dance*. Harvard Semitic Monographs 46. Atlanta: Scholars Press, 1989.

Seux, Marie-Joseph. *Hymnes et prieres aux dieux de Babylonie et d'Assyrie*. Paris: Cerf, 1976.

Smith, Mark S. *The Early History of God*. San Francisco: Harper & Row, 1990.

Smith, Morton. *Palestinian Parties and Politics that Shaped the Old Testament*. London: SCM Press, 1971.

Soden, Wilfrom von. *Grundriss der Akkadischen Grammatik*, 2d ed. Analecta orientalia 33 & 47. Rome: Pontifical Biblical Institute, 1969.

Soggin, J. Alberto. *Introduction to the Old Testament*. Translated by J. Bowden. Revised edition. Old Testament Library. Philadelphia: Westminster, 1980.

————. "Der offiziell geförderte Synkretismus in Israel während des 10. Jahrhunderts." *Zeitschrift für die alttestamentliche Wissenschaft* 78 (1966): 179-204.

Soldt, Wilfred Hugo van. *Studies in the Akkadian of Ugarit: Dating and Grammar*. Alter Orient und Altes Testament 40. Kevelaer: Butzon & Bercker, 1991.

Stager, Lawrence E. "The Archaeology of the Family in Ancient Israel." *Bulletin of the American Schools of Oriental Research* 260 (1985): 1-35.

Stamm, Johann Jakob. *Die Akkadische Namengebung*. Leipzig: J. C. Hinrichs, 1939.

Steiglitz, Robert. "Ebla and the Gods of Canaan." Pages 79-89 in vol. 2 of *Eblaitica: Essays on the Ebla Archives and Eblaite Language*. Edited by C. H. Gordon and G. A. Rendsburg. Winona Lake, Ind.: Eisenbrauns, 1990.

Tadmor, Haim. "The Aramaization of Assyria: Aspects of Western Impact." Pages 449-71 in *Mesopotamien und seine Nachbarn*. Part 2. Edited by H. Nissen and J. Renger. Berlin: G. Reimer, 1982.

Tallqvist, Knut L. *Assyrian Personal Names*. Helsinki: Societas Scientiarum Fennica, 1914.

Thompson, Thomas L. "The Intellectual Matrix of Early Biblical Narrative: Inclusive Monotheism in Persian Palestine." Pages 108-24 in *The Triumph of Elohim: From Yahwisms to Judaisms*. Edited by D. V. Edelman. Grand Rapids, Mich.: Eerdmans, 1995.

Todd, Judith A. "The Pre-Deuteronomistic Elijah Cycle." Pages 1-35 in *Elijah and Elisha in Socioliterary Perspective*. Edited by R. B. Coote. Atlanta: Scholars Press, 1992.

Toombs, Lawrence E. "War, Ideas of." Pages 796-801 in vol. 4 of *The Anchor Bible Dictionary*. Edited by D. N. Freedman. 6 vols. New York: Doubleday, 1992.

Toorn, Karel van der. *Family Religion in Babylonia, Syria and Israel: Continuity and Change in the Forms of Religious Life*. Studies in the History and Culture of the Ancient Near East 7. Leiden: Brill, 1996.

——. "God (I) אלהים." Pages 668-92 in *Dictionary of Deities and Demons in the Bible*. Edited by K. van der Toorn, B. Becking, and P. W. van der Horst. 2d ed. Leiden: Brill, 1999.

Toorn, Karel van der, Bob Becking, and Pieter W. van der Horst, eds. *Dictionary of Deities and Demons in the Bible*. 2d ed. Leiden: Brill, 1999.

Van Seters, John. *Abraham in History and Tradition*. New Haven: Yale Univ. Press, 1975.

——. *The Life of Moses: The Yahwist as Historian in Exodus-Numbers*. Louisville: Westminster, 1994.

——. *Prologue to History: The Yahwist as Historian in Genesis*. Louisville: Westminster, 1992.

Vaux, Roland de. *Ancient Israel: Its Life and Institutions*. Translated by J. McHugh. London: Darton, Longman, & Todd, 1961. Reprint, Grand Rapids, Mich.: Eerdmans, 1997.

——. "Les chérubins et l'arche d'alliance." *Mélanges de l'Université Saint-Joseph* 37 (1960-1961): 93-124.

Vermeylen, Jacques. "Les premières étapes littéraires de la formation du Pentateuque." Pages 149-97 in *Le Pentateuque en question*. Edited by A. de Pury. Geneva: Labor et Fides, 1989.

Volz, Paul and Wilhelm Rudolph. *Der Elohist als Erzähler: ein Irrweg der Pentateuchkritik*. Beihefte zur Zeitschrift für die alttestamentliche Wissenschaft 63. Giessen: Töpelmann, 1933.

Vorländer, Hermann. *Mein Gott: Die Vorstellungen vom persönlichen Gott im Alten Orient und im Alten Testament*. Alter Orient und Altes Testament 23. Kevelaer: Butzon & Bercker, 1975.

Waltke, Bruce and Michael O'Connor. *An Introduction to Biblical Hebrew Syntax.* Winona Lake, Ind.: Eisenbrauns, 1990.

Weber, Otto and Erich Ebeling, ed. *Die El-Amarna-Tafeln. Zweiter Teil: Anmerkungen und Register.* Vorderasiatische Bibliothek 2. Leipzig, 1915. Reprint, Aalen: Otto Zeller, 1964.

Weidner, Ernst. "Aus den Tagen eines assyrischen Schattenkönigs." *Archiv für Orientforschung* (1935): 1-43.

Weinstein, James M. "The Egyptian Empire in Palestine: A Reassessment." *Bulletin of the American Schools of Oriental Research* 241 (1981): 1-28.

Weippert, Manfred. "The Balaam Text from Deir 'Allā and the study of the Old Testament." Pages 151-84 in *The Balaam Text from Deir 'Alla Re-evaluated: Proceedings of the International Symposium held at Leiden, 21-24 August 1989.* Edited by J. Hoftijzer and H. van der Kooij. Leiden: Brill, 1991.

Wellhausen, Julius. "Die Composition des Hexateuchs." *Jahrbücher für Deutsche Theologie* 21 (1876-1877): 392-450; 536-602; Reprint, pages 1-210 in *Die Composition des Hexateuchs und der historischen Bücher des Alten Testaments.* Berlin: G. Reimer, 1889.

―――. *Prolegomena to the History of Israel.* New York: Meridian Books, 1957. Reprint of *Prolegomena to the History of Israel.* Translated by J. S. Black and A. Enzies, with preface by W. Robertson Smith. Edinburgh: Adam & Charles Black, 1885. Translation of *Prolegomena zur Geschichte Israels.* 2d ed. Berlin: G. Reimer, 1883.

Westenholz, Aage. "Some Notes on the Orthography and Grammar of the Recently Published Texts from Mari." *Bibliotheca orientalis* 35 (1978): 160-69.

Westermann, Claus. *Genesis 12-36.* Minneapolis: Augsburg, 1985.

White, Marsha. *The Elijah Legends and Jehu's Coup.* Brown Judaic Studies 311. Atlanta: Scholars Press, 1997.

Whitehead, J. David. "Some Distinctive Features of the Language of the Aramaic Arsames Correspondence." *Journal of Near Eastern Studies* 37 (1978): 119-40.

Whybray, R. Norman. *The Making of the Pentateuch: A Methodological Study.* Journal for the Study of the Old Testament: Supplement Series 53. Sheffield: JSOT Press, 1987.

Winnett, Frederick V. "Re-Examining the Foundations." *Journal of Biblical Literature* (1965): 1-19.

Wijngaards, Joanne. "הוֹצִיא and הֶעֱלָה A Twofold Approach to the Exodus." *Vetus Testamentum* 15 (1965): 91-102.

Wolff, Hans Walter. "The Elohistic Fragments in the Pentateuch." Pages 67-82, 154-56 in *The Vitality of the Old Testament Traditions*. Edited by W. Brueggemann and H. W. Wolff. Atlanta: John Knox, 1982. Reprint of "The Elohistic Fragments in the Pentateuch." Translated by K. R. Crim. *Interpretation* 26 (1972): 158-73. Translation of "Zur Thematik der elohistischen Fragmente im Pentateuch." *Evangelische Theologie* 29 (1969): 59-72.

———. *Hosea: A Commentary on the Book of the Prophet Hosea*. Edited by P. D. Hanson. Translated by G. Stansell. Hermeneia. Philadelphia: Fortress, 1974.

———. *Joel and Amos: A Commentary on the Books of the Prophets Joel and Amos*. Edited by S. D. McBride, Jr. Translated by W. Janzen et al. Hermeneia. Philadelphia: Fortress, 1977.

Wyatt, Nicolas. "Of Calves and Kings: the Canaanite Dimension in the Religion of Israel." *Scandinavian Journal of the Old Testament* 6 (1992): 68-91.

———. "Qeteb קֶטֶב." Pages 673-74 in *Dictionary of Deities and Demons in the Bible*. Edited by K. van der Toorn et al. 2d ed. Leiden: Brill, 1999.

Wynn-Williams, Damian J. *The State of the Pentateuch: A Comparison of the Approaches of M. Noth and E. Blum*. Beihefte zur Zeitschrift für die alttestamentliche Wissenschaft 249. Berlin: Walter de Gruyter, 1997.

Xella, Paolo. "Barad בָּרָד." Pages 160-61 in *Dictionary of Deities and Demons in the Bible*. Edited by K. van der Toorn et al. 2d ed. Leiden: Brill, 1999.

Zimmermann, Hellmuth. *Elohim: Eine Studie zur israelitischen Religions- und Litteraturgeschichte nebst Beitrag zur Religionsphilosophie und einer Pentateuchtabelle*. Berlin: Mayer & Müller, 1900.